TO LIVE AGAIN

CATHERINE MARSHALL was born in Johnson City, Tennessee, the daughter of a minister. Her early years were spent in Mississippi and West Virginia. She was twenty and at college n Georgia when she was first introduced to Peter Marshall, although she had been admiring the popular young pastor for two years. They met at a prohibition rally where they both made ardent speeches for the cause, and a little over a year later they were married. Theirs was a warm and truly happy marriage until her husband's death at the age of forty-six.

CATHERINE MARSHALL

To Live Again

Collins
FONTANA BOOKS

First published in Great Britain by Peter Davies, Ltd., 1958
First published in Fontana Books, 1967

To R.A.W.

© 1957 Catherine Marshall
Sermon material on pages 278 and 284 is from the picture 'A Man Called Peter', produced by Twentieth Century-Fox Film Corporation

Printed in Great Britain
Collins Clear-Type Press
London and Glasgow

CONTENTS

I wish to express my deep appreciation to Frances Jane Munsey, my efficient secretary, whose never-failing patience and good humour have constantly lightened my task; to Harlow Hoskins for his help in typing the manuscript; to Dr Raymond I. Lindquist for the stimulus of his vigorous and able criticism; to Ruth Welty for her fine editorial suggestions; to my sister, Emma Lynn Hoskins, for her culinary help in the chapter on Evergreen Farm; to Samuel G. Engel and Eleanore Griffin for their suggestions on the movie chapters; and to Peter John, who continues to be my senior editor.

I am also grateful to the Fleming H. Revell Company, New York, for permission to quote from *Mr Jones, Meet the Master* by Peter Marshall; and to Alfred A. Knopf, Inc., and the Society of Authors as the Literary Representative of the late Miss Katherine Mansfield, for permission to quote from *The Journal of Katherine Mansfield*, edited by John Middleton Murry. Finally, I should like to express my appreciation to the many friends who have graciously granted me permission to quote from their letters to me and to tell their stories.

Crisis

On the grey morning of January 25, 1949, my world caved in. At 8.15 a.m. my husband's tired and damaged heart stopped beating. Five minutes later the doctor rang. The measured words coming through the telephone receiver were like physical blows from which I instinctively recoiled. . . . " Oh no! Not *that*!" And then a deep breath, like that of a drowning person gulping for air. . . . " How? Why? Please tell me what happened?"

The controlled voice on the other end of the phone went on with maddening deliberation, " Dr Marshall seemed to stand the ambulance trip to the hospital quite well. Sedation soon reduced the pain in his chest and arms. There was no immediate need for oxygen. The night nurse on the floor went by his room shortly before eight o'clock this morning. Dr Marshall seemed to be comfortable—was, in fact, sleeping. So the nurse didn't disturb him.

" Meanwhile, I telephoned one of the nurses on his case during his first attack, and she had agreed to come. Shortly after eight she came on duty. It was she who found him. . . . Dr Marshall died in his sleep—very peacefully."

I found myself unable to speak. I was hanging on to the telephone receiver as if that small black instrument could hold me up.

" Mrs Marshall, do you want to come down to the hospital?" the doctor asked. " What order shall I give?"

When I found my voice again, it sounded hollow, alien. . . . " Please—yes, I'll be right down. Don't let them move him—until I get there—please."

" I assure you nothing at all will be disturbed. Mrs Marshall, may I say—I'm *sorry*."

How can real life seem more like a dream than any dream?

What is reality? Life? Death? Who can tell? A whirling head, a furiously beating heart, unseeing eyes, unsteady legs must somehow walk on into the dream, to be enveloped by it, to feel its clamminess, to protest it. . . . One must pick up life again, even though one feels as dead on the inside as a wound-up tin soldier—mechanically—setting one foot—in front of the other.

At the moment when the telephone had rung, Peter John, our nine-year-old son, had been getting ready to leave for school. He had been standing near-by and had overheard my half of the conversation with the doctor. I had replaced the telephone on its cradle, had stood there for a moment as in a daze. Then suddenly I became aware of a small blond boy there in the hall, looking at me with uncomprehending blue eyes.

Almost instantly, two thoughts surged through me—an intimation of what the news I had just heard meant for this little boy's future, and my own need to feel close to him. I knelt and impulsively pulled him into my arms.

"Peter, the doctor told me that Daddy just died." There were no tears in my voice; I was still too stunned. But Peter John burst into a flood of little-boy tears.

I knelt there holding him close, feeling the warmth of his body pressed against mine. He was quivering. Only once since babyhood had I ever seen Peter John tremble like that.

The incident came back to me so vividly. . . . As an eight-year-old, Peter John had been away to summer camp for the first time. His father and I had received a letter from him written on ruled paper in his big, round, scrawly hand:

Dear Mummy and Daddy,
    I am still very homesick. Could you come and take me home before Sunday? I would like it very much. If you can't would you please come and take me home Monday.

                                        Love,
                                          Peter

We had kept in touch with the counsellors by telephone.
"Don't come," they had advised. "Write your son, but
stay away from him. This often happens. He'll get over
it."

But he hadn't. The homesickness had got worse and
worse. Then he had come down with a summer cold and
had landed in sick bay.

"We'll go to see how he is," his father had conceded.
"But Catherine, we've got to be firm with Peter—no soft
stuff now. He's got to grow up."

As soon as Peter John had seen his father in the infirmary
door, he had leaped into his arms. The little figure in
crumpled summer pyjamas had clung around his father's neck,
his legs wound around him, the blond head buried in the
broad shoulder. Sobbing and quivering—even as he was
now in my arms—he had said, "If—if you—love me—
you'll—take—me home."

Love him? Who could have doubted it, watching that
scene? The rugged-looking Scotsman, his curly hair a bit
unruly . . . his blue-grey eyes moist . . . stroking the blond
head with his big mechanic's hand . . . his carefully-mus-
tered sternness melting like ice in the sun. . . .

"All right, Peter," he said softly, the burr of his accent
softened by emotion. "I understand. We'll take you home.
But you are to stop crying."

"And now," I thought, as I held that same little boy
in my arms, "you will never again hear that voice or feel
that hand."

As I knelt there, the front door opened. It was my
brother Bob and his wife Mary. I sat on the davenport in
the living room beside Bob and repeated all that the doctor
had said. Still there were no tears. The whole thing seemed
utterly unreal. Peter dead! How could Peter be dead?
Surely, God would somehow, some way, still intervene. . . .

He was not to intervene in the way I hoped, but in quite
another way—equally miraculous. Just how miraculous I
was not to realize until much later. I was to be led by that

Power outside myself into areas beyond my knowledge, along the path that leads through and out of the Valley of the Shadow of Death. There would be rocky ledges, steep slopes, slippery places, many a fork in the road where a clear-cut decision would be required. I knew none of the trails: the Valley was untrodden country. Yet by sure steps I would be led through it. I was to discover the Lord as my Shepherd—quite literally and in many practical ways.

As soon as I could get ready, Bob and Mary drove me to the hospital. At my request, they let me go alone to Peter's room, but a young interne insisted on going up with me in the elevator. As the elevator ascended we were silent. Then, as we walked up to the closed door, the interne—his eyes searching my face—asked, " Mrs Marshall, are you really all right? Are you quite sure that you want to go in there alone?"

I nodded. He opened the door and stepped aside. " Then I'll wait for you here in the hall," he said. " Call if you need me."

I was young, had looked on death only twice before. Yet one glance at the still form on the bed and I knew that the man I loved was not there.

But the little hospital room was not empty; I was not alone. For a while there was a transcendent glory. Though I did not understand it then and cannot explain it now, I knew that Peter was near me. And beside him, another Presence, the Lord he had served through long years—years stretching back to boyhood experiences on the moors of Scotland.

" There are some things," Peter had been fond of saying from his pulpit, " that can never be proven by argument, by logic, or by reason; things that are matters of perception—not of proof. There are some things that can never be poured into the cold moulds of human speech." This was exactly the case with what happened to me during that hour in the hospital room.

I was not the only one who witnessed it. As I sat by the

bed, there came a soft tap on the door. Slowly it was pushed ajar, and I saw my closest friend, Alma Deane Fuller, framed in the doorway. She stood there hesitantly, wanting to be with me, yet fearful of intruding. What she saw can best be told in her own words, as she described it to me in a letter the following week:

I don't think you have any idea how transformed you were in that hour. I have never seen you look so beautiful. The smile that was on your face was my first glimpse of the heavenly glory which surrounded every part of Peter's going. I know you well enough to know when something has been added to you, and you were unquestionably filled by a newness and a differentness, and all the love in the world was in your eyes.

That little hospital room was filled with the same power that was in you. It was charged with it. I shall never be able to thank you enough for asking me to come in. It was in those moments that I learned what Christ's power over death is. Glory filled that room. . . .

Having actually experienced that glory, I thought at that moment that I would never again doubt the fact of immortality. In a deep and intuitive way, beyond argument or intellectual process, deeper than tears, transcending words— was the knowledge that human life does not end in six feet of earth.

I was also, minute by minute, learning something else . . . that our God can handle even the worst that can happen to us as finite human beings. Since Christ is beside us, no troubles that life can bring need cast us adrift. This is a knowledge which can release us from lifelong bondage to fear. So I found it.

Yet my realization of the splendour was not to last. At a precise moment, the two vivid presences withdrew. Suddenly I saw Death stripped bare, in all its ugliness. With very human eyes I saw it . . . the face of the man I loved. . . . *There's nothing pretty about death. Those who senti-mentalize it, lie. . . .* Carbon dioxide escaping from the sagging jaw . . . the limp hands . . . the coldness and pallor of the flesh. . . . *No wonder they call us the white race. I never knew that skin could be that white* . . . the finality of it . . . the pathos.

Sometimes when one is walking through moments of high drama, there is a curious detachment. It is as if the mind separates itself from the emotions and stands off to observe. Was it the numbing effect of my grief that for a time gave me an aloofness that enabled me to think, *Every detail of this moment will be for ever stamped on your mind—the sight of it—the sound of it. This is the raw stuff of which life—and death—are made. Now you know.*

Yet of this part of the experience I was not to speak—not for a long, long time. In reply to those who would say, "What a lovely, peaceful expression he had on his face," I could only smile and say nothing. What would have been the point of replying, "But you never saw the expression on his face. That lovely, peaceful look must have been contrived by—" No, no, I couldn't say that. . . .

Or how could one explain that, when we see death starkly, stripped of all our techniques for camouflaging it, when one knows that the beloved person has left the pathetic shell empty, then the shell becomes—well—almost repugnant?

Shivering, I rose to leave the room. I knew that this would be the last time on this earth I would look on my husband's face. An instinct stronger than reasoning, sounder than custom or convention, told me that the inner spirit had taken all the shock it could stand for a while, was standing dangerously close to an emotional precipice. So there in the hospital room, I said my last *au revoir*.

Now there was nothing to do but to walk out. My legs would obey my will and carry me out of the hospital room. I was sure they would. Had they not always obeyed me before?

I sensed that out beyond the door, out beyond the chilly hospital corridor, a new life awaited me. That was the last thing in the world I wanted. But then Peter had not wanted a new life either—not yet anyway—not at forty-six. And already he was embarked on that other adventure.

My heels tapped out a sharp rhythm on the floor. The door clicked shut behind me. Flooding my heart, pounding at my brain, were the whirling thoughts—Now you are all alone, all on your own. What does the new life hold? You are not ready to live without him. You are not trained to earn a living. How are you going to get along?

But part of the whirling thoughts were mistaken. I was not alone, not altogether on my own. It only seemed to be that way. For this was fear, natural enough under the circumstances. But deeper than fear was the sure knowledge that from the moment of Peter's death, God had taken over Peter John and me in a new way.

That this was so became quite apparent during the next few days. A Power outside myself lifted my spirit up and carried me steadily and surely through the necessary mechanics always connected with death.

Many bereaved people have experienced this. Some of them account for it simply as one result of the numbness that follows shock; others say that it is a refusal to accept reality. All of this is true. But there is more to it than that. Even emotional torpor and an inability to understand are nature's gracious gifts for the crucial moments of bereavement. They are like an anæsthetic that enables one to bear the cruel wound that the spirit has sustained.

Looking back, I know that what I experienced was much more than just being stunned. God gave me added capacities. The first was the ability to think of other people and their needs. I found myself especially concerned about the void left in the congregation which Peter and I had served. Such flinging off of egocentricity was unlike me. It was something added. I was not really that mature a person.

Then there was the gift of a series of detailed instructions straight from God. It was not even necessary to ask for them. Like a child, I was taken over and managed. It was as if, at the time of Peter's death, I literally stepped into the radiant Kingdom of God on earth.

I longed to have certain friends near me. It was not necessary to wire or to telephone them. Even as I wished for them, they were on their way to Washington. There was no straining over the planning of the funeral service; all details were as clear as if they were set in type.

It was a service that included our entire congregation, Peter's friends and mine, in a way that few funerals ever do. I was aware that many of those who would be there needed to be ministered to as much as I did. Their minds were full of their loss. . . . 'How are we going to get along without his leadership?' Their faith was shaken. The spiritual crisis would not have been so poignant had not Peter, through his preaching and ministering in Atlanta and then in Washington, succeeded so well in making Christ real to thousands of people, in helping them to see Him walking beside them in the hurly-burly of everyday life. 'And now,' they wondered, 'how does Dr Marshall's early death jibe with all that he himself believed and preached? Does his death somehow cancel everything?'

The service was at eleven o'clock on Thursday morning at the New York Avenue Presbyterian Church where Peter had served for over eleven years. I sat in my usual place —the pastor's pew—with my family around me, Peter John beside me.

My first inclination after Peter's death had been to shield Peter John as completely as possible. How much could a nine-year-old stand? Perhaps he should be sent away to a friend's or neighbour's until the services were over. Might not exposing him to this time of upheaval leave permanent scars?

Somehow I was saved from this false reasoning. Shunt-

ing him off at this time would have left far worse scars than
including him. After all, child or not, he was a person
in his own right, a member of our family. It was my husband who had died, but it was also Peter John's father.
Our son too had emotional needs. One of them was to be
loved, to know that he belonged. He needed to feel, along
with the rest of us, the tenderness at the centre of heart-
break and the warmth of the Christian community. That
was why Peter John was sitting beside me now, solemn but
dry-eyed.

The old church had never been so crowded except on an
Easter Sunday morning. Downstairs in the lecture room
several hundred people listened over loud-speakers. Hundreds were turned away for lack of space. Outside on the
sidewalks, hundreds more stood silent and bareheaded, refusing to leave.

Government workers, Senators, Senate pageboys, the Vice-
President, judges, clerks, typists, secretaries, housewives, the
Negro janitors of the church, the boys from the parking
garage who, still in their uniforms, had slipped across the
street—they were all there, fused into a unity and sweetness
of spirit through which unmistakable spiritual power pulsated.
In the air was a vibrancy, as of the dynamo of the Spirit of
God. Yet there was nothing mawkish about it—a little weeping.

That vast congestion rose and sang together as one voice.
The choir, 110 young people, sang the anthem that Peter had
loved best—part of Mendelssohn's " Elijah " :

> O, Rest in the Lord,
> Wait patiently for Him,
> And He shall give thee
> Thy heart's desire. . . .

Several of Peter's close friends in the ministry spoke
quietly—with humour here and there. How could anyone

think of Peter Marshall without seeing in his mind's eye Peter's flashing smile and hearing his infectious laughter?

One of them, Ed Pruden, the pastor of Washington's First Baptist Church, later told me that the tone of the entire service was changed for him by an incident that had happened just before the service began.

Those who were to take part in the service had gathered in Peter's church study. As the hands of the clock in the bell tower moved toward eleven o'clock, Mr Bridge, the associate minister of our church, asked the seven men to line up preparatory to their filing on to the rostrum.

He consulted a paper in his hand, " Let me see now . . . Dr Pruden, will you go to the head of the line, please?"

There was a moment's silence. Then as Dr Pruden moved to the front of the line, he smiled broadly. As if at a signal, several of the other ministers began to laugh.

A puzzled look crossed Mr Bridge's face. Obviously, he could see nothing funny about what he had said. Under the circumstances, the levity seemed strangely out of place.

But as the little procession moved down the stairs and out toward the church sanctuary, Dr Pruden hastened to explain to Mr Bridge, " You know, once a week, if we could possibly manage it, five or six of us ministers used to have lunch together at the cafeteria just down the street. After we would get in line, pick up our trays and silverware, inevitably the same thing would happen. The group would be so engrossed in conversation that the cafeteria line would move off and leave us. Somehow, I always seemed to be the first one to see the gap in the line. Then, as unobtrusively as possible, I would rush up ahead of the others to help keep the line moving.

" But always Peter would spot me. Then his hearty laughter would ring out, ' There goes Ed to the head of the line, gang. Always afraid the food's going to run out.'

" It was just that when you said, ' Dr Pruden, you go to the head of the line,' each of us could hear Peter's laughter. It was almost as if it were his way of saying to us, ' I see you made it again, Ed. Don't you dare go in there to my people and lead them in any service of mourning over me. I'm still very much alive, still with you—still one of the gang—and don't forget it.' ''

Later in the service, Mr Bridge said the same thing in a different way. The words he spoke were to gather significance for me in the years ahead:

Let me say in a few words and, in very simple words, try to express what we are trying to do this morning. We are endeavouring to establish a new relationship. We have known Peter Marshall in the flesh. From now on we are to endeavour to know him in the spirit just as really as we have known him in the flesh. . . .

Peter Marshall is still, and will continue to be, one of the ministers of this church, though no longer visible to us. The fellowship we have with him will remain unbroken, and may God give us wisdom, grace and strength to join hands with him. . . .

Throughout the service I was conscious of Peter John beside me. I kept wondering what all this could possibly mean to a nine-year-old, what thoughts were going through his mind. . . . Was he perhaps remembering his birthday party less than a week before? At that time, his father had helped with an elaborate treasure hunt.

Each small guest had gone to our garage to find the beginning of the string that was to lead him to his treasure. In preparing this game, the two Peters and I had had great fun taking the strings up the stairs to the first floor, the second, under beds, behind bureaus, into the most unlikely places. In the end, we three had become hilarious watching one another all tangled up in string.

The party had been on January 21; four days later Peter was dead. And now—each year when Peter John's birthday came around, he and I would be thinking of that other anniversary. I reached out for his small hand. . . .

Then the service was over. The family and I walked down the long centre aisle of the church behind the casket. While I was intensely aware of certain details of the scene evolving around me—in particular of the love on the faces of certain close friends as I passed—in another way I was moving as in a dream. Part of my mind and my emotions were still numb, still blocked off.

Of course, the numbness—the dream—could not last. For we, still in the flesh, are clay with feet of clay. And clay belongs to earth. By the following Friday, eight days after the funeral, I had come back to earth with a thud. Peter's death was real—final. There would be no reprieve from the cruel fact. With this realization, the long pull of the healing of a desolated heart had begun.

On that Friday, it was my mother who caught the first fury of my rebellion. She and Dad were still with us; they had planned to stay for ten days.

With my descent to earth had come physical exhaustion. Mother insisted that I go to bed. But there was no need to leave me alone because I could not sleep. So Mother sat in the little needle-point rocker near my bed and wisely let me pour out my torrent of thoughts and the surging emotions that all but engulfed me.

First, I sought to blame myself. Had I done everything possible to save Peter? Had it really been God's will that Peter die? Or was this just another failure on my part? Had I, for example, somehow failed to fulfil the conditions of answered prayer?

Then I remembered that I had been annoyed with my husband for a time and childishly petulant on the last Sunday of his life.

On the way home from church, we had the radio on. Just as Peter had brought the car to a halt before our front door, a radio announcer had mentioned the approaching St. Valentine's Day.

Peter had reached across for my hand. . . . "Will you be my valentine, Catherine?" he had asked gaily.

And I had withdrawn my hand and ruthlessly crushed his small moment of gaiety by replying sarcastically, "Oh, sure! I'll be your valentine, having a gay time all by myself here in Washington while you're in Des Moines. I hear you decided to accept that invitation, too."

For a passing moment a look of pain had crossed his face. The remembrance of that look stung and hurt me now.

Between sobs I told Mother of the episode and verbally whipped myself, "How could I have been like that? What on earth got into me? I'm supposed to be a woman—not a child. How could I have been so immature, so disgustingly petty?"

Other people too were caught up in my rebellion. Grief fanned into flame my resentment against all those who had known of Peter's heart condition and yet had persisted in heaping demands on him. These demands had snowballed from 1947 on, after he had become Chaplain of the Senate.

"How often I've stood by," I said to Mother, "and heard someone say to Peter in one moment, 'Dr Marshall, please don't overdo. You just must take care of yourself. We need you so . . .' And then in the very next moment, plead with him to speak to their pet group. Their organization was always different; their group should always be the exception. How selfish can human beings be?"

Then having struck out at people, I lashed out again at God. "Why? Why did it have to end this way?" I asked bitterly. "Have Peter and I been duped? Has everything that Peter preached been pious nonsense? If God is a God of love and has the power to help us, why didn't He do something about Peter's heart?"

Sorely troubled, Mother watched me and groped for words that might help. Yet she knew her words would make little difference at the moment. It was enough that she was there to listen. She knew that every bitter thought—against myself and other people and God—needed to come up and out.

She understood my need for an answer to my agonizing question . . . where is the God of love who cares about the individual in what has happened? She knew that if this question were not faced and answered, there could be no healing of my bruised heart; that without an answer, I would then be forced either to flee life or to live it on a busy-busy level, dragging an anæsthetized spirit after me. She knew that my great need was still to be oriented to God, centred in Him, so that my life would have an anchor. But she also knew that this could not be forced.

" In God's own time," she told me quietly, " you will get God's answers."

I was a particularly ill-equipped widow. Death had never before invaded my immediate family circle. Moreover, I had consistently evaded it as a fact of human experience. Even as a minister's wife, I had exhibited an ingenuity approaching genius about side-stepping funerals.

It had begun back in childhood. One of my remarks on this subject had become something of a classic in our family.

When I was six, I had an uncle who was killed one December 22 in a tragic automobile accident. Uncle John was to be buried on Christmas afternoon. The noon meal just before the funeral, at which quite a number of relatives were gathered, was anything but gay.

I am told that after I had listened for some time to the solemn grown-up talk about funeral plans, suddenly—during a lull in the conversation—I announced in a clear, firm voice, " Well, I'm not going. I never have been able to get anything out of funerals." That immediately broke up the solemnity.

While this was a silly childish remark, it nevertheless revealed the emotional coloration that everything connected with death had for me even then. It was an attitude that I carried over into adult life.

Peter saw this in me. Once during his first convalescence, he had insisted on telling me about his business affairs. I remembered the scene all too well.

"Get a pencil and a piece of paper, Catherine," he had ordered. "There are some facts you must have down for ready reference in case anything should happen to me."

I had been almost defiant. "I'll put this stuff down to humour you. But I can't stand to hear you talk that way. Nothing is going to happen to you. Don't be foolish. . . ."

My husband's blue-grey eyes had crinkled at the corners with amusement. "You act, Catherine, as if death can be avoided by willing it away. After all, it does come to all life on this planet."

And I had sat there thinking, 'How can any man with a serious heart condition be this objective, get outside himself that much?'

The voice with the burr went on, gently teasing, "In this area, you're like a little girl. One of these days, Catherine, you're going to have to come to terms with the fact of death. But that will have to be in your own way and in your own time. I can't do this for you. . . . Now take this down. . . . My lock box at the bank is 731. All important papers are there. The key is with the others on my key ring. First, I'll summarize the insurance programme for you. . . ."

In many ways, I was still a little girl. I had adored and leaned on my husband. Like many a sheltered woman who has married young, I had never once figured out an income tax blank, had a car inspected, consulted a lawyer, or tried to read an insurance policy. Railroad time-tables and plane schedules were enigmas to me. My household accounts rarely balanced. I had never invested any money; I had been driving a car for only three months. I would never even have considered braving a trip alone to New York.

Now I was faced with all these practical matters, plus many, many more.

There was some insurance, but not enough. I had no idea where Peter John and I would live after we left the Manse. I was not trained to earn a living. I had married when my college diploma was warm from the dean's hand, before I had even earned a teacher's certificate. . . . The adjustment that faced me, therefore, posed a challenge in every way in which a woman can be challenged.

CHAPTER 2

To Comfort All that Mourn

Most people accept intellectually a belief in some kind of life and death. But usually it remains a theoretical belief until death invades one's immediate family circle.

Then, at the time of the funeral, we are handed the victory. The working through of the specific problems that sorrow brings must come later.

Many know that initial victory. As with all God's gifts, we do nothing to earn or to deserve it. Undoubtedly a loving Father knows that without this kind of help, many of us could never withstand the emotional shock, would never even be able to get through the funeral.

At that time, the first need of the bereaved person is for comfort—just plain comfort. In sorrow, we are all like little children, hurt children who yearn to creep into a mother's arms and rest there; have her stroke our foreheads and speak softly to us as she used to do. But, of course, that is impossible; we are grown men and women. Yet the need for comfort remains.

Our God has promised precisely that. . . . " Comfort ye, comfort ye my people, saith your God. . . ." " For thus saith the Lord. . . . As one whom his mother comforteth, so will I comfort you. . . ."

Strangely in my case I was given the beginning of that experience of comfort a few hours prior to my husband's death. That morning Peter had wakened about three-thirty with severe pains in his arms and chest. The doctor had come as quickly as he could. He had insisted that Dr Marshall be taken immediately to the hospital.

As we had waited for the ambulance, Peter had looked up at me through his pain and said, "Catherine, don't try to come with me. We mustn't leave Wee Peter alone in this big house. You can come to the hospital in the morning."

Reluctantly I had agreed. I knew that he was right, though I wanted so much to be with him.

After the ambulance had come and gone, I went back upstairs and sank to my knees beside the bed. There was the need for prayer, for this was an emergency indeed. It could mean only one thing—another massive heart attack. But how was I to pray? Swirling emotions had plunged my mind into utter confusion.

Suddenly the unexpected happened. Over the turbulent emotions there crept a strange all-pervading peace. And through and around me flowed love as I had never before experienced it. It was as if body and spirit were floating on a cloud, resting—as if Someone who loved me very much were wrapping me round and round with His love.

I knelt there marvelling at what was happening. I had done nothing, said nothing, to bring it about. Through my mind trooped a quick procession of thoughts . . . *the Three Persons of the Godhead . . . Father, Son, and Holy Spirit. . . . Sometimes I've known the Spirit within as a nudge, as direction, or reminder, or conscience. . . . Once especially I knew the Son—in that wonderful incident that was the turning point in my long illness. . . . But this is different . . . this must be the Father. . . . Maybe this is what the Bible means by that lovely statement—" underneath are the everlasting arms." That describes exactly what I'm feeling. . . .*

But what did this mean in relation to Peter, his ailing heart, and the emergency that threatened us? I thought it meant that everything was going to be all right, that Peter would be healed. There seemed to be nothing for which to ask God. Surely there was no need of asking for His Presence; that Presence was all around me. So my prayer took the form simply of thanking Him for the miracle that His love could be such a personal love; for His tender care of Peter and Wee Peter and me.

At 8.15 that same morning, Peter had stepped across the

boundary that divides this life from the next. Then I knew that the experience of the night before had meant something far different. I had been granted it so that when the blow fell, I might have the certainty that a loving Father had not deserted me.

Several years later I heard of someone else who had had a similar experience—Rufus Jones, the Quaker. In July, 1903, Dr Jones was on the high seas en route to Birmingham, England, to lecture. He had left his only son, Lowell, whose mother had died some years previously, at a grandmother's home in New York State.

On the night before landing in Liverpool, Dr Jones awakened about two in the morning. In his stateroom there was a strange air of sadness. He lay there wondering what it meant. Suddenly he was all but overwhelmed with a feeling of the Presence of God. Tender, illimitable love filled the room and seemed to hold Rufus Jones in warm embrace. Finally toward daybreak, he fell asleep, still not knowing the significance of what had happened.

At Liverpool a cable awaited him. Lowell had been stricken with an undiagnosed paralysis. Both breathing and speech had been affected.

But just before the end, the eleven-year-old boy had raised his arms and said with wonder in his voice, " Oh, Mother! " Then he had slipped away.

Afterwards Dr Jones said, in describing that night before Lowell's death, " It was the most extraordinary experience I have ever had."[1] Just as I had, he had felt the full power of God's consoling love even before he was aware that tragedy had struck.

After comfort, the next need of the bereaved is for the ability to distinguish between body and spirit. In this age of materialism most of us have had little practice with it.

One friend, whose husband had died six weeks before, expressed this perfectly. " My biggest need," she told

[1] Jones, Rufus, *The Luminous Trail*, Macmillan & Co. Ltd, London, 1947.

me, " is to believe that Bill is not in that grave. If I could be sure of that, I could stand the personal hurt."

I understood her difficulty. The moment I had stepped into Peter's hospital room after his death, I had known that the man I loved was no longer in the body on the bed. That was a patent, indisputable fact. I had thought I would be able to hold on to that conviction. Yet less than two weeks later, I was having difficulty with it.

One morning about that time I was awakened early by the chirping of birds in the ivy outside my bedroom window. Somewhere in that twilight zone between sleeping and waking it seemed that Peter spoke to me. " Catherine," he said clearly, " don't think of me as dead."

How could he possibly have known, I wondered, that since the brief committal service I had been unable to think of him except as dead? In imagination I saw his body lying in the receiving vault. This was a temporary arrangement until a final decision about burial could be made.

Was this really Peter speaking to me, or was it some sort of a subconscious suggestion? I did not know. I wanted to believe that my husband was still alive. But my descent to earth after the funeral had been so abrupt that doubts had come crowding in. At any rate, wherever the brief message came from, it was the precise word I needed at the moment. I could neither forget nor ignore it.

In subsequent days I found myself pondering Peter's statement. If he were still alive, then where was he? What was he doing? With no idea of the answers to those questions, how could I visualize him or think of him as alive?

That brought me to a question my every emotion cried out to have answered . . . what is my relationship to my husband now?

In marriage I had found my identity, my answer to the question, ' Who am I?' As a woman, much of my orientation in life had been centred in my relationship to one man. It is this way with most women.

Then when death cleaves the marriage partnership, the

woman left alone feels that her whole basis for living has
been washed out. She must begin all over again. . . . 'Who
am I now?'

Words that Mr. Bridge, the associate minister of our
church, had spoken at Peter Marshall's funeral service, kept
coming back to me. . . .

This morning . . . we are endeavouring to establish
a new relationship. We have known Peter Marshall
in the flesh. From now on we are to endeavour to know
him in the spirit. . . . The fellowship with him will remain
unbroken. . . .

Those had been sincere though lofty words. Were they
true? For me, the fellowship had certainly been broken.
"Till death do us part," Peter and I had vowed on our
wedding day. The fact was that death had now suddenly and
ruthlessly parted us. Across that chasm, Mr Bridge had
said that we were to build a bridge to Peter Marshall's
spirit.

I could not even imagine how to begin. Thus, I found
my prayers taking a new turn. In a childlike way I began
pleading with God for some glimpse of Peter, for some
knowledge of his new setting, of what he was doing.

The response came in a vivid dream. It was a dream with
a self-authenticating quality. Now, years later, every detail
is still clear. Of no other single dream in my life can I say
that. I also learned from it some of the details of the life
we are to lead after death that have rung true with the
testing of time.

In the dream I was allowed to visit Peter in his new setting.
First I searched for him in a large rambling house with many
rooms and airy porches. There were crowds of people about,
but Peter was not among them.

Then I sought him in the yard. Finally, at some distance,
I saw him. 'I'd recognize that characteristic gesture—that
certain toss of the head any time,' I thought, as I began

running toward him. I found myself able to run with a freedom I had not known since childhood. My body was light; my feet were sure. As I drew nearer I saw that Peter was working in a rose garden. He saw me coming and stood leaning on his spade, waiting for me.

I rushed into his arms. Laughing, he pulled me close and rubbed his nose on mine.

" I knew it was you," I said breathlessly, " by the way you tossed your head. I've come home to you."

Then, resting there in his arms, I felt something strange. Mixed with the tenderness of Peter's love was a certain restraint. He was not holding me as a lover.

My impression was that Peter was bewildered at what had happened, still surprised at his own death. I wondered if the large many-roomed house, the yard, and the rose garden comprised some small part of what the Scriptures call "heaven." I had always thought that people in heaven would be extremely happy. Peter's attitude did not quite fit that pattern.

Then I awakened. The feeling of Peter's strong arms around me lingered, and my cheeks were wet with tears.

Days later I was still pondering this strange dream. Then it began to come clear. Peter had not expected his life to end so suddenly on that gloomy Tuesday morning. He, like me, had confidently anticipated a different outcome to the problem of his damaged heart.

Five minutes after death he was essentially the same person that he had been before death. There had been no dramatic change except that he had shed his physical body as one would take off an overcoat. But the spiritual body in which he found himself—if that's what one could call it—gave him the same appearance as before.

He was being left alone to work in the rose garden to give him time to recover from his bewilderment, to find himself again. It seemed an especially thoughtful and loving touch that in the meantime he had been given work of a kind he had especially loved on earth—cultivating roses.

But it was that touch of restraint toward me in Peter's attitude about which I thought most. I asked God to tell me what was meant.

When the reply came, it was to have considerable significance for my future. A long time was to pass before I would have the courage to share this bit of insight with other widows, especially when their grief was new. For the dead are so terribly silent. The one whose sorrow is fresh longs for nothing so much as the touch of a vanished hand, the sound of a beloved voice. One in whom the wound of grief is still unhealed yearns for the assurance that, if immortality means anything at all, it means that one's love will be untampered with, will be just as it was here on earth.

Yet will the relationship between husband and wife be the same? From Christ's own lips—as recorded in the Gospel of Matthew—we are given quite another thought about this. He spoke in answer to a sardonic question put to him by a group of Sadducees, who did not believe in the resurrection of the body. They posed a case about a woman who in this life had had seven husbands, and then asked the pointedly ridiculous question: "Therefore, in the resurrection, whose wife shall she be of the seven, for they all had her?"

And Jesus answered in part:

> . . . in the resurrection they neither marry, nor are given in marriage, but are as the angels in heaven.
>
> (MATTHEW 22:30)

In other words, Christ seemed to be saying that after death the woman would not be a " wife " to any one of her former husbands. That is, there is no marriage in heaven; one's relationship even to the person one has loved on earth is different then.

Precisely what the new relationship was to be I did not then understand. I did not know what being "like the angels in heaven" would be like, and I was not at all sure I wanted to know. On the whole, I thought it a revolting idea.

Yet I guessed that part of what this meant was that the one who has stepped over into the next life still remembers every tender moment on earth, still cares what happens to those left behind, still wants to help them, still considers this as part of his continuing mission—but that the emotion of his love is intensified and purified. With this purification, as in a refiner's fire, all selfishness and self-seeking, the usual possessiveness that comes with love, and the fire and excitement of physical love—all this is consumed, gone for ever.

I remembered how often Peter had said from his pulpit, "Death has no scissors with which to cut the cords of love." Of course he had been right. Yet it is difficult for us to imagine love without possessiveness, just as it is hard for us to imagine anything more wonderful than physical love.

And yet we have the Apostle Paul, in his famous love poem (I CORINTHIANS 13) setting love at the summit of all spiritual gifts, describing for us in gladsome detail what it will be like some day. It was on this conception of a new kind of love, on a different kind of relationship with Peter, that I had to fix my mind.

In the days following my dream, it was as if God were saying to me, "Because I want you to get this matter straight from the beginning, I am trusting you now with part of this truth. Some of it you will not understand; some of it will be hard for you to take. But I shall never give you more than you can bear. You must not only trust in the truth of anything that comes directly from My Hand, but you can know that what I give will be good."

You are not really trusting God until you are trusting Him for the ultimates of life. . . . So the thought had come to me in a moment of prayer several years before. And what are the ultimates of life? Life and death, health, economic necessities, the need to find one's own place in the world, to love and to be loved.

When life has tumbled in and we sit in the wreckage—stripped, dazed, with all of life's values askew—our hearts are full of questions about these ultimates. We question ourselves. We question life. We question God. We even have moments of doubting the existence of God. . . . How could a loving God have allowed this to happen to me? How am I to get my questions answered, my values straight again?

Like every bereaved person, I too was full of questions—momentous urgent questions. . . . If there is life after death, will we know ourselves to be ourselves. . . .? Will we remember all that has happened in this earthbound life . . .? Will we recognize one another then . . .? But how can there be recognition unless we have bodies of some kind . . .? Do those in the next life know what we are doing here on earth . . .? How can heaven be happy if those who still love us can see our earthly heartaches and tragedies?

Prior to Peter's death, I had never seriously considered such questions. Now they were important. I wanted authoritative answers. If I asked other people or even read books on the subject, I would at best merely be getting other people's opinions.

Therefore, I went directly to the most authoritative source I knew—the Scriptures. And I discovered what I should have known before—that when you and I go to the Bible out of great need to learn what it has to say to us, it is then that we get real help.

My first discovery was that reading what the Bible has to say about death and immortality immediately bathes the subject in the sunlight of normalcy, lifts it out of the realm of the dark and sinister unknown. What a grave injustice we do ourselves when we fail to take advantage of this help and go on through life fearing and wondering!

Then I found out, by both direct word and by inference, that the New Testament reassures us that the next life is not only a fully conscious one with every intellectual and spiritual faculty intact, but that these faculties are heightened. . . .

> For now we see through a glass, darkly;
> but then face to face: now I know in part;
> but then shall I know even as also I am
> known. (1 CORINTHIANS 13:12)

We shall be able to remember, to think, to will, to love, to worship, and to understand so much more on the other side of the barrier of death. Our new life will be no sleeping, non-conscious, or unfeeling existence.

There are many suggestions of this in Scripture. For example, before His crucifixion, Jesus told His apostles, "But after that I am risen, I will go before you into Galilee," and He did. He met them on the shores of the Sea of Galilee (JOHN 21:1), and on the Mount of Transfiguration in Galilee to which He had directed them (MATTHEW 28:16).

After His resurrection He kept saying to His disciples, "Lo, I have told you" thus and so, referring to conversations He had had with them before His death.

In the same way, in Christ's parable of the rich man and Lazarus, He pictures both men as having a fully conscious life after death, of recollecting earthly life with no break in memory. Then there are Christ's words from the Cross. . . .

> And he [one of the thieves who was being
> crucified] said unto Jesus, Lord, remember
> me when thou comest into thy kingdom.

> And Jesus said unto him, Verily I say unto
> thee, Today shalt thou be with me in paradise.
> (LUKE 23:42-43)

Christ's words to the dying thief would have been nonsense had He not meant that after death on that very day, both He and the thief would know themselves to be themselves, would remember that they had suffered together, would recognize each other.

The Scriptures say that we shall have a spiritual body. . . .

> There is a natural body, and there is
> a spiritual body. (I CORINTHIANS 15:44)

This spiritual body will give us much the same appearance that we have had on earth, except that if imperfect or deformed or diseased, all will be made perfect. . . .

> It [the body] is sown in corruption; it is
> raised in incorruption:
> It is sown in dishonour; it is raised in
> glory: it is sown in weakness; it is
> raised in power. . . . (I CORINTHIANS 15:42-43)

Christ's resurrection body gives us some idea of the characteristics of the new body we shall have. For one thing, we shall transcend time and space barriers. . . .

> On the evening of that same day—the
> first day of the week—though the disciples
> had gathered within closed doors for fear of
> the Jews, Jesus entered and stood among them,
> saying "Peace be with you!"
>
> So saying he showed them his hands and his
> side; and when the disciples saw the Lord,
> they rejoiced. . . . (JOHN 20:19-20)[2]

There were appearances and reappearances. . . .

After that, he was seen of above five hundred

2 Moffatt, James, *The Bible: A New Translation*, Hodder & Stoughton, London, 1935.

> brethren at once; of whom the greater part
> remain unto this present, but some are fallen
> asleep. . . .   (I CORINTHIANS 15 :16)

As to my question about how much those in the next life
know of what is going on in this one, a passage like Hebrews
12:1 would seem to be conclusive. It speaks of a long list
of the heroes of the faith—Abraham, Joseph, Moses, Gideon,
Samson, David, all men who had long ago passed off the
stage of history. Then the passage goes on . . .

> Therefore, with all this host of witnesses
> encircling us we must . . . run our appointed
> course with steadiness. . . .
>   (MOFFATT; HEBREWS 12:1)

But we have been taught that life with Christ is a happy
life. Could it be happy if earthly sorrows are known in
heaven? The Bible seems to be silent on this point, perhaps
because we mortals have no basis on which to understand.

But several thoughts came to me. Perhaps those on the
other side see the end from the beginning, and that makes
all the difference. Moreover, we know that the higher we
rise spiritually, the more unselfish we become; the more
we are concerned about others, the more we long to minister
to them. Therefore, is it reasonable to suppose that those
in the next life would be more preoccupied with their own
ease and happiness and less concerned about those they love
and have left behind than we are? I don't think so. In fact,
happiness—especially in the next life—could scarcely come
from oblivion, inactivity, lack of knowledge, or selfishness.

Lastly, I found that the Bible does not ignore sorrow as
a fact of human experience. Some of the loveliest words of
Scripture are for the sore of heart. . . .

> I will not leave you comfortless. . . .
>   (JOHN 14:18)

> . . . he hath sent me to bind up the broken-
> hearted . . . to appoint unto them that mourn
> in Zion, to give unto them beauty for
> ashes, the oil of joy for mourning, the
> garment of praise for the spirit of
> heaviness. . . .   (ISAIAH 61 : 1, 3)

I was surprised to find that a great number of promises
in the Bible are directed specifically to widows, and to children who have had to part with one or both parents.

Yet here is an odd thing—the word "widower" does
not occur anywhere in the Bible. Perhaps this means that
the patriarchs and others who had lost a wife did not stay
unmarried long enough even to get the word "widower"
in the concordance! Or is this just another example of the
realism of the Bible? The status of women during those
centuries made their widowhood a precarious existence. Surely
they needed God's help. . . .

> The Lord will destroy the house of the
> proud; but he will establish the border
> of the widow.   (PROVERBS 15 : 25)

> Yet leave to me your orphans, I will
> save them; let your widows trust to me.
>
>   (MOFFATT; JEREMIAH 49 : 11)

> . . . . thou art the helper of the friendless.
> (PSALTER OF THE BOOK OF COMMON PRAYER 10 : 16)

And this, the most beautiful promise of all. . . .

> Fear not . . . thou shalt not remember the
> reproach of thy widowhood any more . . . for the
> Lord hath called thee as a woman forsaken
> and grieved in spirit . . . with great mercies
> will I gather thee. . . .

And all thy children shall be taught of the
Lord; and great shall be the peace of thy
children. . . .   (ISAIAH 54:4, 6, 7, 13)

The help for the bereaved to be found in the Scriptures is
indeed limitless.

It is not part of God's plan that the sorrowing should languish
in self-pity. I had learned this long before in an entirely
different connection.

During the years when I was in bed with tuberculosis, a
good friend came one day to the Manse to call. Anita was
a tall, stately woman, always exquisitely dressed, who was
married to one of Washington's wealthiest men. She was
also a spirited woman with the gift of a rare discernment.

On this particular afternoon, Anita did not walk into my
bedroom—she marched in. She did not even bother to sit
down.

Standing in the middle of the big room, she cleared
her throat as for a speech. Her eyes were sparking as much
light as the star sapphire on her right hand. . . . " Catherine,
you've been on my mind for days. I've been tempted to
feel sorry for you. I'll be damned if I'll feel sorry for you.
Forgive the language, but I feel just that vehemently about
it.

" Pity wouldn't help you a bit. Besides, why should I pity
you? You have all you need—the strength and the guidance
of God—"

Her words were flung at me like ice water striking my face.
I might have resented them, but I didn't. In fact, when I had
recovered from the first shock of the ice water, I felt
exhilarated, even as Anita had hoped I would.

My thoughts raced . . . All right, don't pity me, then.
. . . See if I care! I'll show you! Enough of this weakness
and secluded life. . . . I'm going to get out of here. And
courage mounted in me like mercury rising in a thermometer in
the sun.

From that visit I learned something important about comfort. During those years, I had hundreds of sickroom calls. Yet that one of Anita's towers like a mountain-top above the others.

Just so, God's way of comforting us towers over man's usual methods. In our attempts to console one another, softness and sympathy loom large. If we think of comfort in terms of a word picture, it would be that of soothing and placating a hurt child: "There now, don't cry." It is true that these qualities, particularly in the very beginning, are present in God's help for his hurt and bereaved children, because He is a God of love. Indeed it was that kind of comfort that I had received from Him in those early morning hours before Peter's death.

Yet now I found the other side of God's comfort. Anita had been close to the truth. God's comfort doesn't walk on tiptoe as in a sickroom; it marches. There is steel at its backbone. It is a bugle call for reinforcements. It makes us remember that the word " comfort " is derived from the word *fortis*—which means strong.

God comforts us with strength by adding resources. His way is not to whittle down the problem but to build up the resources.

I opened my New Testament and found there exactly that concept of comfort. . . .

> Discipline always seems for the time to be
> a thing of pain, not of joy; but those who
> are trained by it reap the fruit of it
> afterwards. . . .
>
> So up with your listless hands! Strengthen
> your weak knees! And make straight paths for
> Your feet . . .
>
> (MOFFATT; HEBREWS 12:11-12)

This made me remember a recurring note in Peter Marshall's

preaching, a note that at the time I had resented, had secretly
refused to accept. . . .

> There are in our day some philosophies growing
> in popularity that teach the attractive idea
> that God always reveals His love by removing the
> distasteful and the unpleasant from our lives.
>
> But where in the Bible do you find support
> for this attractive and alluring concept?
> Certainly not from the lips of Jesus.
>
> On the contrary you are startled to discover how
> plainly and bluntly Christ told His disciples to
> expect trouble.

" In the world ye shall have tribulation.
　But be of good cheer." That is His message.
" Be of good cheer . . . I have overcome the world."

No . . . Christians are not spared. . . .
The calamities of life knock on their door
　　with the same startling swiftness . . .
and the rain falls on the just
　　as well as the unjust.

There is no hint or intimation anywhere in the Gospel
that they who follow Him shall never hunger
　　　　or be out of work
　　　　or be left alone.

No, there is no hint of such immunity. . . .
But there is the promise of something far better . . .
　the promise of deliverance . . .
not from these things . . . but in these things.

There is an air of reality about the Gospel. . . .

It is not a fairy tale in which Cinderella's rags
 are changed into the robes of a queen . . .
but rather a promise in which Cinderella in her rags
 becomes more queenly.

And now in my own dark hour, I found in God's dealing
with me exactly that note of stringent reality about which
Peter had so often preached. God was asking me to grow
up, to take a new step toward maturity.

This element of stringency, a firmness which the New
Testament calls "God's discipline" or "chastening," was
a big factor in the next lesson God provided in my progress
out of grief. I needed a grip on my relationship with God
Himself, a new understanding based not on sentimentality
but on bedrock truth, and just as my relationship with God
was made clear-cut would other relationships, including
the new one with Peter, fall into place. And without this
kind of clarity, God would not have been able to take me
along those rocky paths that lead from the Valley of the
Shadow.

On the second of February, nine days after Peter's new life
had begun, I had awakened early and was propped up in
bed reading. Out of the early morning quietness a voice from
beyond my own thoughts seemed to speak. It had about it the
quiet authority, the take-it-or-leave-it unforgettable quality that
in my experience the voice of God in the depths of the spirit
always has.

"Apparently," the message went, "you did not really mean
what you said to Me."

I knew perfectly well what the statement meant. It referred
to a specific promise I had made to God one anxious afternoon of the previous September.

At that time, four months before my husband's death,
I had known that only a miracle could save Peter. The first
attack of coronary thrombosis had come out of the blue
to an ostensibly healthy and vigorous man of forty-three. This
had been a severe attack, necessitating a five-month convalescence.

For the first few months after his return to an active ministry, Peter had been cautious. But he was a man in whom there was an incalculable zest for life. Writing sermons, preaching, pastoral calling, his Senate duties, playing games with small groups of friends, stamp collecting, all that went into being an avid baseball fan, fishing, gardening—no day held enough hours for all he wanted to include in it.

In the year following his heart attack, I tried reasoning with my husband in an effort to change some of those habits. Our talks together were always calm and rational. Peter did not mean to be unreasonable. He had no desire to flirt with death, and he well knew the danger of over-activity. It was just that in the end his zest for life submerged all caution. Nothing ever really changed as a result of our talks.

Many of Peter's friends also entered into a loving conspiracy with me to try to get him to take more time off from his church and Senate duties. Often even these efforts boomeranged; he was all too inclined to take too strenuously what was meant to be relaxation.

In late June of 1947 one of the church officers, George Hildebrand, prevailed on Peter to join a group going on a deep-sea fishing trip to the Chesapeake. He not only went, but took Peter John along. It was an all-male party.

The day was warm and the sunshine on the blue waters of the Bay inviting. What's more, the fish just weren't biting.

" That water sure looks good," Mr Hildebrand commented, grinning. Then he walked to the bow of the boat, stripped, and dived in.

" Man overboard!" someone yelled. The rest of the party promptly stripped and dived overboard too.

Peter, in the water at 200 yards from the boat, was vigorously waving his arms and shouting exuberantly to the others, " Look at the invalid!"

The skipper was vastly amused by the turn the fishing party had taken. He cupped his hands to his mouth and shouted at Peter, " Boy, if only folks at the church could see their minister now!"

I remember that Mr Hildebrand, in telling me of this day with Peter, had added, "What on earth are you going to do with a man like that?"

The truth was that none of us knew what to do with a man like that.

Peter's attitude toward his own condition had not been improved by the fact that, after recovery from his first attack, there had apparently been no further difficulty. He had not been bothered with any shortness of breath, dizziness, swelling ankles, or arm pains. Some mild symptoms might actually have been a blessing, since he would then have been warned of the true situation. Without any symptoms, he was undertaking more and more.

As out-of-town speaking engagements piled up, I battled my increasing fear for Peter. The second year after his attack, he had made ten such trips; the next year, it had been twenty. And these had been sandwiched in between a constant round of in-town duties, talks, and appearances.

Peter knew full well what my conviction was: that it was only out of the framework of a keen sense of stewardship of his body that we could ask God to take care of his heart. I was not at all convinced that all the speaking engagements came from God.

But all my human efforts had failed to curb my husband's whirlwind pace. I therefore concluded that either Peter's heart would have to be healed so completely that there would be no need of curtailing activities, or his temperament and whole approach to life would have to be changed. Only God could do either.

Nothing seemed left for me but a complete relinquishment of the man I loved to his Lord. It was with this that I wrestled on that September afternoon in Washington, fear and trust struggling for mastery. Then thoughts began flowing to me. It was as if God were speaking in a quiet inner voice in my heart. I wrote down the thoughts:

Trust Me—that's all. Are you really willing to put your

future into My hands? Are you willing to tell Me to manage it as I please? Let yourself trust Peter to Me. It's like trusting yourself to the water . . . It seems dangerous to you to trust him to Me in that way, because you will feel that if anything is done, you must do it. Do you really think that you can do more than the Lord of the Universe? You have scarcely realised your presumption. . . .

Trust—trust—trust—the word had been used over and over. It was indeed like trusting myself to the water. My feeling was like that of a child poised and teetering on the end of a high diving board.

At that time out of the depths of my fear I had made an act of giving Peter's future and mine to God for Him to do with as He pleased. The relinquishment had been as complete as I was able to make it. It had been made in my will, even as my every human emotion had cried out against it.

Practically speaking, this meant that my attitude hereafter would be " hands off." I would stop battling Peter's out-of-town speaking engagements, his ever-increasing Washington commitments. A few days later I told Peter about this decision, and he had been pleased. He was happy to have an end to the conflict between us.

But now, months later, God was saying, " Apparently you did not really mean that relinquishment that day. . . ." The clear implication seemed to be that God had taken the transaction between us, made in my will, at face value, as a covenant, as He always does a promise made to Him by one of His children. I was now being challenged. My bluff was being called. Did I really believe in the existence of God enough to believe that when I spoke to Him, He heard; when I made Him a promise, He accepted it and held me to it?

Had not God promised us that " He healeth the broken in heart, and bindeth up their wounds "? (PSALM 147:3).

This was the God of love speaking. But God's sternness in dealing with me did not seem quite like love. Yet I thought of the many times when it had taken far more love for me to hold my son to what I knew was right than to indulge him. This is the kind of firmness that is even a proof of love. The Bible tells us this too.

> For the Lord disciplines the man he loves. . . .
> It is for discipline that you have to endure.
> God is treating you as sons; for where is the
> son who is not disciplined by his father?
> (MOFFATT; HEBREWS 12:6-7)

Now that I understood how God regarded a promise, I remembered a technique that Peter had often used. It was the method of finding a specific promise in the Bible that applied to one's need and then claiming it as a definite transaction between an individual and his Lord. A favourite quotation had often been on Peter's lips at such a time of claiming. He had written it on the flyleaf of his Bible. It was a statement of David Livingstone, the Scottish missionary and explorer of Africa. . . . " It is a word of a Gentleman of the most sacred and strictest honour, and there is an end on't."

In precisely that spirit I claimed for myself and the son whom Peter and I had brought into the world, this promise:

> And we know that all things [the things we understand and those we do not; the joyous things and the tragic] work together for good to them that love God, to them who are the called according to his promise.
> (ROMANS 8:28)

I did not yet know where the comfort of God's strength was leading me or what I was to do with it. Yet during those days, God was steadily asking me not to fear where Truth would lead. Truth may be painful, but it makes us free. God is not interested in coddling us, but in liberating us for further creativity, for the new life that we are forced to make.

Much of this was hard to swallow, but in its stringency lay its self-authentication. Though my private world had tumbled in, God was still in His Universe.

Did I actually think that the God who had led Peter Marshall from Scotland to the United States, from the Tube Mill to the seminary, who had provided for all his needs when he had no money, who had saved his life on several occasions when it could so easily have been lost—would that God have deserted Peter in death and me in life? Even through the veil of occasional doubt, I knew better.

CHAPTER 3

Turn Around and Face Today

At the Manse out on Cathedral Avenue, papers covered with columns of figures were spread all over the dining-room table. Three men had come to spend an evening with me to talk about business matters. One of them, a young insurance agent, had everything neatly worked out in a series of graph columns.

" It's by far the wisest course to spread Dr Marshall's insurance over a reasonably long period of time. After all, it will be eight years before Peter John goes to college." He was using a well-sharpened pencil as a pointer to the skyscraper-looking graphs.

" Doing it that way, how much income will we have each month?" I asked.

" One hundred and seventy-one dollars a month for the first eight years. That includes Dr Marshall's pension from the Presbyterian Ministers' Fund. Then the monthly income will take a drop."

One of the other men, an engineer, said, frowning, " You're really going to have to be realistic about this, Catherine. That won't be enough to include keeping the car. You should probably sell it."

" And you're scarcely strong enough to hold down a real job," the other friend added. " By the way, what could you do job-wise?"

I began to have a suffocating feeling. " I—I don't quite know. I married right out of college—have only a bachelor of arts degree—not even teacher training. I couldn't be a secretary. I don't know shorthand and I use only my own brand of hunt and peck on the typewriter."

The three men were troubled. They had all been Peter's close friends and were genuinely fond of me. As a breadearning widow, they looked on me as an especially poor risk . . . no vocational training and twelve years in which Peter had sheltered me from business affairs.

" I don't think you realize how desperate your situation is," one friend insisted. " One hundred and seventy-one dollars a month in Washington just won't do it, won't even cover the bare necessities. You're going to have to cut living expenses to the bone."

" And I do think you are going to have to sell the Cape Cod cottage quickly," another added.

The three men left that night the more distressed because they realized that they had failed to convince me that I was now in actual financial straits. They were right. There was in me a stubborn refusal to accept their gloomy forecasts—financial or otherwise.

Yet I had not argued with them, because facts and figures had substantiated all they had said. There the facts were, down on paper in neat columns. How could figures lie? Yet somehow I felt that they did lie.

Alone in my room I stared out of the window into the moonlight shining on swaying treetops. Suddenly I was back in a crowded little tearoom on Connecticut Avenue. It had been a Sunday just after church. My husband, Wee Peter, and I had been having dinner together with Alma Deane Fuller, whom we always called " A. D." She was the friend who, during my illness in 1944, had given up a job on Capitol Hill to keep house for us.

Over our main course, we three adults had been discussing life insurance. A. D. and I had been taking a very lofty ivory-towerlike attitude. Peter had seemed amused at us and a trifle annoyed. But partly he had only himself to blame, because we were still in the clouds where the high-flying phrases of his Sunday morning sermon had tossed us.

" We say we trust God. But then most people go right out and buy as much life insurance as they can afford," I remembered A. D. had said. " Their actions belie their words."

Peter's knife had been poised over a slice of lamb. " But

don't you think God wants us to have a sense of responsibility about our families? Surely business common sense and thrift are right?"

I knew well that this had been a fair representation of my husband's point of view. After all he was a Scotsman! But throughout our married life I had always resented our going without so many things in order to buy insurance.

"Think of George Müller, the founder of the British orphanage system in the last century," I said in a hopelessly stuffy fashion. "The way he sold all his household goods and trusted God for all resources for himself and his hundreds of orphans. Don't you really think, Peter, that if a husband were to die, God could be trusted to supply what a widow needs?"

"I'm not George Müller," Peter had said gloomily.

If a husband were to die. . . . The words were echoing in my mind now. It had happened. How could I have been so glib about it? How had I managed to go through life acting as if I and those I loved were somehow immune to the universal experience of death?

I didn't know. But I recognized how grateful I was now for the love and caring behind Peter's insurance, inadequate though it might be. At least it gave me some feeling of security, something on which to fall back.

And yet, I thought, A. D. and I were right too. There's something missing from the sombre picture the men painted tonight.

The moonlight was almost white. One brilliant star above the treetops winked like a solitaire. Suddenly, standing there at the window, I knew what the missing factor was. My three friends who had meant to be so kind, had reckoned without God.

So now I was up against one of those poignant ultimates of life—the economic one. Immediately I decided on my course. I would refuse to be destitute. I would simply not give in to poverty.

When soon after Peter's death I had claimed that promise that " all things," even those that appeared to be stark tragedy, would " work together for good," I had not expected the good to be limited to spiritual blessing. Working together for good, I had reasoned, would surely be good as we human beings understand it. It must also include the money for rent and clothes and food. A sense of adventure had crept in; it would be exciting to see how God would help me to work out my problems.

But how did one go about trusting God for money? It was to take weeks—indeed years—to get the full answer to that question. But when His grand design for me was revealed in its entirety, it answered so much more than my bare economic needs; indeed, it led me to a new career, a new life.

How He managed it seems like a fairy tale. In my wildest dreams I could never have anticipated what happened. God's plans for His children are always so much more bountiful than our best-laid plans for ourselves. To put this in the classic language of the Apostle Paul, I found for myself that God is still

> . . . able to do exceeding abundantly
> above all that we ask or think. . . .
>
> (EPHESIANS 3 :20)

In the meantime, however, I was having to work through the practical problems that always follow a death in the family. For these, I was not presented with any celestial road map of the way out for the lacerated of heart. Road maps are not God's usual way. I had to learn the path step by step, incident by incident, as I lived it out.

As I look back, certain principles applicable to any bereaved person emerge from those experiences. For one thing, no major decisions should be made in the weeks immdiately following a death in the family. One has experienced deep shock. There must be a recovery from this condition before it is possible to have a firm basis for making proper decisions.

For example, I was fortunate in not having to make any immediate decision as to where my son and I were going to live when we moved out of the Manse, the house that the church provides for its minister and his family. This was a spacious ten-room brick house in Washington's Cleveland Park area.

Six days after their minister's death, I received an official letter from the board of trustees of the church:

Dear Catherine:

We want you to know that the Manse is available to you until such time as it is required by the church. . . . Your continuing there will help maintain ties that were so sadly broken these past few days. . . . We hope that you will be agreeable to this suggestion.

We do not know of course when the church will again require the Manse, but we will notify you at least three months in advance or sooner if possible. . . .

God bless you and keep you—and little Peter.

Very sincerely,
s/ Charles A. Stott
Secretary, Board of Trustees

This generosity on the part of the officers of the church proved important to me in several ways. Familiar, beloved, and once-shared possessions helped to soothe a sore and wounded spirit. All five seascapes on the walls of the bedroom that Peter and I had shared together; the well-worn games in the game closet; the same familiar few blocks in which to walk our cocker Jeff—somehow, this was for me balm rather than added hurt. It gave a sense of continuity to life.

Sometimes one's friends are inclined to feel that a swift change of setting will hasten the healing process. For most people, and for me in particular, this would have been running away. Changing my setting, even removing all physical reminders of my old life, would have left me still the same person.

Next I found that the mechanics connected with death are actually helpful, though they may seem hard. In the very beginning one may feel that these practical activities are an intrusion into grief. The bereaved person looks out on the world with new eyes, marvelling that other people on the streets and in the shops are going on about their business as if nothing has happened, as if everything were just the same.

For a time, during busy hours, one can forget the pain. Then a tiny thing—anything—brings it flooding back. Opening a drawer and coming across a small Christmas card written in a well-known hand; the sight of a distant figure walking down the street, wearing the same kind of slouch hat . . . and suddenly the old stabbing pain is back.

How is it possible, one wonders at such a time, to force oneself to sort out dresser and desk drawers; to dispose of clothes that a loved person will never need again; to listen attentively to the reading of a will; to write cheques; to put one's mind to business and insurance details; to acknowledge somehow the dozens of telephone calls and personal messages, the loving offerings of food brought to one's home, the funeral flowers, the notes of sympathy?

The truth is that the empty heart needs work for the hands to do. I learned that there is a certain therapy in these necessary mechanics, as on the day when I had to go down to the church to clean out Peter's office, so that his successor might have the use of it.

I remember shutting the door and sitting down at his big desk. The flavour of Peter's personality was all around me. Two walls of the room were covered with his theological books. On one wall was a group of etchings—all seascapes —and in their midst was one fine lithograph of the American flag.

From the top of one of the bookcases a bust of Sir Walter Scott stared down at me. Beside the bust was a careful detailed model of John Knox's house in Edinburgh. . . . Once Peter and I had walked hand in hand up those narrow steps into that queer little mediæval house.

I pulled out drawer after drawer of the desk, preparatory to emptying their contents into cartons. Each drawer was in meticulous order. On the desk before me was Peter's date book. Oddly enough, stuck in the front of it was a newspaper clipping entitled, " Would You Live a Longer Life If You Could?"

The book was open to the week of January 23. It was to have been a busy week. Peter's neat, very British handwriting informed me that on Tuesday, January 25, he was to have had lunch with his friend, Harold Folk. That night he was to have presided over the St Andrews Society Burns Night Dinner at the Mayflower Hotel. Instead, that evening someone else had given a eulogy for Peter Marshall. How rudely death had interrupted every plan!

I sat there, half believing that at any moment I would hear Peter's firm step on the stone stairs, see him appear in the doorway, hear him asking me, " What in t'thunder are you doing at my desk . . .?"

Yet it was fortunate that there was not time for me to sit there and turn my dreams into mourning. Work was waiting. The books had to be taken off the shelves, packed into boxes; a decision made about what was to be done with them. The etchings had to be taken down and packed, the desk drawers emptied. As my hands worked that day, there was a strange sweet easing of my pain.

A third lesson I learned was not to try to hide or steel the emotions. Trying to force oneself to be brave will not heal the heart. This is hard for men who are trained to believe that tears are the sign of weakness. But it is for ever true that when the storms of life are savage, it is the tree that bends with the wind that survives. Tensing up, walling up the heart, damming up the tears, will inevitably mean trouble later on, perhaps years later. There is emotional release in letting the tears flow.

This principle I discovered for myself on the Sunday following Peter's death. The question was . . . would I attend church as usual, sit in my customary spot at the New York Avenue Presbyterian Church? The church was of all places most uniquely connected with Peter Marshall. I knew that my absence on that particular Sunday would be completely understood, indeed expected. Yet an instinct told me to take head-on the business of facing up to life.

That Sunday, as I sat in the pastor's pew, someone else stood in Peter's pulpit. Peter had been there preaching powerfully and poignantly seven days before; he would never be there again. Through the entire service, tears overflowed swiftly and silently. I was as embarrassed as anyone would have been, but I was powerless to stop them. I saturated handkerchief after handkerchief.

Sitting beside me was a Chinese woman. In that silent communion that lies at the heart of the Christian fellowship, her compassionate and understanding spirit reached out to enfold me. Words were not necessary. I did not know who she was, I had never seen her before; yet I knew that she understood. The silent message of her love got through to me.

Going to the church that Sunday was one of the hardest things I had ever done, but postponing it would only have made it harder.

Subsequently, I had to follow this same pattern in returning to our Cape Cod cottage and to other places where Peter and I had been happy together. But each step forward I found a little easier than the step before.

I was learning, as I lived it out, still another step in the healing of the broken-hearted. That was the therapy to be found in keeping one's heart wide open to other people.

When a deep injury to the spirit has been sustained, the tendency of the sorrowing is to shut the heart and bar the door lest hurt be heaped upon hurt. Yet isolation is not the way toward mental health. Of course, the newly bereaved person needs periods of stabilizing solitude both for physical rest and to gain perspective. But in between times, he needs to accept as fully as he can the love that flows from friends and family.

The truth is that this spontaneous sympathy from other human beings is only a small token, a pale reflection of the great heart of a compassionate and understanding Father. And God's love is always a healing love. The one who—almost involuntarily—shuts his heart against his friends and lets bitterness creep in is, in a tragic way, insulating himself against that re-energizing love of God.

When my own private crisis came, I certainly knew nothing about the way out of grief. I had never heard that psychologists and psychiatrists consider the matter of establishing new patterns of interaction with other human beings one of the most important laws for recovery. Conversely, they feel that to turn inwards upon oneself at such a time places the bereaved person in danger of emotional suicide.

Part of the miracle of God's direction was the fact that I was enabled immediately after my husband's death to open my heart wider than ever before. For the temperament with which I was born was that of a deep reserve; I was not naturally endowed with the gregariousness and outgoingness of my husband.

Yet on that fateful January 25, within an hour after I had returned home from the hospital, friends began dropping in. One couple who had been particularly fond of Peter, sought me out in my bedroom. I remember that the young wife, her cheeks wet with tears, threw her arms around my neck. "Darling," she cried, "I love you so. We're going to have to stick awfully close together now."

My split-second choice at that moment was made by instinct—not in my conscious mind at all. It was a choice of whether or not I would merely politely tolerate such an overflowing exuberance of love—or really accept it.

In yielding to it, I found a oneness with all human beings, a kinship with all suffering in the world—an authentic glimpse of the kingdom of God actually at work in a given community.

And so I opened wide the door of the Manse. People came with warm handclasps and tear-filled eyes. They brought what they knew best how to make—soup, chicken salad, baked ham, angel food cake, custard, chess pie. And somehow, they found in our home an atmosphere that dried their eyes, that made them loath to leave. The gap of Peter's absence was sorely felt. But the love that flowed like a great tidal wave through the Christian community that was our church family, blessed us all.

The telegrams and notes piled up. They were not only from people of our own faith or nationality. There was, for example, a card saying that money had been given to the Jewish National Fund for a tree to be planted in memory of Peter Marshall; a letter from a friend in the British House of Commons; an official letter of sympathy from the Sisterhood of Adas Israel. Where love is, God is. And He was definitely there in this overflowing human compassion.

Yet it is God alone who can finally heal the broken-hearted. Grief is a real wound, a mutilation, a gaping hole in the human spirit. After all, the ties that bind parents to children, brothers to sisters, and husbands to wives are the deepest of bonds, as real as love is real. Some beloved person has been wrested, torn bodily from one's life. The hurt is none the less real because the family physician cannot probe it; Christ alone is physician to the spirit.

Because we no longer have Christ's physical presence with us, our connection with Him must be through prayer. " Ye have not because ye ask not," our Bible tells us in a shaft of pin-pointed sunlight on the question of prayer. Yet there have been times in my life when I have been unable to ask for myself in an effective way. At such times I have been filled with fear or undue emotional stress. I was in just that condition in the weeks immediately following Peter's death.

That was why I sought out a friend, Rebecca Beard, and asked her to claim for me through prayer the help I needed. Rebecca was a physician who, several years before, had given up her practice to experiment with techniques of spiritual therapy. She was to be in Washington only briefly visiting friends, but she had agreed to see me.

On the afternoon of my appointment, she received me in a small upstairs room in the home where she was a guest. Dr Beard was a big, grey-haired woman whose outstanding characteristic was motherliness.

Soon I was pouring out my heart to her—all the hurt of it, the ineptness and the fear I felt about facing the future alone. As during the church service on the Sunday following Peter's death, the tears flowed copiously.

My friend just let me talk. She said little. She attempted no pat explanation of Peter's death; offered no advice for the future. Sometimes there were tears in her own eyes as she watched me.

Then finally, when the well of my emotion was dry, she said quietly, " As a doctor, I have only one remedy to offer for what ails you. Let's talk to Christ about it."

Her prayer was a simple heartfelt claiming of Christ's promise to bind up the broken-hearted. Then when she had finished, without another word she gathered me into her ample arms. That afternoon it was as if a gentle Hand were laid on my heart.

From that moment the healing began somewhere in the depths of my being. As a wound that heals from the inside out, so the restoration was to come, gently, almost imperceptibly.

I know now that this specific asking for the touch of the Great Physician for my torn emotions was an invaluable step. I also do not believe that this prayer would have had the same effectiveness had it not been made in my presence. Nor can it be as effective if it is a casual prayer, a sort of overflow of good will on the part of one's friends. The prayer for the healing of the broken-hearted must be an appointed prayer act—at a definite time and in a definite place. This is a responsibility that clergymen and Christian friends need to undertake for the sorrowing; they fail us if they do not.

Since death had invaded our family circle, God had been working in me at the level of the spirit. I might have anticipated that. But now, for me as for everyone who is called to walk this trail, God's hand became wonderfully apparent in the world of practical men and external affairs.

CHAPTER 4

Work for the Hands to Do

Peter Marshall had done a lot of preaching in his lifetime
about a practical God who cares about us human beings as
individuals, who " knows folks' names," who is quite as
capable of guiding us in the market-place as in the cathedral.

I had thought this a fine thesis and had accepted it as
true. But now came the acid test; an economic imperative
stared me in the face. Already I had claimed God's promise
that He would bring " good " for my son and me out of
the seeming tragedy of Peter's early death. I had assumed
that this would have to include economic good, else it would
be for the angels—not for widows on this earth. But
the next question haunted me . . . what was the right job?
I did not know. After all, I had had no experience with any
work outside my own home. How could I start all over?

Actually the answer to my prayer was already on the way.
A design was in the process of being woven, though I was
still too close to the warp and the woof to see the pattern.

Only seven days after Peter had begun his new life a
friend had written to me:

. . . the following matter is on my heart and a like
sentiment has come my way from various people in the
congregation. Please forgive me for bringing it up so
soon. I, along with thousands, earnestly hope that you
will see to it that Peter's sermons, his prayers in the
Senate and from his pulpit, will be published. . . .
Spiritual insight pungently expressed is necessary food.
I'm certain you understand that. Old clichés no longer
mean much. Ours is a virile faith needing virile expression. Peter was blessed with such an ability. . . .

A few days later I wrote a former professor of mine at Agnes Scott College, the head of the English department:

Dear Dr Hayes:

Thank you so much for your wonderful letter written the day after Peter died. . . .

I have no idea now what the future holds or what it is God wants me to do. I just hope that I can take this great crisis in my life in the spirit of an adventure, or as Peter expressed it once in a sermon to young people—as going out "under sealed orders."

In the immediate future there is the task of answering between five and six hundred letters, and all through them there runs a request for the publication of some of Peter's sermons. Already I have had overtures from two of the smaller publishing houses. Editing the sermons would probably be of real help to me, in that the work would give me something constructive to think about in the days ahead. I do also have a deep conviction that they should be given to the world. . . .

That conviction grew with each day that passed. It was buttressed by a ground-swell of requests from friends, parishioners, and people whom I did not even know. It almost seemed as if everyone who had heard Peter from the pulpit and had been stirred by his preaching now wanted a book of his sermons so that his words would not be lost to them.

About this time, one of our friends who was similarly enthusiastic was in New York on business. One morning as he was walking down Fifth Avenue he noticed a glass door with the words on it:

THE FLEMING H. REVELL COMPANY
BOOK PUBLISHERS SINCE 1870
NEW YORK, LONDON, GLASGOW

On an impulse he walked in and asked to see the president of the company. The ensuing conversation was soon reflected in a letter to me from that official, William Barbour. He suggested that he or his chief editor, Frank Mead, come to Washington to confer with me about publishing a book of Dr Marshall's sermons. He came himself on February 27 and took back with him to New York some of the sermon manuscripts. Enthusiastic comments from his editor followed quickly in the mail and then an offer to publish.

Putting the Revell Company's definite proposition alongside the two that had already come to me, I had to decide between placing the sermon manuscripts in the hands of a church denominational publisher or letting the New York house handle them. The decision was not difficult. Though I had great respect for the work of the church publishers, I knew that their distribution was necessarily limited, indeed all but confined to church groups. I believed that Peter's work had a wider appeal.

I could not forget all these messages of sympathy and heart-felt letters that had come to me after Peter's death from people of a great variety of religious denominations, Jewish and Catholic as well as Protestant.

And, I reasoned, had not one of my husband's favourite texts been the words of Christ : " I came not to call the pious, but the irreligious "? It was the average man or woman beset with problems who stood on the fringe of the church, or altogether outside it, whom Peter had always yearned to reach. His sermons had so often been slanted towards the average man. So the decision was made; I turned my face to New York.

The notation on my little green date book for Tuesday evening, March 8, read : " Work on sermons." Peter had left some six hundred sermon manuscripts filed in three worn, black-and-white cardboard boxes. The proposed book could include at the most only twenty to twenty-five. The problem was . . . on what basis should I go about trying to choose from the six hundred?

It appeared that my immediate task was to sort the sermon manuscripts into types—Biblical word pictures; those that dealt with modern problems: worry, tension, fear, sex, divorce, health, death; special-occasion sermons; those Peter had preached during World War II; those with a national or patriotic flavour. Some of my contemporaries at the church had offered to help with the reading and sorting.

On that March evening, six of us were sitting around the dining-room table at the Manse surrounded by a sea of papers. The manuscripts were spread in little piles on the table, even on the floor. We found it hard to make progress with the sorting, because first one and then another of us would keep intruding on the silent reading.

"Just listen to this," someone would say. "You've got to hear this!"

> It is the same old brass of wilful
> disobedience coated with the chromium
> of the twentieth century.

"And this. . . ."

> Christianity began as good news. . . .
> We have permitted it to be diluted
> into good advice.

"Oh—but listen to this. . . ."

> In Mathematics, one-half plus one-half
> equals one. . . .
> But this formula does not hold in the
> Church.
> We cannot add two half Christians to
> make one effective Christian.

We could not even be sad about our task, because Peter's humour and exuberance for life kept flashing out at us from the typed pages. Suddenly, someone would begin chuckling. . . .

> Modern politics appear to be related to the
> art of conjuring. . . .
> The skeletons in the nation's cupboard are
> replaced by the rabbits that come out of the
> politicians' hats.

Then another would interrupt, " Do you remember this statement that Peter made during the war years?"

> Evil may be triumphant for a moment.
> But it is always deprived of the results
> of its triumph.
> The conquests of their armies to date are
> hollow victories. . . .
> The flies have conquered the flypaper.

And another one:

> There are some good people who feel that they
> are the custodians of the public morals, the kind
> of person who will come to you—in love, of
> course—and say, " I want to tell you some
> things for your own good."

Yes, I remembered. How often Peter had said to me, " If there's anything I can't *stand* it's people seeking me out to tell me something ' for my own good.' "

Along with the cardboard boxes of sermon manuscripts was a long, slim wooden box filled with Peter's sermons which had been printed locally in pamphlet form. Soon after we had come to Washington the project had been initiated by a group of the church women. The pamphlets had sold for ten cents. During all the war years, they had been distributed free to any serviceman or woman who had asked to be on the mailing list. Consequently, the distribution had been global.

Tom Wharton, a packaging engineer and a deacon in our church, was one of those present that night to help us sort sermons. He seemed to be in a quiet and thoughtful mood. I noticed that he kept pulling printed sermons out of the wooden box and comparing them with typed manuscripts.

All at once he said, "Catherine, would you come here a minute? I want you to see something."

I crossed to the other side of the table, and Tom patted the chair beside him. "Sit down here and look at these two passages side by side."

The pamphlet sermons had been printed in the usual way prose is set in type. . . .

There is a silent uplifting impartation from the Absolute. It does us good to look up and see Orion driving his hunting dogs across the Zenith, or Andromeda shaking out her tresses over limitless space.

It enlarges the self to have studied great architecture; to know great art—the reds of Titian, the sunsets of Turner, the seas of Winslow Homer; to have felt the spell of epic heroisms; to have swung to the rhythmic pulse of Homer; to have known the tenderness of Francis of Assisi . . . to have heard the whirring of angels' wings in Milton's "Paradise Lost"; to have been swept away on the streams of Beethoven's music; to engrave the prologue to the Gospel of John on the heart; and to march with the majestic affirmations of the Nicene Creed.

It does something inside a man. It stretches him mentally, stirs him morally, inspires him spiritually. . . .

But the typed sermons looked different, more alive, almost like poetry . . .

There is a silent uplifting impartation from the Absolute.
It does us good to look up and see
Orion driving his hunting dogs across the Zenith . . .
   or Andromeda shaking out her tresses over limitless space.

It enlarges the self to have studied great architecture . . .
to know great art—the reds of Titian . . .
                        the sunsets of Turner . . .
                  the seas of Winslow Homer . . .

To have felt the spell of epic heroisms . . .
   to have swung to the rhythmic pulse of Homer . . .
      to have known the tenderness of Francis of Assisi . . .

To have heard the whirring of angels' wings in Milton's
   " Paradise Lost " . . .
to have been swept away on the streams of Beethoven's
music . . .

To engrave the prologue to the Gospel of John on the
heart . . .
to march with the majestic affirmations of the Nicene
Creed.

It does something inside a man.
It stretches him mentally . . .
   stirs him morally . . .
      inspires him spiritually . . .

Years before, as a young minister, Peter had been intrigued by the sermon manuscripts of Dr Trevor Mordecai of Birmingham, Alabama, a Welshman whose preaching he had much admired. Dr Mordecai had devised a way of typing his sermons that had assisted him in delivery. Peter had found the idea useful and had adapted it to suit his own needs, carefully teaching each succeeding secretary exactly how he wanted his sermons typed.

The device had two chief characteristics: all lists or series of nouns, adjectives, phrases, or even descriptive clauses were typed in stair-step fashion; and every new sentence was typed flush with the left hand margin rather than being indented.

" The typewritten copies are certainly much easier to read than the printed ones," I had to admit.

"Exactly! Catherine, I feel sure that the book should be printed just as Peter had his sermons typed. In fact, I'd even go so far as to say that doing them any other way would be unfair to Peter."

Such an idea had never once occurred to me. "Let me have time to think it over," I told Tom. "If you're right about this—well—I'll have to come to it in my own way, slowly."

This would, I felt sure, have been just as new an idea to Peter. His stair-step device had been solely for his own use in delivering the sermons orally. Certainly he had never thought of having the pamphlets printed in anything but the time-tested manner. In fact, the publication of the individual sermons was as far as he had ever been willing to go. Steadily, he had resisted the thought of any book publication. " I'm a preacher," had been his viewpoint, " not an author or an editor."

Over the next few days I made more comparisons of passages set up in the two ways and had to acknowledge that in the typed format the words seemed to come alive on the page. The reader caught the emphasis of word or clause that the speaker's voice had supplied in oral delivery. The extra amount of white space made reading a pleasure. And the phrases and clauses fell readily into the rhythm implicit in their meanings. In comparison, the printed pamphlet sermons seemed dry reading.

But how, I wondered, would an old and conservative publishing house receive the suggestion of such a novel typography for the proposed book?

I need not have feared; the event was not in my hands. During this period I was haunted by the feeling that I was treading a path that had been planned for me; that I was acting out a role, the script for which I had not written; that I was walking through doors that another Hand opened for me. I know now that this was no idle imagining. Time after time circumstances and events proved it so.

For one thing, just the right persons began to appear on my horizon at the precise moment they were needed. This was to prove such a stimulating adventure in the manner of human relationships that I had little time to be lonely or to do any nursing of my grief.

On Sunday, March 20, for instance, while I was still mulling over Tom's idea, I had dinner at the apartment of two career girls. One of them, Sara Leslie, a tall, willowy brunette who had come to Washington from Tennessee, had had full apprenticeship training as a printer. I was amazed to learn that this attractive and very feminine girl had successfully invaded such a predominantly masculine field. In addition, she had a great love for all that goes into the making of books.

After dinner that day, the conversation turned to the possibility of printing Dr Marshall's sermons in the unusual format. Miss Leslie was intrigued, eager to help. Through her interest I was brought into contact with a specialist in the field, a man in the publications division of the State Department. He, in turn, introduced me to one of Washington's top-flight designers of fine books, Warren Ferris, then chief typographer at the Government Printing Office.

I soon learned that the Government Printing Office does far more than print Congressmen's speeches and turn out agricultural pamphlets. There, in his office, Mr. Ferris showed me several of the beautiful special editions he had designed. He even set out to introduce me to some of the mysteries of the art of bookmaking. He analysed books for me, discussing the matter of type faces, the quality, weight, and rag content of the paper, the leading, and the margins. I found all of this exciting. And my excitement increased when, as soon as Mr Ferris had seen a sampling of Peter's sermon manuscript, he had endorsed Tom's idea as an inspired one.

Meanwhile, day by day my astonishment grew at what was happening to me. What had I done to deserve such adventure? But then I realized that no one of us ever deserves God's blessings. This realization was, in turn, the soil out of which my gratitude could grow. And gratitude is a sure cure for self-pity—that special illness at the heart of all grief.

Soon, at the fitting moment, there came the next right person on my horizon. I had a visit from our Cape Cod neighbours, the Robert Ingrahams. Earlier in his life, Bob Ingraham had been associated with a publishing business. He now volunteered to assemble for me some opinions of New York professionals in the printing field. That, Bob felt, would give me some expert backing for the coming interview with my publisher.

There was still another link in the chain that was being forged. My conference with Frank Mead, of the Revell Company, was to be on April 21. On the evening of April 20, I had a surprise visit from Glen Clark, an author, teacher, and old friend who had given me much spiritual inspiration in the past. Dr Clark appeared at my door with a timing so precise that only God could have engineered it.

He was a short, stocky man with a fringe of grey hair around a shiny bald spot. His face wore such a benign expression that it gave him a somewhat beatific air.

Since I had had a few hours' notice of his visit, I had prepared several parallel passages from Peter's sermons for him—some in the stair-step manner, some with the usual paragraphing.

My guest sat on the davenport, leaning over the typed sheet and sermon manuscripts spread out on the coffee table

Curled up in a red leather chair near-by, I was fascinated watching his plump, expressive hands as they hovered over the papers.

Finally he straightened up, leaned back in an attitude of complete relaxation.

"You've made the right decision all right."

"But will Dr Mead think so? He comes tomorrow, you know."

Dr Clark leaned back even further, became more contemplative. He put the tips of his forefingers together in a precise gesture, as we used to as children when we playfully made a church, the steeple, and the people with our hands. . . . "Here's one thing—I'm sure of it. These parallel passages you've typed out are too short. I didn't get the full impact of how readable Peter's stuff is until I looked at some full sermons. Don't show Dr Mead fragments tomorrow. Show him complete sermons—typed ones, and the same ones printed in the pamphlets."

Somehow Glenn Clark's visit supplied me with the one thing I had most needed—the conviction that the book project about to be undertaken was God's venture—not mine. Only on the solid foundation of that conviction could my house of faith for the success of the project be built. After that a sense of destiny about what I was doing never deserted me.

Before Dr Clark left that night, he and I had eased the task ahead with prayer. As a result, what happened the next day shamed my small faith. What I had anticipated as being arduous—convincing the publisher to try a radical experiment in design—did not turn out to be difficult at all The interference had already been run; the work already done.

Dr Mead listened carefully. He was in a reflective mood, semed to be absorbed in what I was saying.

"I'll have to check all this with my associates," he said, on leaving. "I can promise you, however, that we shall give the whole matter careful consideration. I'll let you know in a few days."

With more than a little trepidation, I awaited the verdict. Within the week it came. The Revell Company would be willing to publish the book of sermons in Dr Marshall's unusual typography. This proved to be an important decision —more so than it may seem. It was to play a large part in the success of the book of sermons.

On June 9, I wrote to Mr Barbour: " If we can handle this book right, I believe that it is going to hit the country like a ton of bricks. . ."

What Mr Barbour did not know was that I intended personally to see to it that the book was handled right. Like many a sheltered woman making her initial sally into professional life, I went at it hammer and tongs. Certain masculine traits I had not known I possessed came trooping to the forefront to take command. They submerged moderation, balance, and perspective.

I thought that I should keep my fingers on every decision, large and small. Thereafter, until the book was off the presses, someone at the Revell Company received a letter or a phone call from me almost every day. Having acquired a smattering of knowledge from Mr Ferris and Miss Leslie, I worked it overtime.

The type face for the book . . . what would they think of setting it in Granjon or Baskerville? Would they please set up sample pages in both type faces and submit them to me?

And what about the size of the book? They had suggested 8 x 5⅜. I would prefer 9 x 6.

As if this weren't enough, I then went into the matter of the quality of paper to be used. Would they agree to Crocker Burbank " Saturn," wove or laid, 50 pound or its equivalent?

I even suggested a special colour for the binding, for all the world as if this were a room I was decorating.

In retrospect, I know that I went to unbelievable lengths. . . . I had a bright idea concerning the breaks in the chapters. Why not use a tiny stylised thistle design? It would be unusual and appropriate, would give an added fillip—like a bunch of artificial carrots on a woman's hat. Promptly, I had an artist friend submit a sample drawing to my defenceless publisher.

I would stop at nothing. I believed in the book, and everything in connection with it had to be perfect. I developed some ideas about advertising copy and wrote some samples. Would the men at the Revell Company like to see them?

Undoubtedly they would not! Yet they bit their tongues, summoned all their patience and diplomacy, and replied that of course they would. Perhaps they sensed something unusual about the situation. Or perhaps a bit of my enthusiasm and sense of destiny about the book was catching.

They even let me do the proof-reading. I insisted on it! Nor would I do it in less than the best professional manner.

For this task the help of five friends was enlisted. One evening they came to the Manse, and we paired off into three couples—one pair in the living-room, one in the sun parlour, one upstairs.

Then two sets of the galley proofs were divided into thirds. Each couple was given two copies of their third. One read aloud while the other person held a set of galleys and followed it silently, watching for printing errors. We found a few. But now I know that the proof-reader at the Revell Company would undoubtedly have found them anyway!

There remained one big question . . . who was to write the introduction to *Mr Jones, Meet the Master*? This gave me my chance to exercise a little diplomacy. The publisher felt that some prominent friend of Peter's, like Senator Kenneth Wherry or Senator Arthur Vandenberg, should be invited to write it. I refused to believe that Peter's material needed " a name " to launch it. Anyway, I wanted to write it myself.

I knew full well that the men of the Revell Company looked on me as a fond wife without either writing talent or experience, who was bitten with somewhat grandiose ideas. They had a point. I had given them a hard time indeed!

"Would you be willing," I cautiously asked Dr Mead, "to let me put on paper the introduction I have in mind? Then if you like it—fine. If you don't—then you can go ahead with other plans. That way you can't lose."

Probably out of weariness, Dr Mead agreed. One night, sitting propped up in bed, the bed and floor awash with papers, I wrote a seven-page sketch of Peter Marshall, the man, as I had known him. I called it "Here Is Peter Marshall" and sent it off to New York.

Two days later Mr. Barbour telephoned me. There was undisguised surprise in his voice. "Three of us here have read your introduction. We didn't think you—that is, well, I mean, it couldn't be more perfect. Of course we want to use it."

Those seven pages of original writing turned out to be my foot in the door of the publishing world.

Meanwhile, as the editing work on the sermons progressed, I began to experience the deep satisfaction and inner contentment known only to those who have found the right vocational spot for them. It was not that my adjustment to bereavement was complete. In fact, it had scarcely begun. The great void was still there. Half of my personality was still missing.

But in spite of that, it was as if I had come home to my own element. The work of editing, the virility of the sermon material itself, the intuitive knowledge that people near and far would find these messages food for hunger of the spirit, the flashing facets of Peter's personality that shone from the typewritten pages, the feel of paper and pencil in my hands —every bit of it was pure joy. I knew then that many things in the years gone by had been meant as preparation for this task.

During the long quiet days of work on the editing of the manuscripts while Peter John was in school, many a scene out of the past came to my mind all unbidden. . . . My minister father's book-lined study, always the heart of our home, with our friends, the books, lining the walls floor to ceiling on two sides. It was here that our family always gathered in the evening. While mother darned or mended, and father read, we three children did our lessons. I could still see us sprawling full length on the floor; or sitting at one of the pull-out leaves of father's roll-top desks; or in the old leather Morris chair within arm's reach of the *Book of Knowledge*, Stoddard's *Lectures*, the *Harvard Classics*, and McLaren's *Commentaries on the Scriptures*.

Our parents never insisted that we go off by ourselves to our upstairs bedrooms in order to concentrate on our home-work. We did our reading and writing right there in father's study, and the warmth and happiness of the room became a part of the studying itself. Father and mother always near . . . the typewriter on its home-made stand . . . the ferns . . the bird-cage with a singing canary . . . mother's rolls raising on the hot-air register . . . the shades drawn against the winter night. It was here that I started several novels in notebooks that I bought for two for five cents. None progressed beyond the second or third chapters—but my dreams did.

It was in that room that a love for books, for reading them, handling them, collecting them, even the dream of someday writing them, became part of my life.

A romanticist to the core, I delighted in *Just David,* the Gene Stratton-Porter books, and every one of the fourteen volumes of the *Little Colonel* series. On the other hand, I tried the *Elsie Dinsmore* books and found them abhorrent. Perhaps I discovered Elsie when I was too old for her. At any rate, I remember finding her brand of sticky piety offen-sive.

I remembered other moments of childhood. I saw myself standing at my bedroom window looking out, but not seeing the mountain just across the valley. For at that instant a dream was being planted in my heart. I had just finished reading a very girlish book, *Emily of New Moon.* The

heroine wanted to be a writer; I had just discovered that
I did, too. The words I had read haunted me. . . .

" Emily, *why* do you want to write? Give me your
reason."

" I just *love* to write."

" A better reason—but not enough—not enough. Tell
me this—if you knew you would be poor as a church
mouse all your life—if you knew you'd never have a line
published—would you still go on writing—*would* you?"

" Of course I would," said Emily disdainfully. " Why,
I *have* to write—I can't help it. . . . I've just *got* to."

" Oh—then, I'd waste my breath giving advice at all.
If it's *in* you to climb you must—there are those who
must lift their eyes to the hills—they can't breathe
properly in the valleys. . . . Go on—climb! . . ."

At sunset Emily sat in the lookout room. It was
flooded with soft splendor. Outside in sky and trees,
were delicate tintings and aerial sounds. . . .[1]

Outside my window was only my mountain. But Emily
had left her mark.

Soon after that came college and the assignment of my
first freshman term paper. The English teacher had given
us a choice of several writers to study. I had chosen the
British girl, Katherine Mansfield—had chosen better than
I knew. After reading several volumes of her short stories,
I came upon her *Journal*. Every line of it had spoken to
something buried deep in me and had awakened a response.
The way Katherine Mansfield had fingered life, rolled it
on her tongue, so that not one, but a dozen taste buds tasted
it. . . . She had been as a little girl with guileless round eyes,
saying, " See! New shoes!"

The term paper had become incidental. Preparing for it was
not work, it was the breath of life. I had discovered pure

[1] Montgomery, L. M., *Emily of New Moon*, Harrap, London,
1923.

gold and revelled in it. Into a notebook I copied lines from the *Journal* that I especially liked:

> She was the same through and through. You could go on cutting slice after slice and you knew you would never light upon a plum or a cherry or even a piece of peel. . . .

> Throttling, strangling by the throat a helpless, exhausted little black silk bag. . . .

> I keep walking and walking round the letter, treading on my toes and with my tail in the air; I don't know where to settle. There's so much to say. . . .

> The sun has gone in; it's beginning to thunder. There's a little bird on a tree outside this window not so much singing as sharpening a note. He's getting a very fine point on it. . . .[2]

Immediately I had decided that I too would keep a journal —only I would tell no one about it. It would be no mere girlhood diary of daily happenings. In it I would try to put down as accurately and memorably as I could my deepest feelings and reactions to life. A great earnestness about this had carried me through four years and several volumes.

Later on in college I had heard Edna St Vincent Millay spend an evening reading her own poetry, and with her had "looked on beauty bare." Thereafter, for the remainder of my college days I had concentrated on writing poetry; mostly sonnets and sonnet sequences. The poetry club had taken me under its wing. My English teachers had been patiently helpful in criticising what I had written, though they were continually urging me not to take myself quite so seriously.

[2] Murry, J. Middleton (ed.), *Journal of Katherine Mansfield*, Constable, London, 1927.

Graduation and marriage had followed. Peter and I had taken a delayed honeymoon trip to his home in Scotland. The next Christmas I had presented him with a neatly typed *Journal of a Trip to Scotland*, bound in a handsome leather notebook. The writing had been a labour of love and was for his eyes alone. Like Emily of New Moon, I had to keep on writing.

Three years after our son was born, the doctors had discovered that I had an early case of tuberculosis. The treatment was enforced bed rest twenty-four hours a day. My immediate physical world narrowed to the big front bedroom of the Manse. It was a pleasant airy room with five windows, some of them framed with ivy, and the pale yellow wallpaper made it seem always sun-drenched. There was the mahogany Chippendale furniture on which Peter and I had splurged, the deep-blue rugs, the seascapes on the walls —some original watercolours and two Turner reproductions.

Soon I had worked out a daily schedule—meal-times on a tray; hours of absolute rest in morning and afternoon; time set aside for reading; periods of playing quiet bedside games with Peter John. I asked that a little bookcase be moved close to my bed so that writing materials would be near. Propped up in bed again, I took pencil in hand and was soon filling notebook after notebook.

This period turned into a time of soul searching, of repeated attempts to evaluate the meaning of human life in general and mine in particular.

One of the books which had helped me at that time had spoken of the value of probing to find one's precise dreams, one's positive longings—" the soul's sincere desires." The author had suggested that the uncovering of these real hungers —not those superficially laid on by society, but the ones God Himself has planted within each of us—could then become the foundation for prayers sure to be answered. The reasoning behind this had been explained in a simple but impressive analogy—that when God plants the pattern of an oak tree in an acorn, it is certainly His will that the acorn become an oak.

I had understood the value of such an urge toward self-discovery. Among other " soul sincere desires " set down in my notebook at that time had been this one:

> To become a writer who will make real contribution to my generation and to the world.

Into the notebook also went my attempt to analyse and sift my motives in order to find out whether or not this desire to be a writer was truly a God-given dream:

> If I *thought* I wanted to be a writer, but what I really wanted was fame or money, or even that my name would not die after me, then this would be false desire. But such I do not believe to be the case.
>
> The writer dream must be part of my pattern because I've had it since I was a little girl, when my dreams must still have been pretty fresh, as from the hand of God.
>
> I have always loved ideas. I enjoy trying to express them in as accurate and beautiful a way as possible. It gives me real soul satisfaction. . . .

After pondering all this for many days, necessarily long quiet days, I had felt that this dream passed the most honest tests I could devise. And just about that time two verses in the New Testament had leaped up at me as though written in fire:

> And this is the confidence that we have in
> him, that if we ask anything according to his
> will he heareth us:
> And if we know that he hear us, whatsoever
> we ask, we know that we have the petitions that
> we desired of him.   (I JOHN 5:14, 15)

If then the wish to be a writer was God's will for me, He would hear me when I asked for the help I needed; and, if He heard, then this wish would some day be granted. So I had sent that particular dream wafting back toward heaven with the confident awareness that He had already heard.

To it, I had added a petition equally important. It was that God would thereafter send into my life the right persons at the right time for the implementation of these dreams. Never before had I thought to ask for this blessing of the right friends.

But it had finally dawned on me that life in our day is no longer possible on a lone-wolf basis; that one can succeed in any field only as he is a success with the people in that field. I had reasoned that, in order for God's will to be done in the lives of men and women in our time, there would have to be a coming together—a juxtaposition of ideas, persons, and events at the propitious moment.

Having tossed these two dreams heavenward, I had then climbed out of my sick-bed, walked off, and left them. Always thereafter, the wish for their fulfilment had been in me somewhere just under the surface. Yet I had not consciously thought of them again for more than four years.

Yes, it had all been preparation—unplanned on my part. Thinking back on this, I was to discover a thread running through my life, never quite disappearing, never quite grasped until the present moment. But now strange events had placed the pencil back in my hands. Not only that, but since Peter's death I had watched unfolding before my wondering eyes that very juxtaposition of ideas, persons, and events about which I had prayed four years before.

Consequently, there was in me a profound gratitude to God and to other people. To God, because I was keenly aware of His firm hand on the life situation of one widow. To other human beings, because their warmth and outgoing generosity had enabled them to be the channels for some of God's will for me—whether they were aware of being channels or not.

Through this series of events, which I could never have engineered myself, I learned several unforgettable lessons.

I learned that money is really only ideas that had been converted into a form usable in the exchange markets of earth. The corollary is that these ideas must be of a kind that will be of some help to other people. Then the way to pray for economic resources is to ask God for new and creative ideas that will make a contribution—no matter how small—to lighten the tasks or illumine the lives of one's contemporaries.

Thus I learned something of what the Kingdom of God (or the "Kingdom of Right Relationships") really means. ". . . for we are members one of another," the Scriptures tell us. Certainly we are! I discovered for myself the inter-relatedness of all human life; how dependent we are on others for success in any line of work; what an unpayable debt we owe to other men—living and dead.

CHAPTER 5

Open the Hands

It is amazing how a word can have definite emotional tone. Thus, for a long time after Peter's death, the word " widow " was despicable to me—as loathsome as had been the word " tuberculosis " in the early days of my bout with that disease.

To such ridiculous lengths did I carry this reaction that I even disliked to open an envelope addressed to " Mrs. Catherine Marshall." To my emotional-saturated reasoning, the writer of the letter might just as well have printed WIDOW in large capital letters after the name. And how I hated to see the descriptive term, " The late Peter Marshall. . . ." What a silly way of putting it, I thought. Late? Late to what?

Such violent reactions were of course sure signs that I was still not facing reality. For the truth was that I was a widow, whether or not I was willing to accept and wear the various tags appended to widowhood.

My resentment about this took varying forms. One evening one of my husband's stamp-collector friends came to the Manse to call. The man had once been widowed, but had re-married. On the table was the manuscript of the introduction to the book of sermons on which I had been working. My guest was interested in it and was soon picking up some of the typewritten pages to scan them. . . .

Our home reflected Peter's taste. . . . The boy who had grown up near the Firth of Forth, and who at four-teen had run away to join the Royal Navy, never got over his passion for the sea. So we ended up with four sea-scapes in the living room, two large ones in the dining room, five in our bedroom and a few others scattered throughout the house.

His taste in colour was just as decided. Fortunately, we were equally fond of blue. . . .[1]

Suddenly the friend put his finger on the page to keep his place and commented : " I suppose it's just as well that you are getting down details like this so soon. But you won't be talking or writing like this for long. Time not only heals, it erases practically everything. You'll be surprised how quickly your life with Peter will come to seem like a dream, or as if it happened to somebody else in another lifetime."

Then he went back to reading the manuscript while I stood there, stunned, saying nothing, feeling only revulsion for the idea he had just expressed. I certainly did not want time just to form a protective scab over a still grievous painful area. Surely, I thought, it would be far better for the wound to heal cleanly, really heal from the inside out.

And though intellectually I knew that I couldn't live in memories, still who would want Time to come with a big eraser and obliterate every tender remembrance? Doesn't the future always have to be built on the past? Wouldn't real healing mean that what had gone before—the flaws in the weaving as well as the most perfect and treasured parts of the design—would all eventually fall into proper place? In that way and that alone, I thought, could the fabric of my life be all of one piece.

There was as yet no such unity in me. There were even indications that my subconscious mind was still stubbornly refusing to accept the fact of Peter's death.

At intervals of weeks or even months I kept having one recurring dream. It had variations of details, but always the same agonising theme. In the dream, my husband was not dead ; he and I were estranged. There would follow all the emotional torment over such a separation. Always in the dream, there would be a reaching out for Peter, an effort to

[1] Marshall, Peter, *Mr Jones, Meet the Master*, pp. 10-11, London Fontana, 1964.

contact him, to win him back. Then when the anguish was at its height, I would awaken.

The first two times a dream had followed this pattern, I had quickly dismissed it from my mind as being just a dream, of no consequence whatever. But then, when it came to be repeated over and over, like a phonograph needle caught in the groove of a defective record, I began to wonder how to deal with it. I reasoned that my subconscious mind was being forced to come up with some explanation of why Peter was no longer by my side. This was apparently the explanation it had hit upon. I kept wishing that the needle would find another groove, or else get on with the next theme.

But I was not yet ready to leave that particular emotional plateau. The dream recurred often that spring. In particular I remember one afternoon. . . . I had lain down for a nap. Some little girls were playing hopscotch on the sidewalk in front of our house. There was the repeated thud of rocks being dropped by the children on the pavement outside, the sound of a window shade flapping in a lazy breeze from a half-open window. I dozed—then after a while the clatter of a rock half awakened me. My mind, struggling back to consciousness, had sent the message . . . *Something is wrong —terribly wrong.* Suddenly my heartbeat speeded up, started racing. Fear made my mouth dry. Then as I shook off sleep a little more . . . *Peter is gone. . . . No, he can't be. This is just a bad dream, a nightmare. It will pass.*

I forced myself back to full consciousness and wearily turned over in bed. This was a way of waking that was becoming all too familiar. The stabbing awareness, the nightmare quality of a half-remembered fact, the pain that touches every nerve-ending—all this is well known to those who have experienced shock. I lay there trying to assimilate the situation, trying to force myself to look squarely at the facts.

But what is the truth anyway? I wondered. And suddenly I thought that I recognised Truth in that intuitive way

that it has flashed into the human mind since the beginning
of time. . . . *Perhaps it is this life that is the dream. One of
these days I shall wake up and find Peter again and know
that he's not dead at all. Then I shall be what the world
calls dead myself. But meantime, how am I going to force
my subconscious mind to accept the fact that my husband is
gone?*

Part of the answer to that question came through finding
that my recovery from these emotional wounds was in direct
proportion to my ability to stop steeling myself against them
and begin accepting the pain inherent in my personal loss.
I now know that the healing process for any of life's frustrations, disappointments, and sorrows can begin the moment
we stop resisting them. Tightly closed hands are not in a
position to receive anything—not even comfort. It matters
little whether they are hands clenched in rebellion or just
piteously trying to clutch the past.

Just as women have discovered that the pain of childbirth
becomes supportable as they stop resisting it, open their
total being to it, and relax—so it is with emotional pain.
The cup of grief is heavy and it holds a bitter brew. But
one can at least take the cup with both hands and put it
to one's lips at intervals, then, for a while, turn to something else. Somehow the cup becomes lighter, a little more
bearable, its contents less bitter each time the cup is voluntarily grasped.

The voluntary part is important. That is the point at which
the human will enters the picture. I cannot believe that the
mere passage of time will effect a permanent and healthy
repair. Time helps, but there must also be the co-operation
of the will actively assenting to the growth necessary to accomplish the healing.

In the months following Peter's death, events conspired to
bring me to just that point of assent. Many of them were
entirely ordinary and practical. I was not going to be
allowed to take off on any flights of unreality which I might

mistakenly have called "spiritual." The business matters confronting me were calculated to bring me back to earth with a thud.

Peter—to the surprise of all who had known him well—had left no will. Apparently he had thought that since he possessed little other than insurance, making me the sole beneficiary of that took care of the situation. If only he had known how much it left to be taken care of! Yet in thinking a will unimportant for those with a small or moderate estate, my husband was not unusual. I learned later that an estimated 70 per cent of American property owners die intestate.

The first business complication developed when Peter's bank account (we did not have a joint one) was frozen. Consequently, no money could be drawn out even for funeral expenses or immediate needs. All the insurance policies were in a strong box at the bank. That box was immediately sealed by the bank under the Internal Revenue Department's regulations. It took three weeks of cutting red tape before even the insurance agent could get into the strong box "to initiate the collection of death proceeds," as the insurance term has it.

Then I learned that, under District of Columbia law, when a man dies without a will, after all the debts are paid, his widow receives one-third of his estate, his child or children, two-thirds. It was necessary for me to appear in probate court to post an expensive bond and to be made administratrix of Peter's affairs. Everything thereafter came under the jurisdiction of this court. Not even funeral expenses, doctor or hospital bills, nor ordinary household expenses could be paid without the court's approval.

Following this, some of my husband's possessions had to be appraised—his car, his stamp collection, a few power tools. The appraisal of something like a stamp collection is a highly technical matter. It has to be handled by men who know the value of stamps. But all appraisers had either to be appointed by the probate court or specifically approved by them. Such appraisal can be time-consuming, a great deal of trouble, and costly.

I found it hard to keep my mind on these business affairs, because my heart kept intruding. The businessmen who were trying to help me would have found many of my thoughts highly irrelevant. . . . How much are a few British colonial stamps worth? So many dollars and cents? A hundred hours of pure pleasure?

I could see Peter bending over the stamp books spread out on a card-table in our living room. To him the stamps were not just stamps. They were cargo ships on their way to romantic, far-flung places—Antigua . . . Barbados . . . the Cayman Islands . . . Grenada . . . Montserrat . . . Trinidad. The very names were music . . .! The commemorative issues were some of history's most dramatic moments. . . . The stamps were beautiful. . . . "Catherine, take a look at this new St Kitts's ultramarine on blue violet—and this magenta, this carmine rose. . . ."

And sermons? How could sermons be appraised? So much lift and lilt to the human spirit? So much bowing down of the heart in adoration to its Maker? Yet the sermon manuscripts were an integral part of the estate and the next thing that had to be appraised. Obviously how much they were worth commercially was anyone's guess. But even after some arbitrary value had been placed on them, then what disposition was to be made of them? It took several lawyers a little over four months to figure out that one.

It seemed that almost daily, everywhere I turned, legal proof of my husband's death was required. Finally I had a whole sheaf of photostats of his death certificate made. To the uninitiated in grief, this may seem like a small matter. Still it scarcely has a soothing effect on the bereaved.

Then came the day when I had to reappear in probate court to be made Peter John's guardian. Since then, I have been required to give a detailed financial accounting of my guardianship to the court each year. This will go on until my son comes of age. Each year the account figures must be sworn to before a notary public. Each year a fee must be paid to the office of register of wills for the accounting.

The amount of cash in Peter's bank account at the time of his death was not large. Most of this had been given to us as a gift on the occasion of our tenth anniversary at the New York Avenue Presbyterian Church, and had been meant to pay part of our expenses for a trip abroad. Yet by the time the final accounting is made to the probate court, almost every cent of that original sum will have been drained away in legal and court costs.

When I discovered the amazing amount of red tape involved even with such a small estate, I almost ran to a lawyer to get help in making a will of my own. Not only that, but I began urging my parents and close friends to consider the same move. Though in my case there was little to leave anyone, I reasoned that the tiny sum involved in making a will might some day save many times that amount in fees for dealing with quite unnecessary legal technicalities.

Of course, Peter had no idea of all of this. Yet some of his close friends were lawyers. And often he himself had been called on to help the recently bereaved in practical matters as well as spiritual ones. I marvelled that he had never even once encountered some other widow entangled in the same difficulties with which I was wrestling.

Another question of a different kind still waited to be decided. It was the decision as to where Peter would be buried. He and I had owned no cemetery plot. Thus when the suggestion had been made that I make temporary use of a receiving vault, I had gratefully agreed.

Part of the relief I felt about postponing this decision was based on emotion so faulty that even at the time I would have been ashamed to discuss it with anyone. Yet I know now that many sorrowing individuals experience the same set of feelings.

Peter had died in January. Climatically that month is usually the worst time of year in the District of Columbia. In the first shock of my grief every shred of emotion in me protested the thought of placing that beloved body—no matter how tenderly—in the wet, icy ground. I would stand at my bedroom windows watching the cold slanting rain falling on the bare bony branches of the trees, and feel relieved that Peter's body was in a dry receiving vault.

Then at the next moment shame at such a thought would pour through me. I understood quite well that reason did not prompt it. I also knew that it dishonoured the faith I held. Had I not known for a certainty, standing in the hospital room that morning of January 25, that the man I loved was no longer in the shell of a body? Of course I had. It was an obvious fact—indisputable. Yet during the weeks that followed, very wisely I refrained from lashing myself too severely about feelings I could not help. Intuitively I sensed that to castigate myself would merely have been to make matters worse. My ragged emotions needed gentleness, time to catch up.

Part of the shame I felt about these emotions came from the realization that I was but reflecting clearly the trend of my time in its pagan attitude toward death. We give lip service in this regard to what we like to believe is a compassionate Christian approach. We think that if some Scripture is read and some prayers said at a funeral or interment service, this proves that we are Christian. Actually, if we Americans really believed that the spirit of the person is not extinguished by death, we could not then view death as unmitigated tragedy.

We reveal our hand in many small ways. One of them is in our accepted social and medical mores concerning last illnesses. The patient must not be told the true seriousness of his case. Undoubtedly there are instances where this withholding of information is justified and desirable. On the whole, physicians in our day are compassionate, dedicated men who make such decisions thoughtfully.

But have we become so soft and cowardly in the twentieth century that we will go to any extreme to avoid facing up to

the transition called "death"? Are we not really handing
the grossest insult imaginable to the dying when we assume
that they have not the spiritual or character resources to
handle this test courageously and victoriously?

Every modern person would shrink from the idea of
maudlin, falsely sentimental, overdramatic death-bed scenes
of the type described in many a nineteenth-century novel. But
then some of life's experiences, among them birth and death,
are dramatic. And isn't it possible that, by going to the
opposite extreme and forcing most humans to spend their
last moments on this lovely earth in ignorance of what is
happening or in a drugged coma, we are denying them and
ourselves one of life's most precious experiences?

At the very least, we are witholding from them the
privilege of making their last plans in their own way, of
saying the things most deeply in their hearts and minds to
those whom they are leaving behind. On occasion, it has
seemed to me at once ludicrous and tragic to watch husband
and wife—each of whom knew that the parting called "death"
was imminent—keeping up a pretence, each trying to deceive
the other, letting only falsely cheery superficialities pass the
lips when the heart was about to burst with things waiting to
be shared.

I have even heard one physician say after it was all over,
"I wish now that my wife and I had talked things out.
Looking back, our pretence seems stupid, childish. We
fooled no one—not even each other."

The same acting out of our feeling that death is the end
of everything—the final disaster—is shown in our morbid
concern with the cast-off body left behind.

We are assured in the words of the New Testament that

. . . it is the spirit that quickeneth; the flesh profiteth
nothing.   (JOHN 6:63)

If we believed that, then we would know that consciousness

is life; that when the living spirit that looked out through the windows of the eyes has gone, what is left behind is like the chrysalis which the winged moth has abandoned. Therefore, we would find it foolish to make a fetish of the deserted chrysalis—to try to preserve it indefinitely, to spend huge sums of money on it.

Yet out of the science of the preservation of that non-profitable flesh, of which the Apostle John wrote, has been built the huge business of the modern mortician, who deals in profits of a very different kind from any the first-century writer had in mind.

The idea of burying the human body at all originated with primitive pagan man. He believed in some sort of life after death, but subscribed to the superstition that it would be the same sort of material life that he had known on this earth. Hence food, weapons, tools, and money were carefully buried with his dead.

The emphasis on glorifying and trying to immortalize the body reached its height under the ancient Egyptians. Their greatest monuments, the pyramids, were houses for the dead, and embalming was regarded as a fine art during the time of the Pharaohs. For long centuries after that, it was scarcely practised at all. In the Western Hemisphere it was revived by a certain Dr Thomas Holmes, a Brooklyn druggist, during Civil War days. Since that time the preparation of the dead for burial has been made increasingly elaborate and expensive. Now it is carried to such an extreme that the services of beauticians and hairdressers are often required in addition to the work of the mortician.

Peter who, like all clergymen, had seen a lot of funerals, felt strongly that we moderns are on the wrong track in our death customs. He had incisive words to say about it:

> Why, in our day, do we shun the fact of death?
> We try so hard to disguise it.
> We are so stupid about it.

We rouge the cheeks of the corpse and dress
it up in its best suit.
And then we say with ridiculous gravity,
" How natural he looks . . ." as if there
could be anything natural about a corpse!

We, who call ourselves Christians, act in
a very pagan way.
We gaze upon the lifeless, human clay. . . .
We touch the cold cheek. . . .
We line up to pass by the casket and " view
   the remains " as the stupid phrase has it,
as if we had never heard of the soul and never
understood what personality is.
If this thing called death were some
leprous calamity that befell only a few
of us. . . .
If it were something that could be avoided,
then our conspiracy of silence concerning
it might make some sense.

But it is life's great and perhaps its only
   certainty. . . .

This conspiracy to disguise death goes on in a score of
ways. There are, for instance, the expressions we use . . .
the dead are just " asleep"; they have only " gone away."

Then custom dictates that the body must be preserved as
long as possible. To this end, there must be a costly moisture-
proof casket or metal vault. Even the grave must be camou-
flaged. A canopy of artificial grass is laid over it during the
graveside rites.

Much of this is done in an honest attempt to smooth the
way of the bereaved. There is, however, danger in these
deceptive techniques. The danger is that facts not faced,
but pushed down below the level of conscious dealing with
them, tend toward creating real emotional difficulties.

This pagan concern with the body is reflected in the fact that steadily, year by year, the cost of dying is rising as funeral customs become more and more elaborate.

Many times undue and unfair pressure is even brought to bear on the sorrowing, emotionally vulnerable members of the family to force them to purchase an expensive casket, cemetery plot, niche in a mausoleum, or a tombstone which they can ill afford.

We in the United States are now spending more on burials than on seeing that our babies are brought into the world safely, more on funerals than we do on hospitals. The figure has now risen to more than 500 million dollars a year. On top of that, we spend another 60 million dollars on funeral flowers.

One modern nation finally became sufficiently alarmed about the gigantic waste implicit in funeral flowers to do something about it. Since 1921, Sweden has had a national organization called the " Flower Fund." Money that would be spent for flowers is sent instead as a memorial to the Flower Fund. This money is then used for modern housing developments for needy old people. The fund has long been a gigantic success, shedding light and joy into the lives of the still living.

Our own nation has no such plan. Still there is an increasing trend toward making a contribution to a favourite charity in memory of the one who has died instead of sending expensive flowers that will wilt in twenty-four hours. This trend has grown to such proportions that the organized florists are feeling threatened. Hence, during the last year and a half, at least two such organizations have been spending big sums on national advertising, trying to repersuade the American people that nothing can possibly take the place of flowers for comforting the bereaved.

Many times I had seen funeral flowers banked twenty to thirty sprays and wreaths deep all the way to the ceiling of church vestibules or chancels. I felt that it would be wrong to let this happen at the time of Peter's death. Therefore I

asked that, instead of flowers, gifts should be made toward
an endowment fund for students for the gospel ministry at
Columbia Theological Seminary, the school from which Peter
had graduated. Of course, some flowers were sent anyway
—some very lovely ones, and they were deeply appreciated.
But there was not the wasteful display that might well have
been.   The Memorial Fund initiated at that time has been
steadily growing ever since and is a living memorial to Peter
Marshall.

Spring came to Washington early that year. The forsythia
seemed a more brilliant yellow than usual; the azaleas were
punctuation marks of flaming coral and cerise. The Tidal
Basin was adrift in pale pink blossoms. Out in the residential
section of Kenwood, one drove through fairy-feathered avenues
of pink-and-white dogwood and cherry trees.

The weeks that had passed since January had wrought
changes in me. For a time grief had made me tone deaf
to the harmonies of earth. Now I could hear music again.
Hence, Easter had fresh meaning that year. In my heart was
a new peace. It was the kind of peace that comes, not from
the absence of any pain or difficulty, but rather from knowing
that I had gone through flames and had survived the ordeal.

From that travail I had been left with a crucible of conviction that, since Christ is beside us, the worst that can
happen to any one of us in this life need not overwhelm us.
I realized that out in my future somewhere there might be
other sorrows, other crises. But there was also the sure
knowledge that I need never meet any future difficulty alone,
that help from a loving God would ever be available for the
asking, that resources beyond imagining are always at our
disposal—provided only that we are willing to put ourselves in the stream of God's purposes. Thus, that Easter-
time, I knew that we human beings who are still grappling
with life on the planet earth, need have no fear of any
unknown tomorrows. In my heart I could kneel before the

Risen Lord and promise Him to try to live in the present—joyfully.

And so I knew that the time had come to make my decision about where Peter would be buried. I was ready for that step in a way that I had not been in January.

Several trips were made to a cemetery on the edge of the District of Columbia—an uncrowded one set in a lovely rolling countryside. A new and costly mausoleum had been erected on the highest point of ground in the cemetery. The owners were anxious to sell me a crypt there.

I was shown through the mausoleum and told in some detail why the crypt type of burial was recommended. There was a certain atmosphere of luxury in the place—subdued indirect lighting, deep-piled rugs on the stone floor, long rich draperies, soft " canned " music coming over hidden loud-speakers. There were very beautiful stained-glass memorial windows, much marble, and somewhere in the distance the singing of imprisoned canaries.

The crypts were in the walls. It was explained to me that both the humidity and temperature were sharply controlled to ensure the best possible preservation of the human body. There would be, of course, both in the mausoleum and outside, what is called in cemeteries of this type " perpetual care."

In all fairness, I should say that the men dealing with me were courteous and gentle. In my case there was no high-pressure salesmanship. I sensed, however, that particularly because the mausoleum was new, the men were eager to persuade me to bury Peter there. They had no intention of using my husband's name in any overt way in advertising. Still I knew that they would like to be able to say privately, quietly, to future visitors to the place, " Now you probably know that Dr Peter Marshall is buried here—right over there off the chapel floor gallery."

As I stood there in the dim light, with the stained-glass windows making little coloured patterns on the stone floor,

I could see Peter's face—laughing at me. I thought of how he had hated dim light anywhere—the subdued, supposedly glamorous lighting of cocktail lounges and some restaurants, even certain churches and cathedrals. "Who wants to grope his way through life?" he would ask. "God made brilliant sunlight—not this duck-soup atmosphere." I could see him making an elaborate pantomime of striking matches to read a restaurant menu—to the open-mouthed consternation of many a waitress.

Now he seemed to be saying to me, slangily, with merriment in his eyes, "Catherine, leave us not be silly. You're taking this much too seriously. Don't let's make a production out of it. *I'm* not in that box. I dare you to think that I am."

So I knew that the atmosphere of the mausoleum was not for him. It would have mocked him, betrayed him. The fetid, closed-in feeling of the place, its artificiality—no—definitely not. In comparison there was something clean and releasing and right about being buried in God's out-of-doors —January weather or not.

That's how it came about that I chose a spot on a hill in the gently rolling countryside just across the Maryland border. Over the site were the spreading arms of a stately elm tree. From the hillside one could see for miles in all directions —a panorama of a good land.

On a mild afternoon in the late spring, a group of us gathered under the elm for a graveside service. We heard those imperishable words:

Because I live, ye shall live also. . . . Let not your heart be troubled; ye believe in God, believe also in me. In my Father's house are many mansions; if it were not so, I would have told you.

As the words rang out—vibrant with the promise of life— it was a voice with a Scottish burr that I was really hearing. For how often those same words had been on Peter's lips

for other people! And always he had spoken them with
an inflection of his own that had given depth to their meaning. . . . "If it were *not* so, I would have *told* you."

As we turned to leave the cemetery, the plaintive notes
of an ancient Scottish bagpipe lament sounded across the
hills. Among many other kindnesses, some of Peter's fellow
Scots in the St Andrews Society had wanted to pay that last
tribute. The pipers were playing that most soulful of all the
laments, the one with a sob at its heart, "The Flowers o' the
Forest. . . ."

> The prime of our land lie cauld in the clay. .,
> Women and bairns are heartless and wae. . . .
> The Flow'rs of the Forest are a' wede away.
> The Flow'rs of the Forest are a' wede away.

Yet the rugged face that I kept seeing, the voice that I kept
hearing, was impatient with, indeed simply would not tolerate,
any sadness in us who were left behind. Somehow in the
weeks since January, Peter had succeeded in getting at least
one basic lesson through to me. . . . "*I'm* not in that casket,
Catherine. I dare you to think that I am." It was because
I knew that—finally—deeply—that what we were doing that
spring afternoon was bearable for me.

The next time that I visited the cemetery, there was an old
man standing by Peter's grave. Tears were raining down the
deep furrows of his cheeks and falling on the newly gashed
earth. I had never seen the old man before. Whatever had
prompted his visit and had released his tears was obviously
too intimate for intrusion. So I went on without making
myself known to him.

As I drove away, I was thinking about the difference in the
way grave sites affect individuals. I doubted that any tears
of mine would ever fall on Peter's grave because I had no
sense of reality about his being in that particular spot. Therefore, there was no special solace for me there. Nor did I find
it a particularly good place for thoughtful appraisal or medita-

tion—as some people do for the last resting places of their beloved dead.

Even as I headed the car out of the cemetery gates, I was once again hearing that resonant, confident voice:

> We do not well, for this is a day of good
>   tiding and we hold our peace. . . .
>
> It is only when we know Christ that we are not
>   afraid, for there is then nothing to fear.
> Only when one is no longer afraid to die, is one
>   no longer afraid at all. . . .
>
> To be free—free as a bird—simply means
> to be unafraid, in the fullest awareness. . . .
> which awareness includes the recognition of death.
> And when we are no longer afraid, do we begin to
> live . . . in every experience, painful, or joyous
> in gratitude for every moment, to live
> abundantly. . . .

" To live abundantly. . . ." I remembered the promise I had made on Easter Sunday morning to try " to live in the present —joyfully." I thought of the editing work on the manuscript of the book of sermons waiting for me back at home, of the immense satisfaction that work was bringing to me, of the friends who had come as if from nowhere to help me. And I had strong suspicions that Peter himself had had more to do with bringing me to that point of grateful acceptance than I had any way of knowing.

CHAPTER 6

The Woman and the Book

I don't know how the woman sitting behind the green baize-covered table appeared to other people. I do know that on the inside she was at once both exhilarated and bewildered. For I was that woman.

The occasion was the publication-day autograph tea for the book of my husband's sermons that I had edited—*Mr Jones, Meet the Master*. The day was November 28, 1949. The scene was being enacted on the second floor of the Federation of Churches building in Washington.

Two rooms had been thrown together for the tea. The line of waiting people stretched all the way across both rooms and down the stairs. Almost every person in the queue was a resident of Washington who had sat under Peter Marshall's preaching. There had been much anticipation of the day when his book of sermons would be released.

Nobody, however, had expected such a crowd. The line moved slowly because almost everyone had something special to say to me. Out of great gratitude they spoke of my husband. The eyes of some were moist with emotion. Yet many spoke with humour, clearly reflecting Peter's light touch. Often they asked for some special inscription on the flyleaf of the book.

On the table beside me was a vase of flowers, a bottle of ink, the ever-present water pitcher and glass, and a tall stack of copies of *Mr Jones*. Behind me hovered three beaming representatives of the publishing house. At one point in the afternoon a lady spotted Peter John standing near me and asked him to sign his name underneath mine. That started it! Soon Peter John was sitting beside me, busily signing his name in book after book in a large, round, childish scrawl.

After a while, someone brought me a cup of tea and some cookies, but there was never time to sip the tea. I was much too conscious of the patient guests who had been waiting so long, and whose feet, I thought, must have begun to ache intolerably. For four hours the line passed in front of me.

Between saying a few words to each person and autographing the books, there was scarcely any time for thinking. Still, I couldn't help reflecting, somewhat wryly, that the situation was ironic. After all, Peter Marshall was the author of *Mr Jones, Meet the Master*—not I. They were his sermons. What business had I autographing his book? Yet that was what the guests wanted and were waiting for—that personal contact.

It began to dawn on me that I was there merely as a channel—a go-between. Since Peter had begun his new life, I was as close as his friends felt that they could get to him. In a way that I had not sought nor bargained for, I was being thrust into the peculiar position of representing Peter to other people.

In several ways, that publication day was a preview of the years immediately ahead. Certainly there was to be success as the book-world measures success. Three thousand copies of *Mr Jones* were sold in Washington on that one day. Before publication day was over across the nation, the entire first printing of 10,000 books was gone. The day after that the publishing house in New York received by telephone, wire and mail, orders for another 4,000 copies. Paper had already been ordered for the second printing (another 10,000 that sold out immediately), but even with all the rushing possible, it took 13 days to get that printing to the bookstores.

Before those books could be printed and bound, there were advance orders for every one of them. From then on for over a year, it was a mad scramble to get *Mr Jones* off the presses fast enough. The third printing, ready 6 days after the second, was stepped up to 15,000 copies; the fourth, to 25,000 and so on.

In one of his broadcasts, Walter Winchell called *Mr Jones* "the book surprise click." Booksellers began tagging it a "runaway best seller." So new was I to all the commercial aspects of the book world that I scarcely knew what that meant.

Therefore, when just after the turn of the year I received a letter from the Revell Company informing me that on January 8 the book would make both *The New York Times* and the *New York Herald Tribune* nonfiction best-seller lists, I was not as impressed as I should have been. I had never paid any particular attention to the best-seller lists; I knew only that books of sermons rarely do that well. But I soon began to realize that the reception that this particular book of sermons was receiving was any author's or editor's dream.

Yet for me, the real success of the book was measured in an altogether different way—by what the message of the sermons meant to individual men and women. This was dramatized through the mail that began pouring in. On any given day there would be letters from many who apologized for writing and confided that this was their first fan letter. Their letters were direct and simple expressions of deeply felt gratitude. For example, one from Villa Ridge, Iillinois, began :

My dear Mrs Marshall :

On my eighty-second birthday I was given a copy of *Mr Jones, Meet the Master*. For almost seventy years I have been a church member. Yet Christianity as Dr Marshall preached and lived it was unknown to me.

By the time I had finished the book my soul was flooded by a downpour of revelation. . . . I thank God that I have lived to come face to face with the Master through Dr Marshall's living words. . . .

Or from a housewife in Conrad, Montana :

Out of a grateful heart I would thank you deeply and sincerely for making it possible for us " little people " to share the love and wealth of expression of Peter Marshall. . . . Just think! How poor the rest of us would have been if *Mr Jones, Meet the Master* had not been published, if Dr Marshall's own congregations had been the only ones ever to receive these sermons and prayers. . . . And please, would it be possible to publish more sermons . . .?

The title for the book, *Mr Jones, Meet the Master*, had originally been a sermon title of Peter's. It seemed that the publisher and I had made the right choice of title, because running like a refrain through all the letters was the thought that out of the pages had stepped a living Lord. . . .

From Schenectady, New York:

I have just finished reading *Mr Jones, Meet the Master*. This comes to you to thank you from the depths of my heart for publishing this book. . . . From the opening word the book has been hard to put down. . . . For sheer beauty of language . . . the book is unsurpassed. . . . But far beyond that, its real value lies in its amazing ability to bring my Lord into my own living room. . . .

And on heavy vellum paper from Park Avenue in New York came a memorable letter:

This book was like a shaft of brilliant sunlight on the dark path I was treading. Thank you. Thank you. . . .

Very soon, mail began coming from abroad too—from the British Isles, from Ceylon, from a woman missionary— a " hen medic " as she described herself—in Potifunk, West Africa, even a letter written by a young American student in Germany. . . .

Heidelberg, Germany

. . . Peter Marshall really had the stuff on the ball. . . .
I haven't read a book in a long time that's put me to
thinking like this one. Now don't laugh, but I've
decided to take the Man up on a few of His promises. . . .

I could scarcely have read letters like these day after day
without their having a profound effect on me. Daily I
was receiving proof that *Mr Jones* really had been God's
idea and His project. The substantiation lay in many little
human-interest vignettes, as varied as the facets of Peter's
personality, that kept coming back to me. . . .

In Cranford, New Jersey, an elderly woman was found dead
in bed with one hand stretched out resting on a much-
thumbed page of *Mr Jones*. The book had been read and
reread to the woman and had been of particular comfort
to her during her last days. The relaxed fingers of one outstretched hand were lying like a benediction on the words :

> Let us therefore act like believers,
> live like Christians so that we can die
> like Christians
>   with songs and rejoicing. . . .

> For those we love are with the Lord,
> we believe, and the Lord has promised
> to be with us,
>   never to leave us nor forsake us.
>   "Behold I am with you always."

> Well, if they are with Him,
>   and He is with us. . . .
>   *they cannot be far away.* . . .

About that time an American correspondent in the European theatre had to submit to an inspection of his baggage at the Czechoslovakian border. The Communist guards confiscated two articles as being "inflammable material"— a small file of letters to American clergymen and a copy of *Mr Jones, Meet the Master*. In telling me about the incident later, the newspaperman commented: "I can't be too sorry about the loss of the book, because I'm glad the Commies had enough sense to think of *Mr Jones* as inflammatory material. It certainly is! I hope that it wasn't destroyed. Somehow I'd be pleased to think of that particular book being behind the Iron Curtain."

But almost the best story of all came from Asheville, North Carolina. A pleasant-faced, grey-haired woman sitting behind a desk in one of the branch libraries was busy sorting cards one morning. That was why it took a small boy on the other side of the counter quite a long time to get her attention. The child was freckle-faced and pug-nosed, with a shock of blond hair that kept falling in his eyes.

The bobbing up and down at the counter finally caught the librarian's eye. It was the little boy jumping on tiptoe, trying to see behind the counter. The woman looked up and smiled at what she saw.

"What can I do for you, sonny?"

"I'm Dick Beamer. My mother said—would you please send her a copy of *Joe's Mixmaster* home by me? She said I was not to come home without it." The eyes under the tousled blond hair were very serious.

The attendant was genuinely puzzled. "*Joe's Mixmaster*," she murmured half to herself. Some kind of a book on small appliances? A cookbook? But she couldn't remember any title like that. She decided to telephone the child's mother.

A minute later, laughing, she hung up the phone, and reached for a book.

"Here you are, Dick. The customer is always right. Just what you ordered."

The book she handed over the counter was, of course, *Mr Jones, Meet the Master*.

Trips for autographing followed—to Atlanta, Birmingham, New Orleans, Cleveland, Columbus, Boston, Detroit, and Richmond, Virginia. I soon found that the autograph party as such is as American as the hot dog stand or the New York Giants. It is a child of American business promotion.

I soon discovered that all such parties have certain common denominators. The bookstore people are always nervous lest the author's or editor's hand not write fast enough or give out on them. Therefore, they want a pile of books signed ahead of the scheduled hours for autographing. This is also designed to take care of those astute customers who have ordered their autographed copies of the book the easy way —by telephone.

The publisher and the author must lean over backwards to give all the major retail booksellers in any given city equal treatment. If books are signed for one, usually they must be autographed for all. That often means tramping from bookstore to bookstore, meeting the personnel, and signing a pile of books in each store.

At each party, there are always a few individuals who do not really understand what an autograph is. I remember one sweet-faced elderly lady who thrust a book at me, saying, "This one is for a birthday present. I wonder if you would be so kind as to write something special in it for me?"

"Of course, I'll be happy to. What would you like?"

"Well—suppose I just sort of dictate it to you. . . . 'To Aunt Emma Cartwright, who means more to me than—'"

My pen hovered over the fresh page. I asked gently, feeling for words, "Are you sure that you want me to put it just that way? You see, Miss Cartwright is not *my* aunt. Won't that inscription seem a little odd over my signature?"

But the face before me merely smiled more sweetly still and went blithely on, "Oh, my dear, I've known Emma for *such* a long time. She *really* is a dear. You would *love* her. It just doesn't matter a bit that it's over your signature. You go right ahead and put your name *right* there. Emma will treasure it *so*."

After a few such feeble protests and attempts to explain—which I found equally futile in Richmond or in Atlanta, in New Orleans or in Cleveland—I just gave up and dutifully wrote anything that people requested—short of blasphemy or libel. The result is that I have inscribed astonishingly tender and intimate messages for scores of people on whom I've never laid eyes.

It is a rare party, I found, which the average bookseller can handle in orderly fashion. Americans do not like lines; I can't say that I blame them. They would rather crowd around, poking books in all directions, first come, first served. The autobiographer—sunk down in the middle of the mêlée, feeling like a target for bow and arrow practice, gasping for a breath of fresh air, her right arm aching, the flowers on her left shoulder tickling her nose, the corsage pin scratching her shoulder—sits there, writing furiously, her signature getting more and more illegible, wondering if the smile on her face looks as mechanical as it began to feel a full hour ago. She meanwhile has one eye on the bookstore clock and the other on the still-unsigned piles of books which must be autographed before an escape can be made back to the hotel room.

It should not have surprised me that I was finding details of my new life—such as sleepless nights on jerking trains or bumpy plane rides—a hurdle and a challenge. The truth was I couldn't even read a plane or train schedule. During twelve years of marriage, all training and motivation had been in quite the opposite direction. During these years I had stayed in the background—a behind-the-scenes wife. So definitely was this true that there were those in my husband's congregation who did not know whether or not the minister was married, or who, at best, had never seen me.

This was quite in keeping with Peter's ideas and ideals on

the subject of marriage. He took a dim view of feminism. But he was able to articulate this in a way that had attracted rather than repelled most of the feminine sex who heard him. His credo of marriage was spelled out—indeed, spread all over the landscape—in his sermon "Keepers of the Springs." Yet during all his years in the ministry, this had been by far the most popular sermon he had ever preached.

The emancipation of womanhood began with Christianity and it ends with Christianity. . . .[1]

When woman in this country achieved equality with man, it was accomplished only by stepping down from the pedestal
on which Christianity, chivalry, and idealism
had placed her. . . .

So she copied the vices of man—in the name of progress!
But it is not progress to go in a downward direction.
It is not progress to lower moral standards and to lose ideals!
No woman ever became lovelier by losing her essential femininity.

There is no substitute for goodness. . . .
nothing can take place of purity.
To be sweet is far better than to be sophisticated.

America needs young women who will build true homes,
whether they live in two rooms—or ten . . .
whether starched white organdie curtains
hang at the windows—or silk damask.

[1] Marshall, Peter, *Mr Jones, Meet the Master*, p. 148, London, Fontana, 1964. Following lines are from unpublished manuscript. Used by permission.

We need homes where harassed husbands may find peace
understanding
refreshment of body and soul . . .
where children may find the warmth of love . . .
where friends may find hospitality
graciousness
and joy.

Only out of such homes will go men with strength and courage to help the United States build a new and a better world.

To make such homes is, therefore, any woman's supreme contribution to her country and to her generation. . . .

There might well have been some conflict between Peter and me over his strong views on the rôle of women in marriage, had I not discovered early in our life together that putting these ideas into practice brought me joy and satisfaction at a deep level. Such non-feminist ideas meant that I was single-eyed in the marriage relationship. I was not a divided personality. All the talents I possessed, all energy, all creativeness, were poured into the marriage partnership, and no effort was made to channel any part of it in other directions.

For any minister—who must preach twice or three times every Sunday and often prepare several weekday talks—a steady stream of new ideas is the breath of life. Therefore, I handed over to Peter any ideas that came to me or that I stumbled across in reading that might be sermon material, as well as any thoughts I might have on the ever-present church organizational or personnel problems.

Nor was any of this a hardship or a sacrifice. I felt in need of neither credit nor approbation for it. For I was discovering for myself during those years the profound truth of that ancient and inexorable law that " he that loseth his life . . . shall find it."

Would the law have been stated more accurately had its

pronouns been cast in the feminine gender? I don't know; I am no expert in feminine psychology. I only know that in giving all of myself to our marriage, with no reservations—in losing my life in that sense, I found it again in a fulfilment of every shred of femininity in me.

Furthermore, almost three years of ill health had given me a special kind of training in the quiet life. Anyone who has had to go to bed full time finds it an irksome adjustment. I was no exception. The first three months were the worst. Every muscle in my body ached in protest against too much bed rest. The minutes held their breath; the hours dragged their feet. Every inner resource available had to be mustered to fill those halting days. Then, too, all of life looks different, takes on quite another colour, when viewed from a horizontal position.

I finally succeeded in making the adjustment. Some natural bent toward the secluded life rose to meet the need. Rush, flurry, and tension fell away from me. Great chunks of time for reading, undisturbed thought, and making notes filled up pits of emptiness in me so that they became reservoirs of mental and spiritual resources. That was all to the good. The filling meant that, henceforward, all of life could be built on a more solid basis.

How completely the adjustment had been made became apparent when the time finally came for me to get out of bed and pick up active life again. At first, the presence of more than two or three persons in a room tired me rapidly and left me confused, like one who watches a rapidly moving object—galloping horses or a roller coaster—on a movie screen. With relief, I would go back to my quiet room to clear my head, to get perspective again. It took many months to retrain nerves, reflexes, and emotions back to the accelerated pace that most of us think of as normal living.

Then only a little over a year after I had recovered and picked up the threads of normal life again, Peter's death and the publication of his sermons thrust me into the public eye.

It was no wonder that I found the reversal of my position with my husband somewhat difficult. Peter had gone on to greater things. Yet for him, as for all in that other life, death now hid his new mission with a cloak of anonymity.

It is as if at the moment of death the sword of self must be laid down along with the flesh and left outside the gates of timelessness. In that sense, therefore, Peter was now the one in the background; I, the one forced to the forefront.

My reaction to this was that, more often than not, I felt like fleeing. Psychologically, I was still reacting as I had as a child. In the house where we had lived for most of the growing-up years, there had been narrow, curving back stairs off the kitchen leading to the second floor. These proved to be a most convenient means of ready escape. When grown-ups whom I did not relish seeing or for whom I did not consider myself presentable came to the front door, I would bolt up the back stairs two at a time. Thus, so far as my emotional reactions were concerned, during the first few months of the publicity that followed the success of *Mr Jones*, I found myself fleeing up the back stairs again and again.

The secret desire to flee was no passing emotional phase. Nor was it just the kind of fear of public appearances that comes from ineptitude or inexperience. I had been making impromptu talks in my father's church since childhood. During high school days I had won local and then statewide speaking contests. In college, it had been an exciting experience to be on the debating team and to match wits with representatives from other women's colleges, even with teams from British universities—Cambridge and the University of London.

No—this was not simple shyness; the difficulty went deeper. Its symptoms appeared before I was even aware that there was any problem.

A few days before an autograph party in a department store

in Richmond, Virginia, I acquired a bad cold which developed
into laryngitis. By the day of the party I was unable to speak
above a whisper. Since the occasion had been widely pub-
licized and many hundreds of books had been ordered, there
was nothing to do but to appear as scheduled—voice or no
voice.

Appear I did; it was certainly an incongruous situation.
Silent and apologetic, I could only sit there at a little table in
the middle of the book department of the store, trying to make
my eyes and a smile say what my lips could not. The book-
department personnel took turns standing solicitously beside
me, explaining my voiceless plight to the people in the
line before me.

The autographing had been scheduled from two to four in
the afternoon and from seven-thirty until eight-thirty that
evening. In between times, I had dinner at a near-by hotel
with a salesman from the publishing house who had come
down from New York especially for the party.

After we had decided on our orders—I, by pointing and
gesturing at the menu—he asked, "Did you notice that I
skipped out on the party for a while this afternoon? Or
were you too tied up to notice?"

I tried to whisper, "I'm afraid there were too many
milling—" Suddenly, even the whisper died on my lips.

"Better write your words of wisdom—," and he shoved
a pencil toward me and groped in his pocket for a scrap of
paper. "I can see that for once in my life when I'm with
a woman, I'm going to get a chance to talk as much as
I want to—well—anyway . . . whether you noticed or not. . . ."
Here his voice sank to a whisper, too. . . . "I skipped out,
found the nearest Catholic church, and said a little prayer
for you. I even burned a candle. I was worried about
whether you could hold out for tonight."

I wrote on the paper, "I'm touched and grateful. . . . But
why are *you* whispering?"

"Hey! Why *am* I whispering . . .?"

The voiceless autographing party in Richmond would scarcely be worth mentioning were it an isolated incident. The trouble was that, as invitations—not only for autographing, but for book reviews and other types of talks kept coming in—the frequent colds became even more frequent. All too often I would become ill shortly before a scheduled trip for some kind of public appearance.

There was no pretence in this; the viruses that felled me were real enough. Sometimes I would keep the engagement anyway, as I had in Richmond. But usually my doctor would step in and positively forbid the trip. This was embarrassing, because always there had been local advertising of the event, and the cancellation inconvenienced other people. It wasn't any fun several days later to receive clippings from a local newspaper in which a notice had been prominently displayed in a box on the front page:

NOTICE
CATHERINE MARSHALL
is ill and will be unable to keep her
speaking engagement at
Smithfield St Methodist Church
tonight
The meeting is therefore cancelled

Finally it began to dawn on me that the colds and the laryngitis, the viruses and the flu, were much too conveniently timed; the correlation between the illnesses and the public appearances was too high. I knew that this was no conscious ducking of obligations on my part. But pondering it, I had strong suspicions that the colds were the result of some kind of inner rebellion and conflict.

Recognizing the psychosomatic character of the small illnesses was half the battle in eliminating them. The rest was done through prayer, applying a little humour to the predicament, and resolving firmly that when I had made a date, it had to be kept—period! Under this treatment, colds and viruses practically disappeared from my life.

Yet the basic conflict—of which the colds had been but a minor sign—did not disappear so easily. It took a long time for me even to realize what the emotional upheaval was all about. I only knew that it was there and that it was making me unhappy.

Was there in me, I wondered, a deficiency of love for other people that was making me yearn after the back-stairs escape routine? Could the trouble be traced to a despicable lack of gratitude to God for the part I had been enabled to play in the publication of *Mr Jones, Meet the Master* and its subsequent success?

The fact that I could represent my husband to the public had been at first not only acceptable to me but very satisfying. I was glad that I could be used in any way to carry a bit further the work that Peter had begun.

About that time, I read a statement that seemed to underwrite what I was doing. It was a paragraph or two in a book that had been published three years before and was still popular—Rabbi Liebman's *Peace of Mind* :

> When death destroys an important relationship . . . equilibrium will be restored when the bereaved person discovers some situation demanding the same or similar patterns of conduct. . . . We must act as the ambassadors of our departed, their messengers and their spokesmen, carrying out the mission for which they lived and strove and which they bequeathed to us. . . ."[2]

I had no idea whether or not Rabbi Liebman, in this point of view, was really presenting a sound principle. Certainly I had not undertaken the project of compiling and editing the book of sermons with the conscious motive of finding a pattern of conduct that would aid my own

[2] Liebman, Joshua Loth, *Peace of Mind*, William Heinemann, Ltd. London, 1947.

recovery from grief. Still it was good to have this assurance that I had been on the right track.

But the probing went on. . . . Was the difficulty that I felt at this time a rebellion against any intrusion of the innermost citadel of my private life by the public? A covert guarding of the heart's door? An instinctive feeling of—"you may come this close, but no closer." Could it be that all of this together was a lingering emotional mutiny over widowhood—a sign that there was still some grief-repair work to be done? Or was the trouble all this and more?

In time the outlines of the "and more" began to emerge. My ideal inner image of woman's rôle in the world—formed partly by the femininity with which I was born, partly by a Southern heritage, and partly by the years of my marriage—was definitely not that of the career woman. I had spent my childhood in a Deep South Mississippi town. In me still was the child who had revelled in the *Little Colonel* series, replete with the beautiful woman reigning supreme over the domestic concerns of her own domain—in that case, a Southern mansion. Still not far under the surface was the little girl who had never had enough perfume, bracelets, and undergarments lavish with lace to satisfy her; who had disdained playing cowboys and Indians but had adored her dolls.

The aggressiveness and independent attitude necessary to make a sally out into the world of successful careers seemed to me a contradiction of everything feminine I had ever known; therefore, it was emotional anathema to me. Yet now circumstances which I had not sought were thrusting this genuinely distasteful rôle upon me.

While in the midst of strong resistance at the emotional level, I was too much involved to analyse my feelings objectively. Looking back now, I know that this was only the beginning of a conflict that was to go on for a long time and become even more poignant before it could be resolved. There was no clash between my idea of a woman's rôle in the world and the writing itself. Always the pencil in my hand meant joy. My difficulty was that of reconciling myself to the commercial aspects of the book world, to my writing being in any way connected with earning a living. The conflict in me was therefore basically a clash between femininity and the career that pressed in upon me. The woman and the book were in headlong collision.

CHAPTER 7

They Walk in Wistfulness

Every sorrowing person has difficulty in returning to places uniquely connected with the one who has died. So I had found it in going back to the church on the Sunday following Peter's death. So I found it the following summer in returning to Waverley, our Cape Cod cottage.

Since Peter and I had always lived in manses belonging to the churches we had served, Waverley was the only home we had ever owned. The sea almost at the front door; the fogs that rolled in off the Atlantic; the cool nights when the rest of the country was sweltering in a heat wave; the little arm of land that is Cape Cod all but smothered in rambler roses—Peter had loved it all, perhaps because it spoke to him of home and Scotland. The cottage was *his*. He proved it by planning and planting a garden of hybrid tea roses, by building fences, and painting the shutters his favourite Chatham blue.

Our son had spent every summer of his life there. As spring had melted into early summer that year of Peter's death, our nine-year-old was all eagerness to return to the cottage and the seashore. He wanted to leave the day after school closed. I, in turn, could offer no excuse for not going that Peter John would have understood.

Friends offered to help me drive up. As we left the parkways of New York and Connecticut behind and crossed the Bourne Bridge from the mainland to Cape Cod, suddenly I remembered what had been in my mind at the same spot the year before. Peter had been driving. He had been gay and eager to begin his vacation, and had let out an exuberant shout as soon as we had crossed the bridge and were on Cape Cod's sandy soil.

Sitting beside him, watching his face, all at once I had

had a stabbing premonition. I had not even allowed it to jell into thought, but had thrust it from me with the opposite idea, ' One more year—and we've made it—together.' Now, a year later, I remembered.

Our friends stayed with us in the cottage for a few days and then had to return to Washington. With Peter John and me alone, there came a procession of agonizing days. At Waverley I could not dodge the reality of my husband's death. Everywhere I turned there were reminders.

Under the bed were the old white shoes Peter had used for garden work, with his socks still stuffed in them. The shoes would never again walk under the rose arbour and into the garden. On the closet shelf in the front hall was a summer hat with its blue band fading to lavender; the hat was enjoying no trips to auctions or to summer theatre matinées that year. In the waste-baskets were scraps of letters Peter had answered the previous September. They were eloquent with the message, " No one will ever again receive a letter from Peter Marshall." On the table was a game score with neat figures, and beside it, a list of perennials Peter had planned to plant. Now he would do no planting that summer or any summer. In the garage was a pair of canvas gloves, thrown carelessly on the work-bench, still almost in the shape of their owner's hands—but now the gloves were empty.

One evening after young Peter—tired from a whole day of swimming and crabbing—was asleep, I headed toward the beach. A brisk breeze, acrid with the smell of seaweed, was blowing in from the sea. Off in the distance was the blinking lighthouse of Chatham Point. The moon shining on the water and the white sand made it almost like day. Always I had found soothing the rhythmical swish of waves beating on the shore.

' On this particular night of all nights,' I thought, ' I need something soothing.' By that afternoon the cumulative effect of our days on the Cape had reached a climax. The result was a tempest of emotion.

Standing there on the wide beach, a solitary figure in the

night, there was wrung from me an unspoken prayer. . . .
' Oh God, I want to believe that Peter is alive somewhere.
But all I can feel is a great aching void, a gigantic empti-
ness.'

There was no answer at the time—only the cool air on my
cheeks, the still moon shining down, and the rhythmical march
of the waves to my feet.

But back at the cottage sometime during the night, after
several hours of sleep, I awakened. The confusion in my
mind was gone. Clear, rounded thoughts were waiting there,
as if they had been dropped into my consciousness during
sleep. . . .

Once again you have been trying to put feeling before
faith. Because you haven't been able to feel Peter's
presence, you have assumed that he is lost to you forever.

Simply have faith that he is with you whenever you
need him. Assume it—and the feeling and the proof
will come later. Accept this on faith. Accept it though
you have no idea how it can come about.

That was all.

The need was to love and to be loved—that ultimate of
life. Could I, and all those like me who walk the earth
in wistfulness, find the way to trust God even for that?

Yes, I would try.

I thereupon made a quiet little act of receiving the message at face value. Why should I doubt it? I have nothing
to lose, I thought. Otherwise there is only emptiness.

I lay there with one arm under my head, staring into the
darkness, thinking of how Christ had told His closest friends
that it was "expedient" that He go away. Probably, I
thought, they had stifled the retort that had sprung to their
lips. 'Expedient? How could it be? We like being with
You. What could possibly be better than the peace, the joy,
and the satisfaction of Your Physical Presence?'

And then I thought of an incident that had taken place seven days prior to Peter's death. He and I had been visiting friends in a nearby city. Their guest room had twin beds. Some time after the lights had been turned out and we had gone to bed, long after the house was quiet, suddenly I had put out one hand toward the other bed, and had found Peter's hand stretched out in the darkness waiting for mine.

He had whispered, "How did you know that my hand was there?"

And I had answered, "I don't know. *I just knew.*"

So now the space between us was wider, much wider— greater than the distance between any twin beds. It stretched all the way across the eternities that divide the world of the seen from the world of the unseen. Somewhere out in that emptiness, an outstretched hand was waiting for me. The promise of it was implicit in the message I had just received. But so far, I could feel only the darkness and the emptiness. And I missed the reassurance of those strong fingers.

Having resolved to accept the message on faith, I felt that I had done my part. The next move was up to God. In that I was mistaken. Not a single one of us can fly across the Valley of the Shadow; we must walk its rocky paths step by step. Being creatures of free will, we must assent to each step in recovery and live it out.

Day after day that first summer I found that my journey through the Valley was a running battle with self pity. Several of the couples on our street would often take a stroll toward the beach of an early evening. Sometimes seeing them, I would think, 'Here Peter and I were, the youngest couple on the street, and our marriage is over.' Or at a summer-stock performance at the theatre in Dennis, I would see a grey-haired man reach for his wife's hand, and I would wince with a passing pang of self-pity.

Or at a dinner party I would find myself the only single

person there. Always I knew that my hostess had not meant to be thoughtless. It is hard for anyone who has known only an unbroken family to imagine how this particular situation makes the single person feel. Try as I might to overcome it, I would find that being in the presence of couples threw my aloneness into sharpest perspective.

In spite of such experiences, the lonely person often makes the mistake of thinking that physical nearness to other people is the answer. Yet some of the most solitary people in the world live in great cities—London, Paris, New York, Los Angeles. One can feel utterly alone, have no sense of belonging, even in the midst of a jostling crowd.

I remember once when the loneliness of a mutual acquaintance, a widow, was mentioned in a group of her friends. One of those present was a married man. An odd look came into his eyes. " Don't make the mistake," he said, " of thinking that the only lonely people are single people. Loneliness doesn't fly out of the window in the wake of the marriage ceremony. A man and a woman can live in the same house, in fact lie side by side in the same bed, and still be worlds apart." Of course, he was right. Our divorce courts testify that in many marriages no water of life has been found for the thirst of the solitary spirit.

What then is the solution? It must lie somewhere in the realm of relationship. As solitaries we wither and die. We long to be needed; we yearn to be included; we thirst to know that we belong to someone. The question is . . . how can we achieve that sense of belonging?

There is a price to be paid. The first tribute exacted is a modicum of honesty with ourselves. Do we so want to be rid of self-pity that we will allow ourselves no more wallowing in loneliness? How badly do we want to make connection with other people? Do we really want to find happiness again?

In the light of honest answers to questions like these, suddenly we find that we do not ever need to be lonely, unless we choose to be. For there are always others eager to receive our friendship if only we will take the first steps out of our solitary shell.

For several months my family and friends had seen me happily engrossed in the editing, prepublication work, and launching of *Mr Jones, Meet the Master*. What they had not seen was my continuing inner struggle to fill up that great void now at the centre of my life.

The church's Order for the Solemnization of Marriage recognizes the problem by including in the marriage service the poignant words "till death do us part." And Christ once commented in speaking of marriage, ". . . and they twain shall be one flesh." Did He mean that only in the spiritual sense or just mystically? Not at all. Perhaps only those who have lost a mate know the stern reality that those simple words represent.

One takes an arm or a leg or an eye for granted until it is gone. When in good health, one has no reason to be preoccupied with different parts of the body. It's only in pain or disease that awareness comes. Even so, those who have lived through the disseverment of a marriage through death become acutely aware of how real the "one flesh" was. With the death of a marriage partner, there is an awareness of dismemberment. Moreover, this tearing asunder has taken place at such a deep level that its healing will yield to no superficial therapy.

I was still groping to find what that answer might be when one afternoon I went to my doctor's office for a routine cold shot. Most of his appointments were over for the day, and the doctor was in a leisurely talkative mood. He was a tall, fine-looking man close to retirement age whom I had known for years. Having helped me through many a difficulty, he was more inclined to treat me like a friend or a daughter than a patient.

Suddenly in the midst of our conversation he fell silent,

leaned forward in his swivel chair, and looked at me closely. His eyes were searching my face as if trying to see what lay underneath.

" Catherine, enough chitchat. Suppose you just relax and drop that gay mask you've been wearing since you came in here. Now—look at me. How are you? Really?"

I half turned to gaze out of the window at trees tossing in a sudden thunderstorm. The room was quiet now except for the pelting rain against the window panes, the ticking of a clock on the mantle, and the nurses' muffled telephone conversation beyond the outer office door.

Finally I turned back to look at my physician friend. What I was feeling poured out in a rush of words. . . . " Do you really want to know what it feels like to be a widow? God made men and women for each other. Any other way of life is wrong, because it's abnormal. The last few months it's been like having a gnawing hunger, a haunting wistfulness at the centre of life. I can forget about it for short periods—ignore it sometimes. But it's always there —always—and I'm afraid not even you can prescribe any pills that can cure it." Suddenly I became a little defensive, " There now, that's how I really am. Does that answer your question?"

" Partly—I could see all that clearly in your eyes. You didn't need to spell it out. It helps you though to be able to talk it out. Now—there's more. What else?"

" Do widows and widowers simply have to learn to live with this aching emptiness at the core of their beings? Some days it's worse than others. But it's always there. Do we just have to come to terms with it? It seems to me that the immense satisfactions of daily living are gone for ever."

Gently the doctor answered, "No, not for ever. It only seems that way." He paused and his voice became a little stern. " Look, Catherine, you aren't the first person in the world to lose someone you love by death. This too will pass. The world won't always seem formless and grey to you. You'll just have to take my word for it. I've watched many friends, many patients, go through this stage, and I've helped a little—I hope. And it is a stage. You still have a lot of living to do—happy living. Just believe that, even though right now you don't see how."

For days after that my thoughts kept returning to what the doctor had said. I fervently hoped that he was right, that the gnawing hunger of the inner person was just a stage out of grief. But if so, I kept wishing that this particular mood —or stage—would pass.

It was true that the bittersweet wistfulness ebbed and flowed. I quickly discovered that certain things brought it to full tide—a convincing love scene in a movie, a sensuous passage in a book, certain songs, even certain fragrances. For me it was English Lavender, the sweetness of Nicotiana— heavy on the night air of a garden—and, oddly, the smell of fresh tar on a street.

Funerals I could now take with surprising equanimity; weddings I found emotionally devastating. Something about the wedding ceremony touched a deep chord at a level where I had no control over the emotions connected with it. Since it was embarrassing and unfair to other people to weep my way through what was a joyous occasion, usually I made excuses and stayed away. Often I would just drop in to greet my newly married friends at the reception after the cere- mony.

Sometimes the situation that precipitated these floods of emotion caught me unawares. There was the night of a mother-daughter banquet for which I had agreed to make an informal after-dinner talk. Before my part in the programme, a young baritone rose to sing a group of semi-classical songs. The last in the group was "Drink to me only with thine eyes."

I had heard Ben Jonson's words sung and read many times. It held no special memories for me, and I had never felt in the least sentimental about it. As the words of the lyric rose and fell . . .

Drink to me only with thine eyes,
  And I will pledge with mine;
Or leave a kiss within the cup,
  And I'll not ask for wine.
The thirst that from the soul doth rise
  Doth ask a drink divine—

suddenly I felt myself tighten. My hands, hidden under the edge of the table, began alternately twisting the edge of the tablecloth and clutching the evening bag in my lap until my fingers ached.

This won't do, I thought. I'll just have to stop listening. My eyes roamed over the scene before me—the mothers in all their finery sitting with their daughters beside them at the round tables, all listening intently to the tall young singer. I was searching desperately for something not at all sentimental on which to concentrate. Suddenly I spotted a red-headed teen-ager's hair-do. Deliberately, I studied it, trying to decide how some beautician had created the sleek turned-under effect.

By the time the last notes of the song had died away, the tension in my hands had relaxed, the fullness in my throat had disappeared. I was able to get to my feet calmly and even put a little humour into my talk.

In this sort of reaction, I was experiencing what almost every person goes through who has known bereavement or deep disappointment. My doctor had been justified and wise in reminding me—a little sternly—that my situation was not unique. Acknowledging that fact helped, not because " misery loves company," but because there is solace in understanding that there is such a thing as a fellowship of suffering.

After all, millions of other human beings down the centuries have known the snuffing out of their dreams and the medley that is grief—the tears, the feeling of being forsaken and bereft, the loneliness, the self-centredness, the self-pity, the self-accusation, the physical frustration, the wistfulness, the loss of zest for life. Somehow other people have survived it; the rest of us can too.

My doctor made it clear to me that the physical adjustment required in the change from married life to a single life accounts for much of the emotional upheaval, even aspects of grief that may seem to have no connection at all with the physical. He urged that I be clear-eyed about it and not try to explain it away on other terms.

"Honesty, even with yourself, helps", I remember him saying with a twinkle in his eyes. "Those who go through life pretending that sex doesn't exist or that it doesn't matter are either deceiving themselves or they're abnormal. Often these same people think that they are being lofty and spiritual in that attitude. Whereas if I read my Bible correctly, it has a surprising amount to say about the flesh. Above all, Catherine, don't be ashamed of your feelings. You are flesh and blood. Just thank God for that!"

In the years since then, an occasional widow, often shyly feeling her way, has talked to me about this delicate point. Always I knew that human beings and their emotional reactions could not be pigeon-holed. Any generalization in this area would be dangerous. Still I find that the feelings of those to whom physical loneliness is a problem follow a certain pattern, though the timing may vary.

At three months after the death of her husband, the average woman thinks, concerning the physical adjustment, 'This is easy. What's all the hullabaloo about? Why all the insinuations and snide remarks, the lifted eyebrows about widows and their needs? If there's anything to it at all, I must be some sort of an exception.'

At about five months the same widow begins to feel differently. She too may have begun to find it difficult. At six months the battle toward some sort of physical adjustment is on in earnest. The happier the particular woman had been in marriage, the more thoroughly she had adapted herself to married life, the greater her physical loneliness and her need will be.

One self-help book written for widows insists that sexual-adjustment difficulties have been grossly exaggerated, often whipped up to an unnecessary froth, as if the widow concerned enjoyed making a problem where one did not exist. The writer's main contention is that the female of the species is made to respond to specific sensual and sexual stimuli. Withdraw the stimuli and the woman is supposedly then in a state of blessed quiescent peace.

It's a neat theory. But just where within the confines of our modern society can the widow shelve herself these days in order to avoid sensual or sexual stimuli? I do not know the spot. Our society, influenced by Hollywood and the entertainment world generally, and further egged on by modern advertising, does quite the opposite. It goes in for all the stimuli it can manage. Exit the state of blessed quiescent peace!

I have known several widows who have sought and found some release through music. One of these used to sit at her baby grand piano and play and sing her heart out. Through the open windows of a summer afternoon her neighbours would see her, hear her filling the empty house with music. After a while, she would rise, go out into her yard, and search for weeds in the lawn with intensity, pull them out with determination. Then she would go back into the house for more music. It was a good combination—the singing and the weeding—but, as later events revealed, it did not solve her problem.

Other widows or widowers have told me that, from the first, they recognized the physical vacuum in their lives for what it was. Then as time passed, they sensed that the frustration was sinking deeper, through level after level of the personality. The hunger to share life intimately with another human being, the deep need for love, then began to merge in all sorts of ways, sometimes in such devious disguises that the individual did not always recognize the masks it wore.

With a woman, the family cat or parakeet, pet poodle or cocker, the mastiff or German shepherd that had belonged to her husband may become the object of her lavish affection. Those of us who love pets find this quite understandable. Fortunately, however, most women do not carry it as far as the one I heard bemoaning in a horrified tone the fact that her miniature schnauzer "had gone without a bath for three whole days." Or the French poodle I saw in a Washington department store whose owner had lacquered the dog's toenails red, put a rhinestone choker around its neck, and sprayed it with Chanel No. 5.

Most pets will lap up the affection and come back for more, none the worse for it. But when one's children suddenly find themselves all but drowned in a superfluity of love, then the situation is more serious. I have watched children come to feel restricted, even threatened by this smothering kind of love. They may start resisting it—either violently, according to the particular child's temperament, or by fleeing it.

One day, a few months after my husband's death, I wrote a reminder to myself on this point in my journal. . . .

I am now inclined to want to pour out too much love on my child. . . . Any tendency toward smother-love must be resisted at all costs. I must not penalize my child's development because of my own need, and rationalize it as mother love.

A kindred reaction of the bereaved is the loss of all zest for life. The sense of futility about everything is like a thick grey blanket smothering all initiative, stifling laughter, snuffing out hope, drugging energy. The smallest task becomes a gigantic effort. Why cook a meal when there is no one to share it? Entertaining looms as an impossible effort. Why dust or polish the furniture when there is no one to see or care? Anyway more dust will have settled by tomorrow. Why bother about clothes or grooming when there is no man around to notice a new dress or to comment on a becoming hair-do? Why bother? Why go through the motions?

The male is equally vulnerable to this kind of lethargy. As one businessman whose wife had died commented to me, "I have a thriving business and a fine income. But now that Fran is gone, it's all sawdust in my mouth. What's the point of success if you have no one to share it with? Why knock yourself out to make money when there's no one to spend it on?"

Such a sense of futility is often accompanied by desultory daydreaming. It may be a reliving over and over of certain scenes out of the past, or it may be conjuring up fantasies for the future. In either case, it saps energy that should be given to daily tasks, to the rebuilding of life, to the working out of new patterns of action.

Another symptom of physical loneliness for a woman is a new and surprising set of reactions to the opposite sex. One woman commented, "When I was with a man, I found myself suddenly and acutely aware that he *was* a man in a way I had seldom experienced before Jim's death. I found that I had to keep a sharp check on my reactions to men friends, leash my emotions in, lest I give undue response to the most routine and insignificant attentions."

The same woman may find that after this "leashing in," tears are too often just under the surface. This discovery frightens her; probably she has always prided herself on not being the crying type. She wonders if she is actually becoming emotionally unbalanced.

Or she may be horrified one day to realize that she is thinking about sex quite a lot. Suddenly it looms too large. Her own reactions in this regard seem alien to her; she cannot remember having been that way before her husband's death. Secretly, she wonders if she has more than her share of sexual energy or is abnormal in some way.

What has happened is understandable. When one is happily married, the physical aspect of marriage falls into place as but a part of one's total life. That is as it should be. But the soldier lost in the desert can think only of water. The explorer, caught miles from his base in Antarctica, is preoccupied with a mental picture of lolling luxuriously before a cosy fire.

I remember one man who had taught for many years in a men's college saying to me, " After years of observation, I'm not sure but what I think coed institutions are to be preferred to all-male schools. When the boys are isolated from girls, they finally get to the point when they can't think about much *except* girls."

What then? It is not enough to acknowledge that this is a common, perhaps unavoidable dilemma for the single person. What is one to do with the superfluity of creative energy pulsing through his veins? There must be some healthy right answer to it. But what?

The first answer that may occur to the widow or widower is remarriage. The single person suspects—probably rightly —that there is no final perfect solution to the physical problem for the unmarried person.

" It is not good that man should be alone," is the wisdom given us from God Himself in the second chapter of Genesis. We would be foolish indeed to pretend that it is good. When we live alone for any length of time, an inevitable warping takes place. It is only in living closely with another person that we find our own identity and that the rough edges of selfishness are smoothed away. Every widow or widower who thinks about marrying again thinks about it in the abstract long before the thoughts are linked to any particular person. He wonders if it would be possible to fall in love again. And if immortality is at all real, he wonders how the one in the next life would feel about his remarrying?

Other widows and widowers immediately shut the door even on the possibility of second marriage, like a slim attractive woman who came to call on me one afternoon. Somewhere in her forties, she had been utterly desolated by the recent death of her husband.

I sensed that her need at that time was to talk out her

grief. So she did talk—for two hours. Then just as she was leaving she said, "Of course, I know that I'll never marry again. I could never replace Jim."

For days afterwards her words echoed in my mind— "Replace Jim. . . ." Of course not! Not Jim nor anyone else. The mould was broken when each of us was born.

Yet this casual remark revealed something fundamentally wrong with that particular widow's concept of remarriage. The idea that Jim could not be replaced seemed close to the idea that remarriage would somehow be a repudiation of Jim, would betray his love.

Another woman who wrote to me seemed about to reach the same conclusion by a different line of reasoning:

After all, real marriage is a spiritual union as well as a physical one. And two people in a true marriage do indeed become one. My love for my husband has long since been written into my being. Therefore death had no power to disturb that. . . .

But Ted has now been gone three years. A fine man wants me to marry him. I can't seem to get my thinking straight on it.

My sticking point on second marriages is this: Since marriage *is* a spiritual union, too, doesn't the idea of second marriage put an undue emphasis on the physical side of marriage? If one's husband were physically incapacitated, would a woman worth her salt divorce him because the physical was denied? Is death very different from that . . .?

These thoughts are not unusual. No doubt a person like Queen Victoria, who for forty years never gave up mourning her Albert, had many of the same thoughts. The interesting thing is that my correspondent and others like her are being more "spiritual" on this point than the Scriptures. For one of the foundation stones of the Bible is the assurance of life after death. Yet in its clear approval of second marriage, it understands our human need of companionship and recognizes that there is a difference between the physical and the spiritual.

There is another, quite opposite danger—that of thinking that remarriage will automatically mend the hurt and solve all problems. Perhaps this danger is partly the result of what I believe to be a mistaken concept of marriage. It is a concept well dramatized in a Greek legend. Androgynos —a bi-sexed, four-legged, four-armed creature—is said to have tried to scale heaven to challenge the gods themselves. Zeus thwarted the threat by splitting this strange creature in two, thus creating man and woman as they are today. Plato, in his *Symposium*, describes the results:

> After the division the two parts of man, each desiring his other half, came together . . . longing to grow into one. . . . Each of us when separated, having one side only, like a flat fish, is but the indenture of a man, and he is always looking for his other half. . . . And when one of them meets the actual half of himself . . . the pair are lost in an amazement of love and friendship and intimacy, and one will not be out of the other's sight. . . .

It is true that when death removes the one from the other's sight, the one left does indeed feel like half a person. Yet death also dramatizes the deeper truth—that marriage as it is meant to be is not the coming together of two halves, but of two whole mature people, each a separate though interdependent entity.

We who have been bereaved are in a peculiar position to understand this, and with that understanding to take a new step toward maturity. The widow sees as never before that only when she is a whole person does she have enough to contribute to any marriage relationship. She sees that in

T.L.A. E

marriage or out of marriage, she will be lonely unless she is taking definite steps toward finding herself, toward becoming the whole person she is meant to be.

In my case, I was early pushed into asking many of these questions by the vivid dream I had had soon after my husband's death. At that time, my deepest questions had been . . . Where was Peter now? And what was my relationship to him now?

My answer was that as love is progressively purified, possessiveness is dropped out. The deeper and truer the love, the more completely it releases the beloved. The bereaved usually think of this from the earthly side, from a selfish point of view. Not often enough do they consider the fact that the possessiveness inherent in their continuing sorrow fails to release the ones who have gone on into the new life, in a sense holds them bound to the wheel of sorrow.

As my child was growing up, I saw an analogy in my love for him. The highest function of my mother-love would be fulfilled when my love was strong enough to cut the apron strings and let my adult child move off into his own life. I would succeed as a mother only when I had so reared my child that he would no longer have need of me. Yet this is not tragedy; it is growth. This is no betrayal of love. This is love.

But what if the events of life so arrange themselves that the bereaved person does not remarry? The first question that every widow or widower must then face is . . . do I really want an immediate solution to my sexual frustration or my loneliness? Or am I clinging to it? To what extent do I actually enjoy wallowing in self-pity? Am I too fear-ridden to venture into new situations that might offer some creative solutions?

Clear-eyed answers to these questions are essential because help is available when and if we really want it. Moreover, God knows the minute we stop playing around the edges of the problem and really begin wanting His help.

What we must *not* do is to assume that the only right way

to handle the problem of physical longing is to be rid of it entirely, in order to be at peace. Such repression can be a carry-over from an abnormal Puritanism.

Is it possible that we in our day are too enamoured of peace of mind? We can be so peaceful that the edge is gone off living; that we hear no birdsong, see no lavender-tinted sunsets, shed no tears, forget the rough edge of pain, no longer know how to laugh. In fact, when we feel nothing at all, then we are dead.

My experience has been that it is only out of a state of tension that growth can come. It is a strange paradox that we have to be willing to suffer the tension for a time, knowing that it is the bridge to the next step in our lives. Even sexual frustration puts the sparkle in the eyes, the warmth in the voice, the lilt in the step. If we can manage to thank God for it, thank Him that there is still enough life in us to burst the old bonds, however painfully, in order to create something new—then we shall find even the tension a blessing.

The solution, at least for a given period of an individual's life, may be in the rechannelling of the creativity that is sexual energy. This energy in us is always seeking a way to express the spirit that is the real person. Such expression *is* creativity. Sex is only one of life's expressions for it. There are many others—singing, dancing, writing, painting, speaking, cooking, gardening, flower arranging, woodworking, dressmaking, giving a child joy or planting a dream in his eyes.

Yet this rechannelling of emotional energy is tricky. Peace of mind, happiness, contentment, and all their first and second cousins come to us only as by-products. The paradox is that he who tries basket weaving, not because he is fascinated by weaving, but in order to avoid his emotional problem, will end up a still-frustrated person, loathing his baskets.

Thus creativity will satisfy the inner hunger only if the individual finds the natural channel of expression for him. No artificially made work, just to fill up time, will suffice.

For the task will satisfy the inner need only if the total person
—will, body and soul, mind and emotions—can be given to
it.

But the person tethered to loneliness and frustration is likely
to be impatient with an answer like this. " This ' live
creatively ' theory of yours is a stop-gap measure," he replies.
" Not a final solution."

His impatience may be justified. It is true that this is only
a wayside stop on the road to a more complete answer.

The problems of loneliness and sexual frustration are
inextricably intertwined. They who walk in wistfulness have
need of belonging, of being loved for themselves. How
then, is that quality of love found?

Most of us make self the centre of reference. . . . What
do I want . . .? What's in it for me . . .? What will make
me happy . . .?

When we live this way, we treat other people not as persons,
but as things. We use everyone else, as we would a com-
modity, for our own purposes. In doing so, we renounce
life's precious law of relationship.

Even though such a person finds romance, the result will
not be love, but lust. And lust titillates, but does not satisfy.
Moreover, the law of diminishing returns always sets in.
It takes more and more romantic adventures to satisfy less
and less. Thus the belongings that we think we have set
up, often fail us in the end. We are left lonelier and more
frustrated than before.

Many another belonging must fail us too. Death can
snatch parents and relatives from our sides. Even the groups
of friends in clubs and organizations to which we have given
our loyalty, change through the years.

In the period immediately following my husband's death,
I felt that much of the structure of my life was gone. I
tried going down many roads in an effort to find a solution.
I found every road a dead end but one. My conclusion is

that there is only one belonging in the universe on which we can finally depend—our belonging to Jesus Christ.

The reason that many a hungry-hearted person does not know this is simply because he has never entered into the relationship. He is still on the sidelines reading about it, thinking about it, appraising it.

Long ago one Paul, from the Cilician city of Tarsus, after searching down many a road himself, tried to put into words for the rest of us the indestructibility of this final belonging. After cataloguing some of the troubles that can plague us in this life, Paul gave his conclusion:

I have become absolutely convinced that neither Death nor Life
neither messenger of heaven nor monarch of earth,
neither what happens today nor what may happen to-morrow,
neither a power from on high nor a power from below,
nor anything else in God's whole world
has any power to separate us from the love of God
in Jesus Christ our Lord! (ROMANS 8:38, 39)[1]

So what must we do to enter into this highest relationship?

Entering into a marriage relationship is an almost perfect analogy. We want to enter into it. We make a decision. We take a definite step at the moment of the marriage ceremony.

We take that step, even though we know that a risk is involved. We cannot know what the future may hold; we cannot guess all that may be required of us. But we guess that the joys of the comradeship will outweigh the risk.

Instinctively, we feel that there is risk involved in entering into a relationship with our God. How can we know what He may require of us?

[1] Phillips, J. B., *Letters to Young Churches*, London, Fontana, 1955.

But when we guess that the joy of the relationship and having His love in our empty hearts may outweigh the risk and we take the step anyway—that is taking a step in faith.

Then, wonder of wonders, our feeling of the futility that has enshrouded life as in a fog begins to evaporate. Life has structure again. A sense of mission returns. Once again we know that we belong. We have come home to our world.

What does all this have to do with physical longing, sex? Quite a lot. Because sex is not unspiritual; it is part of life. It is only our earthly expression of the spirit that is us, reaching out to love and to be loved, to belong in an intimate way.

And loving is giving ourselves—not just our bodies—but the real us, the essence of us. Not until we have entered into that highest Relationship, do we find a self to give. Only then do we become a warm-hearted person capable of giving love; only then can we receive it.

And after we have entered into this highest Relationship, we discover the best thing of all—that our God is indeed a personal God. His directions could not get through to us before. We could not understand His plan; now we can. We find that His solution for us is designed to fit our special needs and that it is consistent with our earthly happiness.

The answer to all my questioning that summer on Cape Cod seemed to be that a new pattern of action, one tailor-made for me, was just around the corner. It would—at least for the next period of my life—answer the deep needs with which I wrestled.

CHAPTER 8

"Go Ahead and Write It, Kate. . . ."

From where I stood in the doorway, Peter John's room was quite a sight. Three ancient, dearly loved stuffed animals were lying sprawled at his feet, with Jeff, our cocker spaniel, beside them. Some books had been piled up carefully. I could see *The Wind in the Willows* and *Misty of Chincoteague* on top. There was another stack of comic books. A cardboard carton filled with train track blocked the door. Peter was standing in the midst of the disorder, holding a plane model in each hand, his blond hair tousled, a bewildered look on his face.

"What's got you stopped?" I asked.

"Mom, do I *have* to give some stuff away?"

"Yes, you do. The apartment only has four rooms. Your room is small. There just won't be space for all this."

"But gosh! I've gotta keep the books, the trains, and the airplane models."

"The books can be thinned out. Children's Hospital will be delighted to have some. Better get on with the sorting."

"Holy cow! I'm not sure we'll like the apartment."

I was not sure myself. I was finding moving out of the Manse even harder than Peter John. It was no wonder. . . . This was the first move of my new life, that life I had not wanted. The Cathedral Avenue house had been our home ever since we had been in Washington, through twelve happy significant years.

Still, in three days the moving men would be on our doorstep. This was early March, 1950. We were leaving the ten-room Manse for a second floor, walk-up apartment in one of Washington's immense developments. We would still be in the northwest section of the city, not far from the Cathedral Avenue house.

There was the problem of what we would have room for in the apartment, what should be given away or sold, what should be stored. Each decision took its own emotional toll.

But before I had taken down the seascapes, packed the books and linen, the china, the glass, I had asked a friend to take some interior flash-bulb snapshots of our house. . . . The breakfast nook with its yellow organdie curtains and the miniature potted plants on the window sills; the sunroom with its shelves of coloured glass; Peter's big chintz-covered chair by the radio; a corner of the front bedroom. . . . I wanted to be sure that each detail would be captured. Yet—how could I ever forget? These rooms had been the setting for a lot of happy living.

The apartment development had been built on hilly terrain. On moving day four men staggered up the hill and down, then up the two flights of stairs with our spinet piano and numberless cartons of books. They grunted and complained about the books. . . . " Why—so many? Books are—heavy."

I carried the boxes of carefully packed antique glass myself. Peter was just as solicitous about his plane models, all three cartons of them.

The moving men finally dragged themselves up the stairs with the last load and drove away. They had left us with boxes piled halfway to the ceiling of our tiny living room.

Eventually, some order was brought out of the chaos. We finally got to the place where we could walk unimpeded across the living room. But we were still crowded. With every day that passed we were becoming more space conscious, learning what every apartment dweller knows—that space is one of the most beautiful things God ever made.

This was dramatized by the way one of our apartment neighbours stored her extra blankets in the trunk of the family car. The only trouble was that the blankets were not exactly accessible at times when they were ten blocks away in the parked car. Our own space problem resulted in my using the kitchen food chopper in the bathroom linen closet. A thorough search had uncovered the odd fact that a linen-closet shelf was the only place to which the food chopper could be attached.

I also found that the manless household has its unique difficulties. I had no knowledge of how to keep the car in good repair, how to fix a leaking tap or repair a burned-out electric cord, or even how to set a mousetrap. As for emptying a mousetrap—no, a thousand times no! One morning, when Peter John was not there to dispose of the unfortunate mouse for me, I pressed the milkman into service.

Soon Peter and I got to know our neighbours very well. If a baby had wind pains and kept his parents awake, all of the neighbours stayed awake too. If the occupants of apartment C-3 were having a party, the rest of us shared the hilarity. If some of the neighbours went through a period of battling damp bugs or cockroaches in the kitchen, all of us battled bugs. Unitedly we bore with the man who liked to listen to prize fights and wrestling matches far into the night, and the Britisher who religiously tuned in the midnight short-wave newscast from London.

With a front as solid as any Macedonian phalanx, we bore up under the strong smell of disinfectant used in the halls, the wide cracks in the floor, and the vociferous cuckoo clock in B-5.

Peter John appeared to take the change from house to apartment living in his stride. He took his turn at walking Jeff often enough to make up for the fact that even the cocker's quarters were cramped. He thought it very funny that to the other children who lived in our court, I was known simply as " Jeffrey's mother." By careful planning, Peter had found a place in his bedroom for all twenty-eight plane models, though that meant he had to duck, dodge, and side-step on the treacherous path from door to bed.

I noticed, however, that Peter rarely invited any of his friends to our apartment. Often after school, he would disappear for a while. Investigation revealed that on these afternoons he was going back to our old home on Cathedral Avenue. The new minister, Dr George Docherty, Dr Marshall's successor at the church, had by then moved into the Manse with his family. His two boys were considerably younger than Peter, therefore not the playmates he would ordinarily have chosen. But apparently the Manse was still home to Peter. Like a homing pigeon, he kept returning to familiar haunts.

Peter was missing more than the house. I knew that he was homesick for the family fun—the special nonsense game he had played with his father at mealtimes, their work together on the electric-train layout, their discussion of sports that " you, Mom, just don't understand." He was missing, as I was, all the guests, the teas, and church meetings, the constant procession of friends in and out of our old home.

He and I were having trouble persuading ourselves that one woman and one child could still make a family.

That month I received a letter from someone unknown to me. It was from an Edward C. Aswell, editor-in-chief of the trade department of the McGraw-Hill Book Company in New York City. He was writing, he explained, at the instigation of one of the book world's most respected and widely known buyers, Peggy O'Neill of Miller and Rhoads in Richmond, Virginia.

Later, I was to find out more details about what had happened. During a visit to her book department from one of the McGraw-Hill salesmen, she had told him, "I have a message I want you to deliver to Ed Aswell. We've had two very successful autograph parties here for Peter Marshall's *Mr Jones, Meet the Master*." *Mr Jones*, it developed, was one of her favourite books.

The salesman seemed surprised, " But you're not a Presbyterian."

" No, I'm not . . . but *Mr Jones* appeals to all faiths. Well, anyway . . . Mrs Marshall mentioned that she has a lot more sermon manuscripts. . . ."

The message was faithfully delivered. Mr. Aswell suggested in his letter to me that his publishing house would like to know more about those other sermons.

That spring we exchanged letters. I suggested a theme for the next book, a compilation of Dr Marshall's sermons on immortality. But by early June another idea—exciting, frighteningly ambitious—was taking shape in my mind. Slowly, I had come to the conviction that the next book should not be a book of sermons, but Peter Marshall's own story. The sermons had grown out of the life; the story of the life held a message that I felt should not be lost to our time .

Mr Aswell seemed interested in the new proposal. He wrote :

Why don't you write a chapter of the book you have in mind, and send it to me, together with a fairly detailed outline of the entire book . . .? I shall await the sample material with eagerness.

There was no time even to think about the sample chapter until after Peter John's school was out and he and I were back at the Cape Cod cottage. In the early summer of 1950, as in the previous year, the return to Waverley reopened emotional wounds. At the cottage, everywhere I turned, I was reminded of Peter. I tried to handle the situation by keeping busy.

During the New England winter, the paint on our garage doors had weathered. One day I undertook to repaint them. By evening, Chatham blue paint was under my fingernails, even in my hair.

But during all the hours of physical work, I had not been able to turn off my mind and my emotions. Finally by evening, exhausted, I went to bed earlier than usual. But I could not sleep. Suddenly I sat bolt upright in bed, startled by an altogether new idea.

What were the last words that I had ever said to Peter?

Yes, I remembered. He had been lying on the stretcher in the first-floor hall where the two orderlies had put him down for a moment. And as he had looked up at me through his pain, I had said—of course! " See you, darling, see you in the morning. . . ." Why had I never thought of it before? Words began stringing themselves together in my mind, spinning themselves into clauses and sentences.

Suddenly the tears spilled over, as if they had been lying in pools behind my eyes for many months and were now glad of release. I switched on the night light and grabbed a piece of paper and pencil. Words poured on to the paper. I wrote steadily with never a pause, though at times tears blurred my eyes and dampened the pencilled lines. Ten minutes later I fell back against the pillows—emotionally drained.

I could not have known it then, but the ending—the last page and a half of book later to be known as *A Man Called Peter*—had just been written. Hardly two words of what had flowed out that night were ever changed.

Later that week, while I was planting window boxes, sunning and brushing blankets, and getting lawn furniture washed, I was pondering the question of what the sample chapter should be. The page and a half was not enough manuscript to send to Mr. Aswell. Finally one day I sat down and began writing. . . .

> I was twenty and allergic to figures. Unfortunately the required college algebra had figures, lots of them. . . .

My pencil sped along the page. What was being set down were certain lighthearted, gay incidents of courtship days. Immediately, I found myself revelling in the humour of the experiences as I relived them in the writing. So long as I worked on the chapter, a weight was lifted from me; it was almost as if Peter were alive again.

Then I put my portable typewriter on the old drop-leaf

mahogany table that Peter and I had refinished together and laboriously typed out the pages—hunt and peck. The brief ending, written in tears; the single chapter, written in happy memories; and a loosely woven, crude outline of the book were then mailed to Mr Aswell.

I had not the slightest idea what his reaction would be. After a few days I began nervously haunting the little white-frame post office in West Harwich for the editor's reply.

Within the week I found the letter lying in my mail-box. Standing in the middle of the post-office floor, I ripped open the envelope. What I read astonished me:

> July 21, 1950
>
> Dear Mrs Marshall:
>
> Your outline of the book on Dr Marshall, together with your draft of Chapter 6 and the end of Chapter 16 arrived safely a few days ago. I read over the material promptly and was delighted with it. I then had several of my colleagues read it and they shared my enthusiasm for it.
>
> There is not the slightest doubt in our minds, that this will be a good book and a very deeply moving one. It is one we should be most proud to publish. . . .
>
> As for the writing, I compliment you on its sincerity and its deep emotional integrity.
>
> We are now prepared to offer you a contract. . . .

I was exhilarated by such encouragement. Still I marvelled that Mr Aswell had so much faith in my ability that he was willing to offer me a contract before seeing the completed manuscript. How did he know that I could write a book? I didn't know myself. But there it was in black and white. . . . "We are now prepared to offer you a contract. . . ."

So far my only contact with the editor had been through correspondence. Though I knew little about the usual relationship between author and editor, I sensed that there would have to be close teamwork. Thus, before considering a contract,

I decided that my next move should be to meet Mr Aswell.

Peter John stayed with one of our neighbours on Pleasant Road while I made the trip to New York. Going down on the train, I reviewed what I had learned about Edward Aswell. He had been Thomas Wolfe's editor during the last part of the novelist's life. After Wolfe's early death in 1938, Mr Aswell had been responsible for editing and publishing *The Web and the Rock, You Can't Go Home Again,* and *The Hills Beyond.* He had also worked with Richard Wright, Betty Smith, and many others. He had moved to McGraw-Hill only a few years before, and was one of those responsible for building the company's reputation in the field of trade books. And now he wanted to see me. I could only marvel.

The New York, New Haven and Hartford train slowed down at the outer rim of the gigantic, sprawling metropolis that is New York. Now we were going through the slum districts with their forests of television aerials, their pocket handkerchiefs of back yards cluttered with debris, the lines of wash swung out from second- and third-story windows, the children playing stick ball in the streets. As the train got closer to Grand Central station, something inside me began to tighten. Just making a sally by myself into New York was still a new and terrifying experience. And this was one of the nation's largest publishing houses which I was invading. . . .

The McGraw-Hill building on West 42nd Street was an impressive, modern, green-and-chrome structure thirty-four stories high. The executive offices of the trade book department were on the twentieth floor, and my feeling of tension increased as an express elevator whizzed me upward.

I did not have to wait long in the reception room. A secretary took me past a battery of clicking typewriters to a quiet corner office. There I met the editor—a greying, balding man with alert and kindly eyes. He was friendly, easy to talk to. He soon put me at ease. We talked for over an hour. I shared with him some of my ideas on the proposed biography of Dr Marshall. Mr Aswell, on his side, told me about his philosophy of books in general. From time to time he would go to the bookshelves that covered one wall and pull out some recently published book to make a point more vividly.

On another wall was a large original cartoon by Thurber, a memento of one of his earlier publishing experiences. As the editor and I talked, we could look over the whole lower part of New York. The two walls of windows were wide vistas, like live murals of the city. Looking west, there were the Lincoln Tunnel, the ocean-going liners at their berths, and across the river, the mist-blurred New Jersey hills. Looking south, there was the Battery, the Statue of Liberty, and the Bay beyond.

During the conversation with Mr Aswell, I had an intuitive feeling that in him I had found the right editor. Even so, I did not sign the contract that afternoon, but took it back to the Cape to study it at my leisure and to check it with other people. After the contract was changed in a few details and signed, it pledged me to deliver the finished manuscript of a biography of Peter Marshall to the publisher by May 1, 1951—ten months hence.

That fall, the day after Peter John's school started, I got out the outline of the proposed biography that I had sent Mr Aswell during the summer. I cringed (as I thought Mr Aswell must have) at the romantic title—*Heathen in My Heart.* Terrible! Couldn't be worse! The outline itself was a rough one. . . .

CHAPTER 1—" Under Sealed Orders "
Peter Marshall leaves Scotland as a quota immigrant. . . .

CHAPTER 2—" The King Is in the Audience "
This shows P.M.'s unique and dramatic approach to Christianity . . .

CHAPTER 3—"Sagging Balconies"
A personality sketch of P.M. as man and preacher. . . .

Something more basic than sketchiness was wrong with this. "P.M. leaves Scotland," "P.M.'s unique and dramatic approach," "A personality sketch of P.M." . . .

Suddenly I felt the necessity of asking myself some pointed questions. . . . Why am I writing this book? What am I trying to accomplish?

I saw immediately what was wrong with the outline. The hero of the biography had to be God—not Peter Marshall. What I was to write was no ordinary Horatio Alger story of the successful immigrant. What Peter Marshall alone had done was not important; what God had done through him—a man with faults like the rest of us— was important. Jesus Christ would have to tower as the central figure of the book if the biography was to be anything more than a wife's recollections. I saw that the life of no human being has lasting significance apart from his relationship to God.

The need of all of us—whether we realize it or not—is to know whether there really is a God, and if so, to know Him in a direct and personal way through Christ. When we know Him and understand something of His love for us as persons, then we can trust and follow Him. Only then shall we lose the pang of our loneliness and our heart hunger.

The life of this one man then, this fallible man, Peter Marshall, could be used to answer the average person's questions about God and how He deals with each of us.

I discarded the old outline and started over, asking myself two questions about each chapter . . . What is the theme, the cohesive idea? And what will this chapter tell about God that people really want to know?

CHAPTER 1—"Under Sealed Orders"
Does God still guide people today as the Bible says He did in other ages?

CHAPTER 2—"Singing in the Rain"
Can God still provide material help in our day . . .?

Such an approach to the writing of a biography was unusual.
I knew that. But then the non-professional writer either
has to be himself completely or else a slaving imitator of somebody else's techniques. I didn't even know enough to be an
imitator, so I was nothing if not individualistic.

That fall, if a space man had paused in an interplanetary
flight to peer in through a window of our second-floor
apartment, he would have stared at a curious sight. . . . A
woman propped up in bed writing, with scrapbooks and
papers cluttering the bed and the floor; pencil smudges on
her face and hands, on the floor beside her a cocker keeping
sleepy sentinel. On one side of the bed was an olive-green
filing cabinet: in a corner, a dictating machine. Sometimes
the woman would jump out of bed to get a cookie or an
apple; at other times, to search the file for a missing
paper.

During my long illness several years before, I had learned
to write in bed. I had discovered then that my thoughts
flowed more easily when my body was relaxed. The bedroom, however, was scarcely the ideal place to work. Papers
were everywhere, even among my lingerie in the dresser
drawers. Most mornings there were from four to twenty-
three pre-school children playing lustily under my windows.
Then there were the ever-ringing telephones. And, of course,
the cuckoo clock in B-5.

Each forenoon, Monday through Thursday, I began work
at nine. By twelve-thirty or one I would be limp, written
out for the day. The afternoons I saved for revision, interviews with people close to Peter, and reading the longhand
manuscript into the dictating machine. A part-time secretary would then do a typewritten copy. This, in turn, would
undergo several revisions.

Experience soon taught me not to work on an evening
if I wanted to sleep. The mind can act like a high-powered

machine. Start it going, and it's hard to turn off. Moreover, I found that I needed to see my friends in the evenings. With the continuous work that a book entails, a change of pace is necessary to keep one from going stale. Fridays were reserved for my housework and weekly grocery shopping. Saturdays I devoted to my son.

Two factors enabled me to take my writing schedule so seriously. The first was the signed contract resting in my files. At moments when I wondered whether I was merely indulging myself with delusions of grandeur about being a writer, I would remember that I was legally pledged to deliver a finished manuscript by May 1.

The second was my continuing sense of destiny. There is no bulwark like the conviction of being under orders. Without that, I would have fallen by the wayside a thousand times.

A series of events vindicated my faith that Someone Else's hand was on the project, and that His help was always available. At one point I needed some detailed information about Peter's stepfather. He had died in Scotland one week after Peter. Mother Janet, my husband's mother, was still living, but her memory often failed her on early details. There was not time to take a trip to Scotland to gather information. It seemed as if all possible sources had been exhausted.

Then one night an English couple whom I had met casually invited me to dinner. In the course of an enjoyable evening with them I felt an urge to tell my host about the facts I needed. Suddenly he interrupted me excitedly.

" Surely, you couldn't be speaking of Peter Findlay?"

" Yes, certainly. Why?" The atmosphere in the room became electric.

" I worked beside him in the same office at Stewarts and Lloyds in Glasgow for years. I knew him well. What do you want to know?"

That night I went back to our apartment as excited as a child on Christmas Eve. There are over 800,000 residents of the District of Columbia proper. It's a safe guess that the man to whom I had been led was the only one of the 800,000 who had ever worked in the same office with Peter Findlay. It was as if God were saying, " I'm in this with you. Let this little incident give you courage when the task seems too big for you."

I needed that courage, because sometimes I grew very much afraid. For example, the chapter about Peter Marshall's early life was still unwritten. I was uneasy about it. A straight narration of facts, dates, places would make dry reading. For this chapter I had to describe events that had happened long before I had known Peter. But how could I write vividly, except out of experience—mine or someone else's? I had no background to help me understand a Scottish boy growing up in an industrial suburb of Glasgow, and later, working as a machinist in a tube-works.

Once again, in a childlike way, I asked God for help. My answer came in a long-distance call from one Jim Broadbent. He was coming through Washington soon, he said. Could he see me? Jim Broadbent was a cousin of Peter's who had known him always. He was a world traveller and adventurer, long associated in business with the Anglo-Iranian Oil Company. It was he who had first turned Peter's thoughts toward the United States.

There was no doubt that Mr Broadbent had the information I needed. Among the writer's treasured raw materials is the anecdote lifted right out of life. First-hand stories provide those graphic details which allow the reader to see, feel, hear, even smell a scene. Many interviews had already taught me that some people have the feel for the good story and the vivid detail, while no amount of prying can get it out of others. I held my breath, hoping that Jim Broadbent would, miraculously, turn out to be one of those tale-spinners.

On the afternoon he arrived, I saw at once that he was the rugged, unself-conscious type. Of above average height, sturdily built, he gave an impression of repressed vitality. His Scottish accent filled the room like a buzz saw.

The Scot is by nature clannish; he will do anything for
"his ain folk." Jim's warmth toward me suggested that he
had already taken me into the clan. He would probably have
given me anything, even half of his oil shares. When he
found out I wanted reminiscences, he settled himself, put
his feet up, lighted his pipe, and prepared to spend the afternoon. All he asked, he said, was a spot of tea later on.

"Tell me what Peter was like as a young boy," I began.
"What did he look like?"

"Tall . . . shot up too quickly . . . shock of curly blond
hair, inclined to be unr-r-ruly, never slicked down . . .
stubbor-rn as a MacDonald or a MacTavish . . . idealistic
. . . impetuous."

Only a few questions were needed to keep him going.
Jim Broadbent had a photographic memory. More than that,
detailed descriptions began pouring out—how a Mr Ash,
Peter's foreman at Stewarts and Lloyds, had looked; the
picture of Peter's tidy boarding-house room; the look of an
iron bedstead; the iron, cold to the fingertips in the Scottish
winter, the quiet ticking of an old-fashioned clock on a wall,
with Peter's kilts hanging on a peg under it. . . .

Bit by bit, the missing pieces of my "Under Sealed Orders"
chapter were falling into place. Excitedly I took notes, at the
same time soaking up the atmosphere of the scenes Jim
described. I could not have imagined a more adequate answer
to my plea to God for help than was Jim Broadbent. Once
again I had been put in contact with just the right person.

But God's help is not limited to such dramatic episodes.
Some of it has to be of the everyday, run-of-the-mill variety.
As a housewife trying to write a book, I needed some help
in craftsmanship and professional writing techniques.

One day in the course of an informal talk in a Washington church, I mentioned my book. Afterward a slightly built
woman of middle years came up to introduce herself. "I am
Ruth Welty," she said, extending her hand. "I wonder if
you would give me your address? I'd like to write you."

In a few days the note came. . . .

Dear Mrs Marshall:

Last Wednesday afternoon I asked for your address in order that I might send you several thoughts. . . .

Your book, I feel, will be an interpretation of the great soul, Peter Marshall. You will relive your association with him, in order that *he* may live for thousands now and in the future.

For the next few months you will not be living in 1950 at all. You will be tempted many times to flee Washington and the many demands made upon you by people who do not understand what it means to write a book. But your source materials, your familiar tools are here, and so you will try to be both the writer and the sweet, accessible adviser. May you have the strength of twins . . .!

You probably have many literary friends. But I'm moved, nevertheless, to suggest that if you should desire impartial comment on your manuscript, or want to discuss it in process, I should be happy to cooperate with you —gratis. It's all part of the Father's work.

> Most sincerely,
> (Miss) Ruth Welty

The offer in the last paragraph of the letter was an unusual one. But who was Ruth Welty? She had apparently never known Peter or me and had never been connected with our church. I put out feelers among my friends; no one had heard of her.

Finally I telephoned Miss Welty. She explained that in the past she had done editorial work in one of the government agencies and had herself once written a play that had been produced on Broadway. Recently she had retired from government work.

"I wrote you," she said, "under a sort of inner prompting. If I can help with criticism, I'd like to. Naturally, you'd be free to take or leave my suggestions. And I couldn't accept anything for the work."

I protested . . . " But that wouldn't be fair."

" That's the only way I'd agree to do it."

" But why?"

" Well, you see, I believe that there's a sort of reservoir of good will in the world. I call it a spiritual blood bank. Those in need can draw help from it. But the reservoir can be added to only through good deeds done without personal gain. I may not have too many more years. I'd like to feel that I've added my bit. That's all."

The spiritual blood bank idea was new to me and sounded a bit odd. I thanked Miss Welty but hung up without committing myself.

I was still so unsure of myself as a writer that the wrong kind of criticism might bog me down completely. Mr Aswell had warned me about that. " Get a first draft down on paper," he had said. " I don't even want to see it until it's finished. Critical work will come later."

How could I know what Miss Welty's criticism would be like? I wanted help, but the right kind. In my dilemma, I again tried prayer, asking God—quite simply—to tell me what to do. After several days, there came the quiet assurance that my unknown friend's " compulsion " about contacting me had been authentic, that I should accept her offer. I waited a few more days. Still it seemed clear and right. Finally I dared to accept her offer.

I need not have doubted that God could give me specific guidance on even such a technical matter as this. Miss Welty took the manuscript several chapters at a time. She sent them back with pages of typewritten suggestions . . . page ———, line ———, my suggestion is . . . She caught poor sentence structure, fuzzy writing, dangling modifiers, misspelling, bad transitions, places where I had taken too much reader knowledge for granted. Never did she tear the manuscript apart in a destructive way. She gave encouragement when it was needed. Always she made it clear that it was my book; the final decisions were mine. In short,

I had been sent the perfect adviser—expert, prompt, business-like, kindly.

By then, some four months' work had taught me a little about the process of creating. A person writing a book cannot wait for times of inspiration. Usually the spurts of inspired writing come as dividends from hours upon hours of grinding labour every day.

Another encouraging result of the daily writing schedule is that the work gains momentum with time. Any interruption in the schedule decreases this momentum. Thus I always found it harder to get started on a Monday morning. After a vacation longer than Friday to Monday, it would sometimes take me days to get under way again. I discovered what many writers know, that it was well to end a day's work in the middle of a paragraph, even in the middle of a sentence. Then one's mind is forced to carry the unfinished work until the next work period, and the picking up is easier.

The other side of the writer's schedule is that it can imprison one. For me, much of writing involves catching on paper those will-o'-the-wisp ideas and impressions that come up suddenly out of the subconscious mind. They can rise up at odd times, ruthlessly interrupt sleep, work, even periods of relaxation. Often I would get an idea while walking Jeff along the woodland trail behind our apartment. Then I would rush home to get it down on paper. Or I might wake up in the night with a full-blown sentence in my mind. I soon learned to keep a pad and pencil on my nightstand.

I found that listening to music—different moods of music—affected the feel of what I wrote. In the same way, I had to screen what I read because different authors affected my own style. Did I want to sound faintly tinged with Shakespeare or Edna St Vincent Millay? *Time* magazine or the King James version of the Bible? A gushing society column or a terse Hemingwayesque novel? It was tricky.

Sometimes it was annoying to have authorship become so tyrannical. I did not always like having to follow docilely where it led. For example, by December I had written the ending of the book, five chapters out of the middle, and some scattered passages. I had no idea what the opening chapter should be. The book still had no title. All this irregularity frightened me. Surely most books, I thought, must be written in orderly and chronological fashion, from the first chapter to the last.

Finally, in despair, I went out and bought a book on how to write nonfiction. The author was a professor in a western university. Eagerly I began to read. The author said that a real writer would discipline himself to outline his book completely before starting, that this was the only way he could know where he was going. I had tried. But my outline was still sketchy. So I gave myself E for effort on that.

The author then recommended doing an abbreviated version of a biography at top speed—say in three days. This version, which would merely hit the high spots, could then be used as another type of outline. I found the idea unappealing. Besides I didn't have the three days to spare. So I decided to pass that one up.

Sooner or later the reader is going to tire of your style, the writer contended. I had strong suspicions that he had something there. For one thing, I had already tired of *his* style, and there were mornings when I all but gagged over my own. I read on eagerly to find out what to do. One might give the reader a change of pace by quoting from some other author—but make it a good author, the book warned. I could just see lengthy quotations from Shakespeare or Dickens interspersed with excerpts from Peter Marshall's sermons.

At that point I tossed the book on how to write a book across the room and told Jeff that he could chew on it. It was not for me. I'd have to do the biography in my own way.

Even so, I became increasingly unsure of my own way. I

was getting material down on paper. But what if it wasn't good enough or written well enough?

At first, I shared my fears with no one. I was ashamed to confess them to Mr Aswell or Miss Welty. Finally I mustered up the courage to take what I had written to a friend whose judgment I trusted. "Will you read it," I asked, "and give me your candid opinion? No flattery, no soft-pedalling. I want it straight."

He gave it to me straight. "You're writing too objectively, too factually. Your stuff lacks warmth. You still haven't gotten inside the man Peter Marshall. He—he just isn't here." And for emphasis he thumped the manuscript.

This was devastating. Yet I knew it was true. The difference between a book that would be as dry as dust and one that really lived would be the presence or absence of a strong glow of emotion. Not trumped-up emotionalism but honest emotion.

I asked myself . . . how does one write without emotionalism but still reach the reader's heart as well as his head? I hadn't the remotest idea. I was at a dead end.

This was a major crisis. My discouragement was so complete that my daily output slowed to a trickle of words on a page. What if I just didn't have what it took to write a book? Indeed, it now seemed rank presumption that I had ever thought I could write.

One morning I awakened shortly before six. Everything was quiet. Miraculously, even the baby overhead was sleeping later than usual. This would be a good time, I thought, to try to get some answers. And I had to have answers— or throw in the sponge.

Because I meant business, my praying that morning was at least honest, if not exactly phrased in theological language.

. . . "Dear God, I believed that You told me to write this book. In that belief, I undertook it. But what I've done so far is no good. I'm whipped, helpless. What can I do now?"

s? Your problem is helplessness? The words
echo. I remembered a verse in the New Testament
about that. I turned to it and found that I'd already under-
scored it. . . . Jesus was speaking:

Without me ye can do nothing. (JOHN 15:5)

Was helplessness, then, not such an unusual state? Could
it be that we human beings actually are helpless, but most
of the time don't know it? Could the realization of it be the
first step out? Could our inadequacy become our greatest
asset when it becomes the open door to God's adequacy?

I remembered that the clearest response I'd ever got from
God had come out of the most abject helplessness of my life.
It had been the turning point of my long bout with
tuberculosis. One by one every resource had failed—the
healing powers of nature, the prescriptions of medical science,
even my belief that God could heal me. When my dejection
had got down to the emotional level—which had meant bitter
tears—and when I had presented it to God as all I had left
to give Him, then I had received my answer—His presence
—and health.

Could it be that it was only out of an emotional as well as
an intellectual realization of my inadequacy that I could get
outside of myself enough for God to help me? Though I
did not get all my answers that morning between six and
seven, I had glimmerings.

A few days later a friend came to Washington. She was
the wife of an Episcopal rector whom I had met three years
before. I knew her as a courageous experimenter with prayer,
a tiny woman with a wonderful sense of humour. I spent
part of an afternoon with her. We had talked about some
of her latest discoveries about prayer, and I had told her
about my book. As I was rising to leave, she asked, " How
would you feel about our having prayer together about your
writing?"

" I'd be so grateful." I sat down again.

My friend's prayer was short and informal, though its content was startling. Her request was specific. " Oh, God," she prayed, " write this book through Catherine. She and I join now in asking You so to write it, that the words will reach out from the printed page to touch the emotions of all who read. Then use these emotions as a springboard to divinely directed action. Amen. So be it."

I was astonished. I had shared none of my thoughts about getting emotion into the writing with my friend. How had she put her finger so surely on the heart of this particular petition? Coincidence? I didn't think so. I felt that the Spirit of God had directed her prayer.

Then in another early morning hour I received a more complete answer about the way in which my friend's prayer was to be fulfilled.

The summer before at Waverley I had asked God to tell me what a widow is to do with her surplus emotional energy, with the great vitality which she used to spend in love for her husband. Now, though I saw no writing in the sky, through an inflow of vivid thoughts I came to know what His answer was for me. " There is a definite connection between strong emotional writing that will touch the reader and your own need of an outlet. Find the connection and use it. The book is My project. I did tell you to write it. For this particular period of your life, use the creative energy that I've given you for My purposes for the book. Allow Me to channel it in a steady stream into your writing."

This made sense. The pieces fitted together. I gave the request back to God. When God has dictated the prayer, it is easy to have faith that the prayer will be answered. That January marked the turning point for the book. After that, the writing was lifted to another level. God took over; more than ever I felt myself only an instrument.

Emotion did rise in me—rich and deep—and flowed into the words that sped across the pages. There was much pure joy. Peter Marshall had been an exuberant man, and one with many lovable foibles. It was fun to get the foibles down on paper, to relive many a funny scene. Sometimes I enjoyed the work so much I felt self-indulgent. I had all but forgotten the frustrations of the previous summer.

There were other times when feeling what I wrote was costly. That was true during the week I worked on the chapter about my husband's death. Not only did I have to re-experience every vivid detail, but there was the necessity of restraining the emotions. Complete communication in writing depends, at least in part, on discipline. Trying to avoid both sentimentality and diffuseness was as exhausting as reining in a pair of runaway horses. By the time the week was over, I felt as if my spirit had been ploughed and harrowed.

My part-time secretary was a fine and eager sounding-board for each chapter as it was finished. Several afternoons a week she typed on a card-table in our living-room. From the next room, I would sometimes hear her chuckling as she worked. Or on the day that she was typing "See You in the Morning," I went to the doorway to ask her a question and was astonished to find her crying unabashedly, tears rolling down her cheeks and dropping on the typewriter keys.

As the spring progressed my project became more and more absorbing. Miss Welty had been right. I wasn't living in 1950 at all. For the first time in my life I became so absent-minded that my friends grew alarmed. "There are times," one of them said, "when you just don't hear what I'm saying to you."

The absent-mindedness reached a climax the day I drove through two red lights—one on Connecticut Avenue and one on Wisconsin. I discovered that it isn't wise to say to a District of Columbia policeman, "I'm awfully sorry, officer. It was my fault. But you see, I'm writing a book."

The officer in question pushed his cap back and scratched his head. There was a quizzical look in his eyes. Then he let loose a blast of sarcasm that all but blistered the paint on my car. "Yeah, lady? I've heard all kinds of excuses in my time. Sure—oh—*sure*. Writing a book, huh? Well, I'm

standing here conducting the National Symphony—. Tsh!
Tsh! Us artistic people have so-o much trouble!"

Then there was the evening I made biscuits without either
baking powder or salt. At dinner I noticed that Peter John
seemed puzzled as he bit into one of them.

"What are these?" he asked.

I thought he was trying to be funny. "What d'you think?
Biscuits, of course."

I had not yet tried one. After the first mouthful I decided
it might be wise to hire a cook until the book was finished.

My eleven-year-old turned out to be one of my best critics.
He couldn't be bothered reading the manuscript, but he
listened to it on the dictating machine. He would make
serious comments, as if he were a senior editor.

"Mom, come here. Listen to this." I came, forced to
listen to my own recorded voice:

> Finally, I would come out, with a toidy seat in a
> laundry bag flung over one shoulder, a Sterno stove with
> cans of baby food—assorted spinach, peas, and prunes
> —in one hand, juggling with the other Peter John
> Marshall himself. Then wedged in between boxes,
> bundles and suitcases, Peter would drive off, muttering
> that he really did not think a few days away from the
> office was worth all this, and that this car might not be
> a truck, but it surely drove like one today. The car
> was so loaded, the rear end was hardly off the ground—

My son snapped off the machine. "It's the last sentence,
Mom. Since when does a car ever ride with its rear wheels
up in the air?"

I was duly abject. "You're absolutely right. I can't
imagine how I missed that. Thanks for the correction."

The completed biography was due in New York on
May 1. All through March and April I watched the neatly
typed pages piling up in an old typewriter paper box.

On the 29th April I wrote the short preface:

"It's all right, Kate. Go ahead and write it. Tell it all, if it will prove that a man can love the Lord and not be a sissy. . . ."

Then on the last day of April, I walked to the post office to mail my manuscript. It seemed to me that the man on the other side of the window was handling my precious bundle much too casually—as if the box contained a few yards of calico and not my life's blood.

"It will have to go first class," I told him. "It's manuscript—not merchandise—" That should teach him!

It didn't teach him a thing! Carelessly he slapped on some stamps and then tossed the package over his right shoulder into the nearest mail hamper.

I walked out with a let-down feeling. Then I discovered how tense I had been and how tired I still was; how drained and yet how glad. For good or bad—I had done it. I had written a book. . . .

Suddenly that particular set of feelings seemed like familiar ground. Then I remembered. It's the way I had felt just after Peter John was born. That's it! Writing a book is so much like having a baby. No wonder I had wanted the man at the post-office to handle my precious bundle with gentleness!

CHAPTER 9

Like a Thank You to a Friend

In the spring of 1951, I had written to my editor:

> . . . I am planning on going to Scotland the middle
> of July, coming back in mid-August, provided this will
> not interfere with anything important about the book,
> such as seeing proofs.
> Let me explain that Dr Marshall had a family
> jaunt to his home in Scotland all set up for the Summer
> of 1949. Because he had so looked forward to giving
> this trip to my mother and father, it seems like unfinished
> business. Therefore, if at all possible—I would like
> to carry out the plan for him. . . .

It pleased me to know that the trip would still be Peter's
gift. For without the royalties from his book of sermons,
Mr Jones, Meet the Master, our going abroad would not have
been possible.

There were other reasons, however, for the return to
Scotland. All his life Peter John had heard about his father's
native land. It would be great fun to show it to him,
to have him meet his cousin Jennifer, who was just his age,
and his Aunt Christina. Peter's mother, Mother Janet,
seemed delighted that I planned to bring him. She could
never seen enough of " her laddie "; Peter John was the living
perpetuation of her Peter.

Then, too, in my book I had written of many incidents
that had occurred before my husband had come to the
United States. I had written about still living people, some of
whom I had never met. I had written of his family. After
having been married to a Scotsman, I well knew that

Americans and Britishers could have quite different points of view.

I felt strongly that, while the book was in the proof stage, when changes were still possible, the early chapters in question should be discussed and checked with Peter's family. A wife, though she sometimes may think so, is not the sole owner of her husband or her husband's memory. Others had loved Peter, had shared him with me.

Our sailing date was set for July 14. My publisher had managed to get *A Man Called Peter* processed as far as the galley proofs. Page proofs would have to follow by air mail. Thirty-six hours before we were to sail, I was still going over the proofs and had done no packing. In the end, a miscellaneous assortment of clothes was thrown into a bag.

Our party of four never knew how we managed to board the *Queen Mary* in time. As the giant ship slipped from her pier 90 berth, I stood on the afterdeck, still breathless, almost too limp to feel anything. " Never again," I vowed, " will I let myself work under pressure like this for the homestretch of a book."

During the quiet days at sea, I lived in the immediate past. I had my first chance to evaluate the weeks just gone by. Once the manuscript had been mailed to the publisher on April 30, events had moved swiftly.

During the first week of May, Mr Aswell had telephoned me. . . . " I took your manuscript home with me. I've read it twice. As much as I believed in it, it far surpasses my expectations. Could you come to New York soon? Say, some time in the next few days?"

" For a conference about revision?"

" No, not that. No real revision is necessary. Just minor corrections. If you and I could sit down together, we could do the job in short order. Then we'll go to press."

I had been almost too surprised to speak. " But—but— you can't do that. I mean—it isn't polished. It needs lots of work. This is only the first draft. I mean—I thought you'd ask me to rewrite whole chunks of it."

Mr Aswell had laughed at my bewilderment. "No—no. Beyond a point a book can suffer from too much revision."

I had a mental picture of my editor grabbing the pages of manuscript from me and rushing for the printing presses. "But—but—I've written it so hurriedly. Eight chapters since February."

"Let me explain. You know, I'm married to an English-woman. There's an old British Army term she uses a lot. Not too elegant—but graphic. 'Spit and polish.' Well, you want to 'spit and polish' your book. A natural enough feeling. . . . But just take my word that it needs precious little. Now—when can you come to New York?"

The necessary changes had then been made in one after-noon. In between handling things like . . . page 167, will Americans know what a *glaikit lump* is . . .? page 173, who is Miss Marmy . . .? page 175, spelling . . . page 239, wolf has a bad connotation . . . my editor had made some interesting comments.

He had admitted that it was unusual for him to ask for so few changes. "But then my experience with this book has been different from the beginning."

"How do you mean?"

"Hard to explain. It's had a different feel about it. As I told you over the phone several of our editors have already read the manuscript. Maybe I shouldn't tell you this . . . but frankly, we've all been amazed. We didn't quite expect what we got."

My heart sank. "You mean it's worse in some spots than you expected?"

"Quite the opposite. You haven't had any training in writing. How did you know certain techniques? Instinct? That doesn't answer it. There's an unknown quantity here." And Mr Aswell had looked at me with frank curiosity in his eyes.

The "unknown quantity" had, of course, been God. But I had been shy about parading my own deep convictions. Besides I had a horror of sounding stuffy, pious. What had happened had been quite simple, though wonderful. Out of my helplessness, a book had been written through me. I knew my limitations. The period of black discouragement in the middle of writing *A Man Called Peter* had brought home to me my lack of ability. Had I not almost rung down the curtain on the book because of it?

Yet the last eight months had taught me that God, always the Creator, helps us with our creative tasks when we ask Him to. Should it have surprised me to find that this could be very practical aid—in my case, help with sentence structure, transitions, and craftsmanship generally? It shouldn't have appeared surprising. All too many people still think of God as interested only in their morals and church attendance.

The next step had been that the people at McGraw-Hill had asked if I would put in an appearance at the June sales conference to talk about *A Man Called Peter*.

At eleven o'clock on the morning of June 4, all of the company's sales, promotion, and advertising personnel, together with the officials and editors of the trade-book division, had been gathered in a conference room on the top floor of the McGraw-Hill building. I had slipped inside, curious and a little nervous, and had taken a seat near the door. The men were grouped around an immense mahogany table, discussing sales techniques.

The talk had whirled and eddied around me. I had tried to listen but couldn't follow the thread of the commercial book world jargon—" quantity order discounts . . . back list titles . . . prepub offers . . . stuffering." So I had used the time to try to size up the people at the table. It wasn't easy. The salesmen, each of whom was responsible for a specific section of the country as his book-selling beat, were obviously of all ages, of every imaginable background. I guessed that almost every religious faith and denomination—as well as men with no religious affiliations at all—were represented there.

I had expected book salesmen to be a hard-boiled lot, interested not at all in the product but only in making the sale. How wrong I was! When I was introduced and rose to speak, I found them easy to talk to, responsive, obviously enthused. In chatty fashion, I told them some of the behind-the-scenes details of the writing of *A Man Called Peter*—of the last pages being written first; of my favourite writing position propped up in bed; of my son's stern editorial criticisms—and then something about my purpose in writing the book.

Later on that day I learned that copies had been made of my manuscript and that all of the salesmen were being given a chance to read it. This was a revelation. I had not dreamed that even a book which they thought had a chance of success would be given such serious, individualized treatment.

After getting back to Washington, I received a letter from Mr Aswell that left me glowing:

> You will be pleased to know that by now all of the salesmen have read *A Man Called Peter*. Their enthusiasm for your book is without parallel in my experience. They are realists, these men. Their experience has taught them what is likely to sell and what is not. With complete unanimity they confirm the hunch I have had from the beginning that this book is going to be bought, and read, and cherished by thousands upon thousands of people in all walks of life.
>
> Prediction, I know, is always hazardous. . . . Yet already this book has the unmistakable feel of success about it. . . .

Thus, I sailed for my husband's native land with a feeling that something momentous was in the wind. Perhaps *A Man Called Peter* would indeed be read by the wide audience I had pictured. At least this was my publisher's guess—and he backed that guess with a first printing of 75,000 books.

By July 21, we were on our way from London to Glasgow by train. As the *Royal Scot* left the grimy industrial city of

Carlisle and sped toward Gretna Green and the Border hills, I saw the heather bending before the wind, the black-faced sheep, smoke curling from the chimney of a stone cottage nestled in the shoulder of a hill. It began to look like the Scotland I remembered, the Scotland that Peter Marshall had so proudly shown his bride back in 1937. . . .

Then the Border country became mountainous, craggy, desolate. The *Royal Scot* crawled upward between jutting rocks and tumbling streams. Once Peter John excitedly called me to a window to see a sandy-haired shepherd with his dog. He stood by a mountain path staring at the chrome and blue monster that shattered his solitude.

In half an hour we would be pulling into the Glasgow station. I imagined that Peter's eighty-one-year-old mother and his sister Chris were probably already there waiting for us.

All at once, with no warning, as if a spring had released it, a freshet of tears overflowed. I put my head down on the table before me and sobbed, crying as I hadn't since that first Sunday in church after Peter's death, when the Chinese woman had opened her heart in silent sympathy. I was as surprised as the rest of the family, because I had had no feeling of holding emotion in check. The intensity of it shocked me.

Then it was over. This trip to Scotland was the last and biggest hurdle of going back to places fraught with special memories. But my tears were healing tears, and the experience was actually another big stride forward.

When Mother Janet saw us on the station platform, she tried to enfold both Peter John and me in her warm arms all at once. As she looked into my face for the first time since her son's death, I was the one who comforted her. And because of what had happened on the train, I was emotionally prepared for the rest of our visit.

Peter John, who was sometimes not too talkative around grown-ups, found his tongue within minutes after he had met Jennifer. On the way out to Airdrie, where Mother Janet

lived with Chris and her family, he shot a running barrage
of questions at his blonde cousin. Some of them provoked
lively discussion; some made wonderfully little sense. . . .
Why is a pence so much bigger than a shilling . . .? Why
is all your ice cream vanilla . . .? Do you play Monopoly?
You have a set? Good! I suppose yours has British money.
. . . When I was a little boy, one of my favourite stuffed
animals was a wire-haired terrier named Airdrie. Isn't that
funny . . .? Could you help me find a store that sells British
soldiers? I'm looking for a set of the Black Watch. . . ."

At Airdrie and elsewhere in Scotland and England where
we wandered, the page proofs of *A Man Called Peter* followed
me with dogged determination in four separate chunks. They
had to be returned promptly, sightseeing and shopping not-
withstanding. It appealed to my sense of drama to deal
with them as I sat on a rock by a trout stream in the Trossachs,
in a hotel room in London, in an inn on the Isle of Wight.
I thought doing the proof-reading in such romantic spots
ought to give my book a special flavour, like garlic rubbed
on the salad bowl or a hint of rosemary in the soup.

One July morning I sat on a wall above the ramparts of
Edinburgh Castle looking over the latest spate of page proofs,
while my parents took Peter John on the 10 a.m. tour of the
storybook fortress. The view was so good that it was
distracting. When I turned sideways, there were the Princes
Street gardens with their manicured flower beds, the flower
clock, and the Sir Walter Scott memorial.

Before me in the cobblestoned courtyard, a pantomime
was taking place. A lady tourist, dressed in flashy tweeds, was
about to take movies of the guard on duty. Dressed in his
Argyll and Sutherland kilt, with his chest thrown out, the
guard was colourful camera material. At first he didn't see
the photographer. Then when her camera started whirring, he
threw his chest out still further, tilted his cap at a ore
rakish angle, and tried to look stern. At that point, I dropped
the proofs, and took a picture of both the tweedy lady and the
Scots guard.

On August 14, we sailed for home. I had had satisfying talks with Peter's family about the book. I had had the fun of playing guide to my mother and father and Peter John, showing them many of the places Peter had shown me thirteen years before—Robert Burns's village of Ayr, Sir Walter Scott's home at Abbotsford, historic Stirling Castle, John Knox's house in Edinburgh, the Trossachs at the edge of the Highlands . . . and the page proofs of *A Man Called Peter* had long since been sent back to New York, for better or for worse.

Peter John was triumphantly bringing home his own strange booty—a hard roll off the *Queen Mary* (to see how long it would last); a bottle of different coloured sands from the Isle of Wight; a wall plaque of Tam O'Shanter and Souter Johnny ("Tam lo'ed him like a vera brither"); a toy reproduction of a London double-decker bus; a set of the Black Watch soldiers and also the Queen's Bays—the Second Dragoon Guards.

It took us four hours to get through customs, but they didn't find that hard roll.

My first conscious thought on the morning of October 5, 1951, was—Publication day! This is publication day . . . I had looked forward to it for so long!

Yet, in retrospect, I can't imagine what I expected. Church bells to toll? Headlines in the *Washington Post*? Booksellers to put placards in their windows? People trampling one another in their eagerness to read *A Man Called Peter*?

Actually, as the day progressed, not a thing happened. October 5 seemed no different from any other day, except that I did receive a routine telegram of congratulations from the publishing house. Having dealt with green authors before, my friends at McGraw-Hill undoubtedly knew what a let-down feeling publication day can bring.

Every author, green or not, is anxious to see the first reviews of his book. I was no exception, though I was equally curious about reader reaction. The reviewers who mentioned the book at all were kind enough. My chief impression, however, was that the publication of *A Man Called Peter* had caused very small ripples indeed in the world of book reviewers.

It was kindly reviewed by Clarence Seidenspinner in the *Chicago Herald Tribune*:

The best stories are those that really happen. None of the novels concerning the ministry, written during the last few years, touches the heart and appeals to the mind in the way that Catherine Marshall does in telling the story of her husband's life. . . .

The *Boston Herald* called the book " luminous and moving . . . a dimensional portrait. . . ." A reviewer in the *Houston Chronicle* wrote that " no matter what your religion . . . you cannot help but thrill to this story." *Newsweek* said nothing about style or craftsmanship, spoke only of the biography's content.

A. Powell Davies in *The New York Times* wrote:

It can scarcely be claimed that any man's wife is well equipped to be his most objective biographer. . . . Nevertheless, Catherine Marshall writes extremely well. Those who do not accept her religious viewpoint will nevertheless admit that she presents it with grace and charm. . . .

And Alvin Morris in the *Des Moines Register* said:

There is more than either Peter Marshall or Catherine Marshall in this book. There is God—God not in abstract idea, but in life. This is the story of a man who served God with all his heart because he knew Him, and yet sought Him with all his heart because he felt that he

did not sufficiently know Him. It is this paradox within
the man that accounts for the true greatness of Peter
Marshall. . . .

You will be sorry when the story is over; only
you have a feeling that it isn't over. You know that
the last chapter of *A Man Called Peter* cannot yet be
written.

A reviewer in the *Saturday Review of Literature* commented about what he called my " Palmer method of English."
(I hope it has become a little less Palmer as time has passed.
. . .) The only thorough panning I got was to come a little
later from a British newspaper under the headline, " Unfair
to Peter " :

It is sometimes necessary to be harsh if only to persuade
some women not to repeat the mistakes other women
have made. Mrs Catherine Marshall, for instance, wrote
Peter Marshall's biography. It is selling well in the U.S.
Why it was published here I do not know. . . .

Mrs Marshall has written an embarrassing book about
a good man who deserved better. The sermon extracts
are very ordinary. Peter Marshall could do much better.
We even have the last words Mrs Marshall ever spoke
to her husband. We have them in italics " *See you,
Darling, see you in the Morning. . . .*" I'm sorry Mrs
Marshall wrote this book and I'm sorry this note is
cruel.

But Peter Marshall was a good minister of the
Gospel and a man who would have been acutely embarrassed by this kind of emotional nudism. She would have
been wiser and kinder to allow some good friend of
Peter's to write a small book on a good man. But she
was not. The good and wise Peter Marshall is a shadow
seen through the substantial presence of his biographer,
who never stands aside. The book might be called

"A Woman Called Catherine"; but we have *A Man Called Peter*, by Catherine Marshall.[1]

J.G.

I soon learned that there are two barometers of reader reaction. One is the actual sale of the book as gauged by the bookstore re-orders to the publishers and the best-seller lists. The other is the author's fan mail or lack of it.

On October 28, within three weeks of publication, I opened my Sunday *New York Times* to find that *A Man Called Peter* had a toe hold on the non-fiction best-seller list. By the end of the next month, it had climbed to fourth place. Through subsequent months it vied with Rachel Carson's *The Sea Around Us*, Millis and Duffield's *The Forrestal Diaries*, Tallulah Bankhead's *Tallulah*, Norman Vincent Peale's *The Power of Positive Thinking*, the new Fannie Farmer *Boston Cooking-School Cook Book*, and the new Revised Standard Version of the Bible.

The climb up the lists were exciting to watch, heady wine for a new author. Every Sunday morning I would rise early, slip on robe and slippers, and grab the papers, wondering who my nearest competitor would be that week—Tallulah or Dr Peale. Then, juggling a cup of coffee in one hand, I would curl up in an easy-chair to study the lists more carefully. Was Tallulah creeping up on me? Was Fannie Farmer faltering? Peter and Dr Peale were neck and neck. . . . It was a lot of fun.

On April 23, 1952, seven months after release, I received a wire from my publisher:

> YOUR BOOK GOES TO NUMBER ONE ON HERALD
> TRIBUNE BESTSELLER LIST OF MAY FOURTH.
> CONGRATULATIONS.

The *Reader's Digest* published a condensation of the book. Then the U.S. Information Agency asked to do its own con-

[1] *British Weekly*, Aug. 21, 1952.

densation for publication abroad. I was particularly pleased, because the books the Agency chooses for possible foreign publication are supposed to portray the best in American life.

A Man Called Peter was to be translated into many languages. In August, 1952, came the first of the foreign editions, that published in London by Peter Davies Ltd. The public demand throughout the British Commonwealth was phenomenal and within two years the sales were to reach nearly a quarter of a milion copies.

In America, the book sold and sold. The sales passed the 180,000 mark by the end of the first seven months. Meanwhile, *Mr Jones, Meet the Master*, out more than two years, had sold some 230,000 copies.

At the end of 1952, *A Man Called Peter* was still going strong. *Time* magazine's round-up, "The Year in Books," for its December 15, 1952, issue said:

> The year's true bestseller was the Bible . . . the new Revised Standard Version. . . . Next to the Bible on the bestseller list stood Catherine Marshall's warm, clear-eyed biography of her husband, the late Chaplain of the Senate, *A Man Called Peter*.

This was just another indication that something had happened with the sale of books in the United States. Fiction was not doing well; religious titles were selling in phenomenal fashion. Columnists wondered whether this was a sign of some sort of a religious revival. Or was it due to the uncertainties of the international situation? To the continuing cold war? Or to fear of the atom bomb?

I had to believe that there was more to it than fear. Could it not be that the public's taste for religious books indicated that a thirst for answers to the riddle of life was at an all-time high?

The sale of religious titles was three and a half times as great in 1947 as it had been in 1937. In February, 1953, as an example, the four top titles on the *New York Herald*

Tribune's non-fiction list were all religious : *A Man Called Peter*, Murrow's *This I Believe*, Peale's *Power of Positive Thinking*, and the new Revised Standard Version of the Bible. A quarter century earlier this would have been unthinkable.

Eugene Exman, religious editor of Harper & Brothers, analysed this phenomenon of religious-book buying in an article "Reading, Writing and Religion" in *Harper's Magazine*[2] about that time. He suggested four reasons . . . an element of fear, the fact that science has failed us as the god we once thought it was, a renewed interest in psychology, and the one-world consciousness that has been forced on us.

Whatever was behind the interest in religious books, it was obvious that one of the reasons for the success of *A Man Called Peter* was that it had hit the country at the right time. I took this to be one more sign that God's hand was on the book.

All of this was heartening. But figures make arid reading. Much more heartwarming was reader reaction as it came to me through the mail. Every day my mailbox was stuffed with letters. Though fanmail had poured in after *Mr Jones* was published, this seemed different, more personal. Something had been added.

Whenever I think of the letters, I see a procession of pictures. . . . A blind woman in Atlanta, laboriously typing a letter, with many mistakes. Often she had not known when she had reached the edge of the paper. . . . A sixteen-year-old girl writing on pink paper at four in the morning. . . . A Senator dictating his letter in his office where scores of autographed photos looked down from the walls. . . . An interne in his Baltimore rooming house. "I'm in the eye section of Johns Hopkins Hospital. . . ." A Boston shoe manufacturer, en route to Washington by train, reading in his roomette until almost dawn. . . . A soldier near the front lines in Korea, sitting on an upturned keg, laboriously printing his letter. "I'm not sure you will ever receive this. . . ."

[2] May, 1953.

An Iowa housewife writing in her farm kitchen. . . . A Japanese girl in her college dormitory room. "I am a foreign student from Tokyo. In the bitter experience of World War II, we lost our house and all our possessions. . . ." An Illinois business man. "I handle auto parts. For the past several years I have been groping for God. Don't misunderstand me. I'm not particularly emotional. . . ." A prisoner in the Insular Penitentiary of the Philippines. "I am a terrible sinner, but I am trying to seek and know God like your Peter did. Humans like you can help me. . . ."

What did these correspondents, of all colours, races and backgrounds, have in common? Nothing. Everything. They had each read a book. But it had been more than reading a book. Often it had been an experience in worship. Something had stirred in their hearts. Haltingly they expressed it. From border to border of the United States and from all around the world they shared their hopes and fears with me. Their common humanity blended into a common longing. And as I read their letters, I felt wrapped around with that common humanity—warm, precious, pulsating.

As 1951 passed into 1952, an increasing amount of my mail bore foreign postmarks. There were as yet no foreign editions of *A Man Called Peter*. The book was being mailed from this country to far corners of the earth, from friend to friend, passed from hand to hand. And so I heard from

A man from Hrisey, Iceland;
A family in Johannesburg, South Africa;
A man writing from a hotel room in Brussels, Belgium;
A woman in Taechung, Formosa;
A couple in Haifa, Israel;
A woman with almost undecipherable handwriting in Lausanne, Switzerland;
A missionary in Ceylon;
A girl in Nagercoil, India . . . "I am an Indian.
An American friend loaned me the volume. . . ."

A boy in Paget West, Bermuda;
A man from Lisbon;
A woman in Dublin;

and on and on.

I noticed that our postman often had a quizzical look on his face as he delivered our mail. One morning I happened to meet him at the door. He pushed his cap back on his head, shifted his pack to a more comfortable position, and started shuffling through the pile of letters in his hand. As he gave me one stack, I thanked him and started to shut the door.

"Wait a minute—there's a lot more." He sighed and continued to shuffle. "I don't mean to be nosy, but what goes on here? Are you starting a Lonely Hearts Club or something? The men at the Friendship branch of the post office say—well—they're puzzled too." He handed over another fistful.

"It is quite a pile! Well, it's like this . . . I wrote a book. Some people have read it and—well—they write to tell me so."

The postman stared at me, his mouth hung at half-mast. "Some people—*some*. . . . Umph! Well, lady, I dunno— See ya when I stagger back tomorrow—"

During the writing of *A Man Called Peter*, I had hoped that it would help ordinary men and women with their everyday problems. The prayer for the book that my friend, the wife of the Episcopal rector, had prayed that afternoon had been a request for specific results. She had asked that the printed word reach through to the emotions of all who read, that the emotion would become a touchstone for action.

As the letters continued to come, I saw that those twin dreams for the book—mine and my friend's—were being fulfilled to an extent that I had not dreamed possible. Someone with a knotty problem in his life had read the book. He had laughed and wept. He had come to know one Peter

Marshall. But far more important, out of the pages had stepped a living Lord. Somehow the Spirit of God had spoken directly to his particular needs.

Was his problem alcoholism, a mental breakdown, bereavement, the adjustment of a man to the armed services, a shaky marriage? I had not written of those problems specifically. Yet the reader seemed to get insight into himself and his needs. Often he was able to solve his problem.

Delightedly, he wrote to tell me about it, sometimes in crude longhand on ruled paper, sometimes in neat script on engraved stationary. Often the writer was self-conscious, not sure how to begin, fearful lest his sharing be an intrusion. Yet each had something he so wanted to say that, without being aware of it, he wrote with the freshness of newly turned earth on a spring morning.

In letter after letter, the heart showed. And I, reading these letters, often with a lump in my throat, knew full well that I, the author, could take no credit for such results. -It was God's doing. I could but thank Him and marvel at the stories that came back to me. . . .

A dark-haired boy on duty in sick bay was reading a book. Most of the patients were asleep, and the big carrier off Eniwetok was quiet. Only the groan of the ship's plates as she rolled slightly and the scratch of the doc's pen broke the silence of the night.

The doc was writing his wife back in Akron, Ohio. "Not really much to tell Mildred.—What's the book, Don?"

"*A Man Called Peter.* Got it this afternoon in the ship's library."

"How d'you like it?"

"Okay, so far."

When Don had finished the book, he wrote to me:

Dear Catherine. . . . Hello there!
   Please forgive me for being so bold to call you

Catherine, but I feel as if I have known you for a long time. This is a sort of fan letter I guess, but it's really more than a thank you to a friend. . . .

Your book was read in still of night in sick bay. Two of our boys were injured seriously in swimming when an LST accidentally ran over them. It was then we turned to God. Strangely enough I had started your book the night before.

Your Peter came alive and very real to me, and with Peter you brought God along . . . or Peter and God came hand in hand. All this sounds trite and artificial I know, but this is what I've been thinking.

Several of the boys here are reading your Peter and now stop and think. This helps when our thoughts get all jumbled up, and there are no emotional outlets. . . .

And from a college dean in the Deep South:

Last week a tragedy struck our campus. A student died suddenly during class. This had a subduing effect on the innate gaiety of our young people.

The day after the funeral, I read to my English class Peter Marshall's sermon, "Go Down Death." The students sat quiet and attentive. The message got through.

Thank you for sharing *A Man Called Peter* with the rest of the world. . . .

There was a letter I shall always treasure from Babs, who was a minister's wife in a small Iowa town. She wrote me one January 3. Her miracle of a changed heart had happened, she said, on New Year's Eve. "As I closed the book," she wrote, "I knew I could never be the same person again."

The story started back in college days. During that period, the young girl was a romantic and an idealist. She had a long list of qualifications laid out for her dream man.

Every night she knelt by her bed and prayed, "Oh God, if You will just send me this man to love, I'll do anything You ask me to."

It happened; the man appeared on her horizon. He had all of Babs' requirements, plus a few she hadn't thought of. Dennis was an industrial engineer with Eastman Kodak Company. He had a fabulous salary and what seemed like an unlimited future.

They had a deliriously happy first year of marriage. Babs was looking forward to the building and decorating of their first home. After that, she planned to have a baby.

Then Dennis began to talk about going into the ministry. At first Babs couldn't believe that he was serious. She hoped this was a passing fancy and that the idea would die a natural death. She thought, "When I promised God back during college days that I would do anything He wanted if He would send me the right husband, I surely didn't mean this." How could Dennis even think about giving up his wonderful position with its great future?

Yet after a nine-month struggle the young husband quietly but firmly informed his wife that there was no other way for him—he felt compelled to answer the call.

The couple went to the McCormick Theological Seminary in Chicago. Babs postponed having the baby and took on a secretarial job. Financially things were not so good, but otherwise they came through with flying colours. "Surprisingly the three years of preparation for the ministry were the happiest of our lives," Babs confided to me. "We were sharing everything and made lifelong friends."

Finally Dennis was ordained. He was offered a call to the Iowa Church. They went there with high hopes, one card table, and a $1,000 debt. The church had paid the last minister $1,800 a year; they stretched a point and offered Dennis $2,400.

Babs had the baby—a daughter, and then two years later, a son. The church work flourished, and Dennis became more and more absorbed in it. Too often Babs had to stay at home with the children alone. Dennis seemed no longer to have time to talk everything over with his wife as once he had. The month the young minister was out on church business every night and was home only one afternoon, Babs' resentment boiled over. She raged, "This isn't any marriage. Am I married to a church or a man?"

On both sides barriers went up; lines of communication went down. Whenever Dennis suggested that he and his wife pray together as they used to, Babs would stiffen and change the subject. Dennis felt pulled in two directions. Where did his duty lie? The quality of his preaching and his contacts with people suffered as the conflict grew.

On New Year's Eve there was to be a party and watch-night service. Babs wanted very much to go, but at the last minute her baby-sitting arrangements failed. Her husband was sympathetic but could offer no other solution and went off without her. Babs' mind was full of rebellion and self-pity. "Thirty and too young to be put on the shelf. . . . Once again the church comes before me . . . it always does. . . . It just doesn't matter to Dennis how lonely I am. . . ."

After the children were in bed, Babs settled down to her solitary vigil. She sat before the fire in the living-room —bored, restless. And then her eyes fell on a book on the table. Its title was *A Man Called Peter*. It had been a Christmas present. Unable to think of anything better to fill the long hours till midnight, she opened it and began to read.

Her letter told the rest of the story:

Somehow reading your book, something in me melted. I felt so ashamed when I thought what I could be and haven't been. All at once I saw myself clearly. The demand in me, the pettiness, the self-centredness. In those hours, I grew up. That night Dennis and I knelt down together and with unashamed tears turned it all over to God and started a fresh chapter in our marriage. I have never known such serenity or felt the Presence of God so continually.

May I thank you for being willing to write this book—
for sharing all the beautiful memories you and Peter
had with people like me. . . .

There were other true incidents. One concerned a college
boy who suffered a nervous and mental breakdown. He
turned ruthlessly against those who loved him best, particularly his parents.

His parents could afford fine doctors and psychiatrists.
But the experts were unable to help because the boy had
withdrawn completely into himself. He would not even
talk to the psychiatrist.

Institutional care was recommended, but his mother still
insisted upon keeping him at home. The withdrawal grew
worse. After two years, the young man would scarcely leave
his bedroom. He even insisted that his meals be served
there.

A family friend thought that reading *A Man Called Peter*
might be of some comfort to the heartbroken mother. On
one of the rare occasions when the son ventured from his
room, his mother noticed that he kept eyeing the book in
her lap.

Something about it intrigued him, she thought.

But she knew that if she suggested that he read it, that
would be the last thing he would do. Then her love
gave her a rare insight into his twisted temperament. She
hid *A Man Called Peter* underneath the cushions on the
davenport. The next morning the book was gone. Apparently
her son had found it and was reading it.

He stayed in his room for the next twenty-four hours.
Then, the following morning when the father and the mother
were eating breakfast, their son appeared in the doorway.
He had shaved and was immaculately dressed. There was a
smile on his face and a new look in his eyes.

"Good morning, Mother," he said. "Hello, Father. May
I have some breakfast?" He chatted happily over his bacon
and eggs as if the three of them had dreamed the last two

years. Later, the mother, using the excuse of a check-up but really overwhelmingly curious about the sudden change, took her son back to the psychiatrist. The doctor was frankly astonished.

"What's happened?" he asked the mother.

"You'll never believe this. A book did it."

"For God's sake—what book?"

"A biography—*A Man Called Peter*."

It was the mother who divulged the story.

The minister who lived near Wapwallopen, Pennsylvania, knew that the General Store near-by stayed open each night until 9.30. Just before closing time one evening, he walked up the creaky wooden steps of the store, nodded pleasantly to the two farmers still lounging on the porch.

The interior smelled agreeably of crackers and soda pop, but no one seemed to be around. Finally the minister called, "Anybody here?"

After a minute the proprietor came out from the back room. 'About seventy,' the clergyman guessed. The old man had been crying and was obviously embarrassed to have anyone see him with bloodshot eyes.

"Been readin' a book," he explained. "Maybe you've heard of it—*A Man Called Peter*. It's a good'un—sort of got me. You know about my wife adyin'—"

"Yes I do. That's really why I'm here. Your daughter asked me to drop by."

"Mighty nice of you, Reverend, to come and see me—"

I heard about the minister's visit and a whole lot more in a letter the old storekeeper wrote me—one of the nicest letters I've ever received. . . .

Your book came at a time when I needed it most. It just about saved my life. My wife died Dec. 26, '52. I just felt I couldn't go on living without her. . . .

I started to read it Thursday afternoon. I cried so much

while I was reading it, I was ashamed to go in the store when a customer came. . . .

One of those who saw me was our minister. He's a Lutheran. I told him what I was reading. . . . But I also noticed a tiny bit of moisture in his eyes, so I didn't feel so ashamed any more.

Sometimes I had to laugh through the tears, like where you spoke of the turkey hash. That's one thing I don't like either—stuff all chopped up—like that. . . .

I hope you'll excuse my mistakes and a stranger writing to you like this. But you don't seem like a stranger any more. . . .

Respy yours,

P.S. Someone said that man is like a tack—useful if he has a good head on him and is pointed in the right direction. . . .

One morning the first letter on the pile was from a teenage girl in Atlanta, Georgia:

. . . I feel, and I know many teenagers who feel that Dr Marshall's ministry was not cut off with his death, but rather extended and augmented.

You see, Mrs Marshall, through this book, the lives of many young people have been changed. Many of our problems, trifles as they may seem, have been solved within the pages of this book. Yet we are too young to have seen or heard Dr Marshall. . . .

On down the pile was a letter from a minister in Ohio:

Then with the sudden passing of Dr Marshall, I felt that God must care very little for His work to take one so effective. But now I think I know " Why."

His ministry is now far wider than ever it could have been. . . .

In those first weeks after Peter's death, I too had asked why. I had asked it desperately, confusedly, almost every hour of every day. Why did this have to happen to me? Why did the one I love have to die so soon? How can you reconcile a God of love with all the tragedy in the world?

I had received no answers then. That had left me with the alternative either of trusting God blindly on the assumption that He would give me some answers in His own good time, or of letting go all faith in the love of God. I knew that the latter would have netted only total darkness, abysmal grief.

Therefore, out of no answer I had reached for the only answer. I claimed that extraordinary promise that God has made to His children in the midst of tragedy.

All things work together for good to them that love God. (ROMANS 8:28)

I asked Him to work His miracle of bringing "good" out of Peter's death.

Almost two years had gone by. Now, in the wake of *A Man Called Peter*, part of God's answer came into sight. Over and over my correspondents expressed it for me.

God moves in mysterious ways. Had Peter lived, you would never have written this book. Then I—and thousands like me—would never have known of his life. . . .

Did this mean then, that it had been God's will that my husband die at forty-six of a heart attack? I did not think so. With all my heart I believe that a loving Father wills health, happiness, love and joy for His children. But on this imperfect earth, we rarely achieve these goals. In fact we stumble into hole after hole. Given our stubborn wills, our limited spirits, our refusal to listen to God or even the message of our consciences, we often make a mess of our lives. Our fondest dreams come crashing down in wild desolation.

Then what? It is as if God says, " Never mind. I understand. Even as you sit in the midst of your wrecked playhouse, don't despair. The mess can be cleaned up. Hand the grief, the failure, the disappointment, over to Me. I'm the only One who can take the broken things from life's rubbish heap, and by a divine alchemy make them better than they were before. Try Me and see."

Isn't this the meaning of the Cross? An old hymn expresses it:

> In the Cross of Christ I glory
> Towering o'er the wrecks of time. . . .

Yes, that's it! Wrecks . . . the wrecks of our lives, the wreck we make of our world—that's what the Cross towers over, as a symbol that something can be done about the rubble of frustration, poverty, war, disease, heartache.

I could not believe that Peter's early death had been in God's ideal plan. There is a difference between God's ideal will and His permissive will. But given a set of circumstances which ended in death, then God was able to step in and turn those circumstances upward to an alternate plan—toward breathtaking good.

CHAPTER 10

The Reservoir of Love

Every human being needs love. Most of our troubles spring from the lack of it. Like thirsty men in a desert, we perish without it.

In one way, love had been withdrawn from my life at the time of my husband's death. By the beginning of the year 1952, as one result of the publication of *A Man Called Peter*, love in another form was being returned to me a thousand-fold. I first became aware of it through the avalanche of fan mail.

Typical was a letter from a seventy-year-old woman from Boulder, Colorado:

Dear Catherine,
   I know you won't mind me calling you Catherine, for since reading your book I feel you are a very dear friend. . . .

Or the same thought expressed by a high school girl in Aurora, Illinois:

. . . I had never heard of Peter Marshall until I read your book, but now I feel as if I have known him all of my life. And I have the same feeling about you. . . .

Friendship and love can follow only in the wake of the heart's articulation. Mind must speak to mind; spirit to spirit. Somehow, this had happened in *A Man Called Peter*.

Out of a sense of compulsion, I had written a book, written it almost solely on the instinctual level, from the heart. At the time, I could not imagine how the public would receive it; for all I knew, few people would ever read it. The immense popularity of *A Man Called Peter* was as much of a surprise to me as to anyone else. I could only marvel—and marvel some more.

Letters from readers made it abundantly clear that one of the secrets behind that popularity was that heart had spoken to heart.

A Marine in Korea wrote:

> Reading about Peter's life has definitely changed mine. I want you to know that . . . Mrs Marshall, your spirit has touched mine all the way over here in Korea. I love Peter and you and Wee Peter with a love that only Christians can know. . . .

Those who read *A Man Called Peter* took it personally. There was a surprising identification with the Marshall family. This transcended all barriers of creed, dogma, or nationality. A Japanese man wrote me from Nagasaki:

> I've just finished your book *A Man Called Peter*. First I started to read it with a dictionary in hand around Christmas. Then I forgot I was reading in a foreign language and stopped looking up words. There existed no longer the barrier of language. I was happy with you, I was desperate with you. I have sobbed and cried with you, and now I am filled with the same bliss and gratefulness and happy memory that you are. . . .

> What a dearest friend of us, Peter Marshall! The impact of him will not let me go again to despair or hatred of other men and myself. I found in him a fellow-Christian who really understands the daily presence of God in our common life, a G.G.P. who encourages and understands my enthusiasm to volley ball, table tennis, Japanese chess, and photography. . . .

The identification was so complete that our family jokes

became the readers' jokes. For example, a girl in India picked up the two sentences from *A Man Called Peter*— " Peter John requests that he not be called Wee Peter any more, since he is growing so big. So he suggests that he be called Big Peter and that I be called Enormous Peter . . ." and closed her letter with " I do hope you and ' Big Peter' are doing well."

In the same way, readers from across the world often remembered the birthdays, anniversaries, and special occasions of our family. A native of Taipei, Formosa, wrote:

As the third anniversary of your dear husband's Heavenly Birthday draws near, I wish to send you this little note to remind you that friends over here remember. . . .

Reader friends even hugged "Enormous Peter's " foibles to themselves:

St Paul, Minn.

Dear Catherine Marshall:

You have shared the personal life of a great man with the public who loves him in a tender and beautiful way. I have just finished reading and re-reading *A Man Called Peter*.

I have wept over many of its pages, chuckled over others—especially that part about the boiling of his egg. Would you please let me know—did you ever get that egg boiled just right?

So complete was the identification that many a reader all but took Peter John and me in as members of his family. One man wrote from Buenos Aires:

I sail ships under the Swiss flag. My home is in Lausanne, Switzerland. . . . By the way, tell Peter John

that we have five children, the third one just his age,
another boy called Peter. We would love to have you
and your Peter visit us sometime. . . .

A letter from a teen-age girl contained an invitation:

Dear Mrs Marshall:
. . . I know you are a very busy woman, but would it
be possible for you to attend my graduation in June?
I am asking you early. You could stay at my home.
I'm sure my Mother wouldn't mind. Graduation is June
26th. . . .

Sometimes the family feeling got surprisingly cosy, as from
an eleven-year-old boy:

Dear Mrs Marshall,

. . . I pray each night to God that you would sent me
a letter, and you did. . . .
. . . I thank you again for writing to me and I am
senting you one of my school pictures. Now I have to
go for I have an ingrow toe nail in my toe, and I have
to soke it.

Then came a continuous stream of letters, telling me of new-
born babies named for Peter Marshall. . . .

Spring Valley, N.Y.
Dear Mrs Marshall,
    I think you would be interested and maybe pleased
that I named my new son after Dr Peter Marshall,
whom I met and fell in love with when I was fifteen.
I shall always remember the two weeks he visited in my
hometown, and will always remember Dr Marshall as
a wonderful man with beautiful curly sandy hair and a
Scottish burr. . . .

I would be delighted if you have a picture of Dr Marshall you could send me to put in Baby Marshall's baby book. . . .

At first I tried to keep track of Peter's namesakes—one in Spring Valley, New York; Warner, New Hampshire; Tarrytown, New York; Marion, Mississippi; Oak Park, Illinois. After a while the book-keeping overwhelmed me. Only God and Peter finally know the latest count on how many little Peter Marshalls there are.

As these letters poured in, the world began to seem like one big family. Then came the realization that my growing family of correspondents was making demands. And one has to give time to one's family. This came home to me very soon, because so personal were all the letters, so warm, so human, often containing such remarkable stories of lives lightened and lifted, that I wanted to answer every one. That alone meant changes in my life. The first was that it was no longer possible to get along with a part-time secretary and a bedroom office.

Therefore, in March, 1952, Peter John and I moved from the apartment into a house. The most pleasant bedroom, one with a bay window, was turned into an office. Open bookshelves with cupboards below were built, floor to ceiling, on three sides. At last I had a place for the books which had always overflowed the apartment. The cupboards were big enough to house the boxes of Dr Marshall's sermon manuscripts and the voluminous scrapbooks that had been such a help to me in writing *A Man Called Peter*. Now I even had a place for the olive-green filing cabinet; no longer did it have to stand beside my bed.

There was also a place of special retreat for Peter John. He appropriated part of the third floor. There he unpacked the toy soldiers he had brought back from the British Isles and lined them up in brigades and regiments. He papered the walls with baseball pictures and favourite pennants. From the ceiling he hung his fifty-odd plane models. Now that he had space . . . space . . . space . . . he set about constructing more models—adding dozens of ships to the planes.

But often during those days, our new home seemed like a glass house. The telephone rang constantly. Out-of-town visitors appeared at the front door without warning. There were requests for autograph parties, speaking engagements, magazine articles, pictures, interviews, radio and television appearances; for awards, even honorary degrees. The demands from my reader family piled up and up. My private life was in danger of being squeezed to extinction.

My publishers tried to help in various ways. To meet the requests for autographing, they suggested that I sign the end sheets before they were bound into the books. This meant that, instead of my making dozens of personal appearances, pre-autographed books could be mailed to the bookstores. The end sheets would arrive at the house in bundles of several thousand to sit in the front hall, mute testimony to the work ahead.

Only those who have tried to sign their way through a pack of paper several feet high can know what an uninviting, even terrifying task this is. After the six hundred and fifty-seventh signature, I always began to wonder if my mind might not start playing tricks on me. At any moment I might misspell my name or sign someone else's. Instead, the signature would only get larger and larger, more and more scrawly. Of one thing I'm sure. No autograph of mine could possibly be worth anything to posterity. There are too many of them!

The typewriter in the new office was in use eight hours a day by my new secretary Peg Bradley. Many of the requests were more amusing that earth-shaking. But since they were important to those who made them, they could not be ignored. . . . Would I please autograph the enclosed scrap of material. It was to be embroidered for one square of a " famous names quilt " and would then be auctioned off. An organization wanted some personal possession to auction off—costume jewellery, a scarf, a pair of gloves, even an old hat—always for a worthy cause.

Women's groups were always wanting my favourite recipe for a cookbook they were printing. Usually I would send them Mother Janet's recipe for steak and kidney pie, the one that began . . . "First you inquire at the Flesher's for two puir wee sheep's kidneys and a half pound o' steak, cut 'em up, brown the pieces in a wee saucepan with a wee pat o' butter. . . ." I thought that this would lift any cookbook out of the doldrums.

That book I had mentioned in the closing pages of *A Man Called Peter*—*The Case of the Perfumed Mouse*. . . . Did I know the author and where could it be obtained? The bench Peter John and I were sitting on in the picture on the back of the book jacket—could I send a detailed drawing or pattern for it? My fan-mail friend wanted to copy it for his back yard. Would I select the beauties for a high school annual?

How was our dog Jeff? An unknown fan-mail friend, a dog lover, had fallen in love with our cocker. If I would send a picture of him, she would like to do a pastel of Jeff. The artist was as good as her word. After a few weeks, the picture came. It was beautifully done, artistically framed. Jeff's doggy personality had been faithfully captured. To this day, he is the only member of our family whose portrait hangs in our home.

Of course many requests were more serious. It was surprising to me how many teen-agers had read *A Man Called Peter*. Some of their letters were difficult to answer. I soon discovered that teen-agers have a positive genius for pouring earth-shaking questions into one sentence with the calm expectation that all of life's problems can be solved pronto in an answering sentence. Letters like this one from Greer, South Carolina, could throw me into a tizzy. . . .

Dear Mrs Marshall:
    In our English class we are studying individuals who

have attained success. I'm writing to ask you, if you would please tell me, "What makes an individual great?"

Or one like this would have me walking the floor:

Dear Mrs Marshall,
　　I am a senior in high school and have decided to write my theme on Peter Marshall. Would you please answer these questions for me:
　　1. Where did Dr Marshall get his ideas for his sermons?
　　2. What did he think of the crime wave going on in the teen-age world?
　　3. Did he have any important likes and dislikes?

I found it difficult to restrain myself from putting tongue in cheek and answering to (1) from life; and (2) he was against it; and to (3) yes, several.
　　Still the teen-agers came on. . . .

　　　　　　　　　　　　　　　　　Phoenix, Arizona

Dear Mrs Marshall:
　　I am a seventeen-year-old Junior in high school. . . . This is a personal question. But did you ever wonder why God called Dr Marshall home at such an early age? Will you please write and tell me why or why not?

Often friends asked me, "Do you get many problem letters?" My answer was—not as many as Mary Hayworth or Norman Vincent Peale, but always more than I could adequately handle.
　　Every type of difficulty was represented in these letters—financial problems; marital and divorce questions; parents with the heart-break of a mentally deficient child; childlessness; questions on courtship; the problems of people who wanted to immigrate to the United States; illness and

how to pray about it; and always and always, bereavement.

The last-named was a reflection of the fact that there are over 100,000 new widows added to the population in the United States each year. The total has now reached almost 8 million. Add to this the war casualties, the toll of about 40,000 killed on our highways each year, the deaths caused through cancer and other diseases. The net result is that the agonizing problem of bereavement is all around us, threatening us at every turn.

Isn't it odd that, in a century where medical advances have prolonged longevity, we are more conscious than ever of our mortality? Life seems like a golden gossamer thread, precious, beautiful, but snapped, so easily snapped—finally, irrevocably.

Many who had seen that thread snapped wrote letters in which they stripped all bandages from sorrow's wounds. As I had shared intimate experiences with them, so they wanted to share with me. They paid me the priceless compliment of believing that I would understand. . . .

Hibbing, Minn.

Dear Mrs Marshall:

I too, lost my husband, and know all the anguish, heartache, and loneliness that only such a bereavement can bring. I want to tell you how it happened. . . .

There must be many others who feel maybe this waiting and longing wouldn't be so terrible if our faith were so deep that we would never doubt that we'd be reunited in the hereafter. Won't you please write us about your husband's teachings on the life to come?

Yes, I, too, feel Lou's nearness. I feel it when I sit alone, out at our cabin at the lake—a beautiful place he built and loved. But I want to see him, touch him, talk to him. Will I ever?

I would read a letter like that and see the world's anxious, sorrowing heart bared before me. For we never see the bared heart in generalities, only in particular. The letters always gave the specific—the three-year-old crushed beneath the wheels of a truck; the tiny boy who had died of sleeping sickness; the couple who had wanted a baby for so long, only to have the young husband die two months before the child was born; the widow who had lost her only daughter.

What can one say? How does comfort come? I found it hard to minister to the troubled individual whom I had met only in the sentences of a letter. For all those sorrowing people who wrote me, I felt something so unbearably tender that even now I grope for the words to describe it. And I knew that what I felt was but a spark blown off the altar of the love of God.

God loves these people. God cares about the three-year-old dying under the wheels of a truck. He yearns over each of us. He stoops to help. That was why a Man who was yet God died on a cross. These things I know. It is of the love of God for each of us that the grieving most need reassurance.

And yet, and yet—over and over the letters posed questions hard to answer, containing in a few sentences all the tangled skeins of the problem of evil in our world. . . .

Dear Mrs Marshall:

Last September 27th, we attended our church picnic at a local park. My young sons, David 13½, and John, 9 years, were playing baseball. I went over and leaned against a eucalyptus tree to watch them play. David saw me and left the game to run over and tell me something. On his way, he passed a microphone that had been set up on the damp ground to announce some games. As he passed, he reached out and touched it. He was instantly electrocuted. There before my eyes, my handsome, tall, blue-eyed son, with his gleaming potential for greatness, was turned to clay. Nothing could be done for him; my David was gone. . . .

I have found no benediction to my grief. My child has been deprived of his life on earth, of his chance at fulfilment. God has placed desolation on me, and I can only respond with desolation . . .

There is no pat answer to such a letter. Nor to this one. . . .

Buffalo, N.Y.

Dear Mrs Marshall,

. . . My wife passed away suddenly and wholly unexpectedly last April 25. She loved life and the living of it with the same fierce intensity that she detested dirt, evil, ugliness. . . . She was a brave and gallant soul if there ever was one. . . .

And now for my question . . . I cannot believe in personal immortality much as I yearn to. . . . My faith is too weak to accept it, just as my reason is so strong to rebuff the belief. Do you believe in it?

If I have presumed too much in writing, just ignore this letter. . . .

How could I ignore such a letter? But my problem was how to compress into a few sentences my personal reasons for a belief in immortality.

And still the letters came, like this one from Highland, Ill.

Dear Mrs Marshall,

You and I have a great many things in common. May I write you about it . . .? Our little girl, Nancy Lee, only four and a half, left us so suddenly, so unexpectedly. . . . We did not know that a slight fever would, in a few hours, develop into the dreaded bulbar polio, so swiftly to silence the gay laughter.

The great pain of this loss quickly bound its heavy chains about my chest, scarcely allowing me to breathe. This lasted months, each morning awaking to an awful emptiness. . . . Oh, Catherine, she was beautiful with big brown eyes so full of love and laughter.

If it were not for my deep faith that my little one is waiting for me to come, I couldn't stand this thing called life. . . . I know you must feel the same deep hurt with me this Yuletide season. The songs, the snow, the very air are poignant with memories that keep a deep hurt throbbing. Do you have any suggestions at all as to how I can stand this day after day . . .?

As I would read letters like this, often I would have the sinking feeling that some who wrote to me nursed the secret hope that I could send them by return mail some magic prescription that would solve their problem. I sympathized. How many times I have wished for that kind of an answer to my own problems!

Yet in all truth, life is not that simple. Christianity is a day-by-day walk, not a shot in the arm.

There are solutions—plenty of them. But in my experience, they have come only when I have been willing to open my total life to receive them.

Always, whether the problem was bereavement or something else, I felt that my answers were inadequate. I am neither a minister nor a trained counsellor. There were times when I, forgetting that Christ alone can be the Burden-bearer, tried to shoulder other people's problems and all but went down under them.

Apparently to some readers the closing pages of *A Man Called Peter* had given the impression that I was scarcely human, that my brush with death had been all victory. A Britisher expressed this by saying, " Your references to God seem a little too glib, if I may express it so, for those who, like myself, have experienced a great loss. . . ." And an American woman wrote, " After finishing your book, it somewhat surprised me and others to whom I have talked about it, that you could so readily find resignation. I haven't found it that easy. . . ."

It wasn't easy. It never is. I had travelled the same road

that everyone travels. The searching, sometimes bitter, always poignant questions that others ask, I also had asked. Then out of the university of my experience, I reasoned, might it not be of some help to other people if I were some day to retrace my slow steps along the way out of grief—perhaps in a book?

One summer morning at Waverley, a happy bobwhite had awakened me early, his loud clear notes ringing out over the garden, hanging almost visibly in the still air. Lazily I opened my eyes to see a pink hollyhock nestling against the window-pane. Outside it was a typical foggy Cape Cod morning, but the sun was trying to break through.

A good day to start on the window boxes, I lay there thinking. Peter John and I had arrived at Waverley the afternoon before. Planting the boxes had always been one of my first tasks for the summer.

I put on shorts and a blue denim shirt and went to get the pots of coral geraniums and vines. The planting was messy work because last year's dirt and dried roots had to be dug out and new top soil put in. To reach two of the boxes, I had to use a step-stool. Since the ground was uneven, my balance was precarious. Soon there were dirt smudges on my face, and a brisk sea breeze that had sprung up had my hair blowing in all directions.

About an hour later, I heard a car stop in front of the house. Surely they can't be coming here, I thought? Too early in the season to have visitors.

I was wrong. Out of the corner of my eye, I saw a young man looking at the cottage, opening the blue gate, starting up the curving flagstone walk. Then he was beside me, looking at me curiously

"Are you—is this 'Waverley'—the Peter Marshall cottage —are you—" He looked at the shorts. "You couldn't be. . . ."

Carefully I climbed down from the step-stool and pushed

a wisp of flying hair out of my eyes. "Yes, I'm Catherine Marshall." I held up grubby hands. "Sorry I can't shake hands with you."

"We asked at the flower shop in the village— They told us where to find you—I hate to disturb you like this—during your vacation and all— I'm Stanley Benton; this is my wife Flora—we're from Logan, Ohio—first time we've ever seen New England."

I invited the young couple into the cottage. Mrs Benton paused in the doorway of the living room. Her eyes were taking in the white organdie curtains, the old-fashioned Christmas lights with ivy in them in the windows, the procession of Scottish Highlanders marching across one wall. "This is the house you wrote about! I remember your writing about the Highland Regiment with their kilts swinging. Look—Jim, there they are! You can't possibly know what it means to us to see this—"

My guests were delightful people. Mostly it was Stan who talked. I wouldn't have missed hearing his story. . . .

"I worked my way through Emory University in Atlanta— with Flora helping me, of course. You may remember that Dr Marshall was down there in 1944 for a week's preaching mission. Flora and I went to hear him on the last night. We were thrilled!

"Then I went into the ministry—ended up in Ohio. Well, when I heard about Dr Marshall's death, I couldn't understand why God would take away someone who was doing such wonderful work.

"So when your book came out, I only read half of it. It hurt too much. It went back on the shelf unfinished.

"Later I had a tough problem to solve. One evening, on impulse, I grabbed the book off the shelf and took a beach chair to the back yard. Flora was busy with something else and, as it turned out, I was glad to be alone. I needed to be by myself to let the tears flow unheeded.

"That night I found the answer to 'why . . .' Why had God let Peter Marshall die? Immediately I knew that it was because Peter's ministry was far wider now than it could ever have been before.

"I knew a lot more too—that the One who wrote the book and guided it into the hands of so many readers was greater than the man who preached the Word.

"I've had a lot of discouraging moments in my ministry. A minister's dreams are often crushed, his church programmes stalemated. You know, it's positively uncanny, though, how through the years, every time I've just about thrown in the sponge, this man Marshall has crossed my path again.

"I guess the biggest thing I want to say to you is—well —thank you for reminding me Who still runs the universe."

That summer a constant procession of people came by to see Waverley. Not all of them rang the ship's bell on the front door; some merely stood in the road, whispering and taking pictures.

I kept thinking that all this must be temporary. Surely life would soon return to normal, the mail would slough off, and I could go back to occasional secretarial help. But when nothing of the sort happened during the following fall and winter, I began to see that the situation would not adjust to me. I was going to have to adjust to the situation.

Sometimes one instinctively flees a superfluity of love. There is always the fear of being stifled by it. So the question was . . . could I open my heart wide enough to accept all the overflow of affectionate good will? Could I let it warm rather than constrict me?

I was able to make only a partially satisfactory adjustment. For one thing, I began to resist lectures and personal appearances. At the time the resistance seemed justified. I was a housewife who had written a book. My life had always been a quiet one. During the months of writing *A Man Called Peter*, it had been a secluded life. It was little wonder that I was again finding painful the transition to the public eye.

There was much inner conflict over the requests for speaking engagements. I knew full well that as a Christian I did not belong to myself, but to God, for any way He wanted to use me. Usually that involves people. And in my case, it could mean speaking.

Yet my son was my sole responsibility. He needed me, and I could not, did not, want to leave him to take to the road. Besides, it was the writing I enjoyed most, and that I could do in the morning while Peter John was at school.

Then, too, there were far more requests than one human being could fill. I never understood why there are so many such groups except that the United States is organization-happy. And each organization has a monthly meeting. And apparently the American eagle would scream, and never stop screaming, if each meeting did not have a speaker. It was difficult for me to fit into this pattern. I was simply not an organization person and had a poorly concealed horror of becoming tagged as a lady lecturer.

Other tags were already securely tied to me. I was a clergyman's widow and had written a book in which God was central. Therefore, quite rightly, the public cast me in a religious mould. There was only one trouble. I soon found that the public's concept of religion is not mine. I see life as all of one piece. To some people, religion is an isolated compartment, so narrow as to be stifling. Perhaps that is why so many flee it.

For example, if I were invited to a motion-picture party, inevitably it would be for such a picture as " The Robe." When friends who were travelling in Europe would send me postcards, they would carefully pick pictures of churches or cathedrals. Often publishers would send me books in proof, asking for a comment. Never once would it be a novel or even a so-called " secular " book; always, the latest religious tome. Television and radio people were always contacting me around Christmas and Easter when they were eager for programmes with religious themes.

One incident was typical of many. I had accepted an invitation for an after-dinner talk at a men's banquet in a

Southern city. "Make it light and gay," the banquet chairman said. "Not too serious."

That was fine with me. I was looking forward to it, relishing the idea of letting myself go for once.

Three days before the engagement, the chairman telephoned. "Our wives want to hear you too," he explained. "So we've decided to adjourn after dinner to the church auditorium. Your talk will be there."

"I can't win," I complained to my secretary as I hung up. "I accepted an invitation for an airy, informal talk. Now it has to be part of a church service, and they will expect it to be deadly serious."

A letter from an unknown friend about that time said:

Dear Catherine Marshall:
    You and I have so much in common. I don't smoke either. I don't drink. I don't swear, nor play cards, nor dance the rumba. I feel so close to you. . . .

Reading this, I couldn't help thinking of Peter Marshall's reaction to such a negative approach to Christianity. To this type of person, he was inclined to reply, "Well, now that's fine. But there's a difference between being good and being goody-goody. You have to be good for something. You don't do this, and you don't do that. What *do* you do?"

For me, the mould began to confine. Life when Peter was alive had never been so narrow. Why should it be now? During this period, I thought I understood how adolescents feel. Often their rebellion is caused by too much pressure to do this or not to do that.

Of course, this invasion of privacy is experienced by every person who catches the public's eye. It takes several forms, one of which is the feeling on the public's part that the well-known person—whoever he may be—belong to the public. Thus the President of the United States becomes "Ike," and his wife, "Mamie." Their souls are scarcely their own. Americans feel free to criticize them and openly to discuss every known detail of their private lives—Mamie's bangs, Ike's golf game, even the way he may be spoiling his grandson.

How Princess Grace of Monaco spends her days, the colours in which Princess Caroline's nursery is decorated, the latest news about Queen Elizabeth and her dashing Philip—all this becomes bridge-table conversation in a thousand homes.

In a small measure, I too experienced this. Though in my case the public was lavish with its good will, I nevertheless received quantities of well-meaning free advice. . . .

Dear Catherine Marshall,

I saw you on *I've Got a Secret*. It was a surprise to me that you are so young. Were you a lot younger than Dr Marshall? Wasn't it fortunate that the Panel did not guess your secret . . .?

I must say, though, I was shocked that you would appear on a programme advertising cigarettes. I thought better of you than that. . . .

Sometimes the advice took a practical turn. . . .

Dear Mrs Marshall:

I want to tell you how thrilled we all were out here in the Midwest to see you on *Person to Person*. . . .

When you showed Dr Marshall's 500 sermon manuscripts, it looked like they were in a wooden cabinet. If they are, don't you think for protection they would be safer in a fireproof cabinet? I do think you should tend to this right away. . . .

No detail was too small for the American public to notice. . . .

Dear Mrs Marshall,

I must confess to my disappointment in your interview on television with Ed Murrow, the little mention you made of your late husband, Dr Peter Marshall. . . .

Maybe I was expecting too much, but I did not even
see a picture of him in your lovely home. . . .

Living in a glass house opens one to inevitable criticism.
As always I found that a sense of humour helps. It wasn't
too difficult to apply the humour to some of the free
advice. One day, after a small informal talk in Washington,
I received an anonymous letter. It must have been from a
man, because it read . . .

Dear Mrs Marshall:
  I heard you speak yesterday for the first time. . . .
If I may be excused for my bluntness, I think you should
put more Sex into your presentations. There is a quality
about you that I feel you are " putting the wraps on "
so to speak.
  I believe maybe you are too self-effacing. You are
a good-looking young widow, and I think you should act
the part.

                          Sincerely,
                            An Admirer

Or on another day. . . .

Dear Catherine Marshall,
  On October 24th this year, I shall be 74 years young.
I am still quite vigorous. I feel sure that I have many
years ahead of me still. Perhaps some of this is due
to the fact that every day I have a workout in a gym
down the street from my home.
  Day before yesterday, I chinned myself 14 times,
yesterday 16. When I have worked up 20 times, may I
come up to Washington and see you . . .?

Along with humour comes a sense of proportion. Many
of my correspondents, I realized, did not think of me as an

individual but as a symbol. By remembering that, I could keep some sort of equilibrium. And the warm and affirmative responses so outweighed everything else. People in many countries had read *A Man Called Peter*, and through some divine chemistry they had glimpsed the love of God. Inevitably, that great warm love had drawn them—American or Japanese, British or Indian, Swiss or Australian.

Dear Catherine Marshall:

Since you and Dr Marshall entered our home through your book, I have thought of you often. I can't help wondering how you are getting along? Is it sometimes lonely for you . . .?

Mr Jones, Meet the Master and *A Man Called Peter* have something that reaches way into one's heart. They're unforgettable, so they're always travelling, never resting on my bookshelves.

You made me want more than anything else in the world to know Jesus and to have faith in Him. Your writing has made it the most desirable quality one might ever have. . . .

And I, reading letters like that, could but conclude that if any words of mine had increased by even a little the reservoir of love in the world or pointed others to the Source of that love, then who could mind—even a glass house?

CHAPTER II

Is there Life after Death?

One emphasis keeps recurring in many of the letters that come to me. A typical expression of it was in a letter from a young widow:

> On June 28th, my husband died. I couldn't see why he couldn't have been spared at least long enough to see our baby. . . . For I am writing this from the hospital. Last Friday morning a little girl was born to us. . . .
>
> Your book gives a person the thought that you think that Peter is still alive. Do you think my Erwin is alive too? He was just a farmer, but he loved God, and he loved the land. . . . I could be comforted and contented if I could be sure that Erwin still lived. . . .

This groping to believe in life after death is the need of every bereaved person. Some can accept immortality on faith without questioning. Others would like to believe; they hope it is true, but can get no further than hope.

I, too, have had the same need of reaching beyond hope to proof. My search was made in several directions.

The philosophical approach did not greatly interest me. For instance, some contend that immortality is an instinct buried deep in the race; therefore, immortality must be a fact. Others use the argument of analogy pointing to seasonal death and rebirth in nature. Or the juridical argument . . . sometimes good people suffer and the evil prosper; therefore, there must be another life to equalize these wrongs. Then there is the moral and ethical argument . . . the higher and more worthy a man, the more incomplete his life seems. Since he cannot achieve his ideals this side of the grave, he has a right to expect to achieve them on the other side of death.

None of this is proof, at least to me.

I have found more conclusive the evidential testimony piled up through the ages. I do not mean spiritualism, but these experiences that have come—unsought—to thousands of people.

Sometimes a person crossing the threshold between life and death gives those watching a glimpse of what lies beyond. The universal testimony in these instances is that death is nothing to be feared; that there is beauty—often rapturous music, reunion with those who have gone before, recognition, warmth and love—on the other side.

A man recently widowed wrote me of just such an experience. . . .

In June, 1952, my wife of nineteen years was taken by coronary thrombosis. . . . I left the house at 1 p.m. . . . When I returned at 5.30, she was lying on the bathroom floor. There were no good-byes. She was gone.

It was probably between 1 and 2 a.m. before I got to bed and to sleep that night. However, at very early dawn I began to be conscious again of the world around me and of another world. Our bedroom is an enclosed sleeping porch at the rear of the house with windows on three sides.

Margaret had loved the out of doors along with music and birds.

How can I try to describe to you my experience of that dawn?

All I can say is that Margaret was there and I was there at a little distance observing it all. As a Navy officer during the war, I found myself thinking of the ceremony when an admiral is piped aboard. It was as if the boundaries between earth and heaven were obliterated and Margaret was being piped aboard. She was entering her heavenly home in a blaze of glory with the birds singing that morning as I have never heard them sing before or since. It was as if ten thousand angels were crying " Joy! Joy! Here comes Margaret! Everybody out! Everybody out! Here comes Margaret!"

Strangely, my dominant emotion was not grief, but a thankfulness that I had had her for nineteen years and a fierce and uncontrollable pride in having been her husband. Only one word can describe my mood at that time—exultation. . . .

Another letter I received records a similar testimony, only in this case, the dying man was pulled back from crossing the threshold:

In 1944, came my first heart attack . . . in 1949, a second. This time I almost slipped through the velvet curtain that shuts out our sight of the world to come. Now I know that death is not to be feared; the pain ceases, you know what is happening, but it does not matter; you sink into a soft velvet restful blackness and consciousness is gone.

I want you to know that your husband did not suffer. One just slips through the curtain, leaving the tired, worn body behind.

Since my experience, I am convinced that consciousness is the only reality. By this I mean self-awareness, the persistence of the I-ness of the individual, the mind, the soul, the spirit, the character, the non-material elements that distinguish one person from another. . . .

As a little girl in Canton, Mississippi, I had a brief glimpse of the continuation of this I-ness into the next life. It came through the eyes of a dear elderly friend whom I called " Auntie Chamberlain." She was a wealthy New York aristocrat who had come South to be near a married daughter. She was often lonely, and my parents befriended her. Soon she was spending every Wednesday and every Sunday in our home.

Auntie Chamberlain was tall, and as a girl in finishing school had been taught to walk erect by practising balancing a book on her head. The head held so proudly wore two braids of hair encircling it, and always around her neck there was a narrow velvet band, sometimes clasped with a diamond brooch, sometimes an amethyst one.

She gave me fluffy dresses, hand-embroidered by nuns in a convent. At other times, her gifts would be beautiful editions of carefully selected books, and she taught me to love and care for them. . . . " A book is a friend and has its own personality. Treat it with consideration. Always wash your hands before handling it." She taught me precision in the use of words. . . . " Never say ' lost ' when you really mean ' misplaced.' Any article that is recovered was only ' misplaced.' "

But Auntie Chamberlain's greatest impact on me came at the end of her life. She had suffered a stroke and was bedridden in her apartment up Peace Street. Often my mother would ask me to take her some soup or custard or delicacy. Holding the offering carefully, I would walk along the uneven brick sidewalks, under the arching trees, to Auntie Chamberlain's.

On one of these occasions, a few days before her death, I saw her suddenly sit up in bed, speak the name of her long-dead husband, and throw out her arms in glad reunion. Caught up in the drama taking place before me, I knew I was witnessing something that was no hallucination. I've never been able to forget the reality of that scene.

There is another type of experience, equally unsought, that has come to people in every century. This constitutes a body of evidence that we cannot laugh off or disregard. . . .

In a hospital in Atlanta, Georgia, a young wife, the mother of two small children, lay desperately ill. Her doctors, feeling that the end was near, had summoned her relatives. Hers was a loving and closely knit family. Her father had died several years before. But all the rest of the family had come —her husband, her mother and her husband's parents, brothers and sisters, and several aunts.

Suddenly the young woman, only thirty-five, in great pain, became hysterical. "I don't want to die," she screamed. "I don't want to leave my children. Why can't somebody help me? I don't want to die."

Her screams tore the emotions of those who loved her. They tried to comfort her, but nothing they could say helped. The hysterical sobbing only grew worse. Nurses on the floor heard and summoned the resident physician. He rushed to help in the only way he could—he gave her a hypo to plunge her into unconsciousness.

She was out for seven hours. When the drug wore off, her devoted family was still huddled near, loving her, praying, hoping they could find some way to help.

But the sick woman woke with a smile on her face. "I'm sorry I acted so badly," she said. "Everything's all right now. I've seen Dad. He came and told me there's nothing to be afraid of. He promised that he'd stay with me every minute and hold my hand. Don't worry about me. I'm all right now."

There were no more hysterics. That night the girl slipped over into the next life. There was a smile on her face and one hand was outstretched.

If such experiences are valid, why do only a few people have them? No one knows. Sometimes they must be granted —as in the case of the young mother—because help is desperately needed. In other cases, it may be that some have the gift of a type of spiritual sight, even as others have an ear for music or a talent for mathematics. I have known several people with this gift. One of their character-istics is that they are not necessarily spiritual people as church people usually mean that term. That is, they are anything but otherworldly. The ones I know have in common a robust sense of humour, a twinkle in their eyes, and give the impression that their feet are planted firmly on earth.

One such friend, Olga Worrall, must have been born with the ability to see into the world of the spirit because she first noticed it at the age of three. As a young girl she decided to give the gift to God for His use. She has never taken a cent of money from anyone for it. She uses it only to give other people the confidence that at death there is no interruption to life. At times she has been able to help even clergymen to anchor their hope of immortality in the utter confidence of sure belief.

One of these is a minister whom I know and who told me of this incident himself. . . .

Several years ago in Baltimore, Lynn Youngman, a student at Goucher College, became ill with lobar polio. The minister some years before had regained his own health through prayer. Lynn was a member of his church and her case lay heavily on his heart. He believed that she could be cured, and night and day stormed heaven in her behalf. He also asked Olga and her husband Ambrose to pray. They did, though they had neither seen nor met the girl. But one morning while in prayer, they came to know that Lynn would not recover.

The next day the girl died. The minister felt that he had failed her and sank into a state of black spiritual discouragement. His depression lasted for days.

Some time after that he brought another person in need to see Ambrose. While the two of them were in an upstairs room, the minister, very tired, stretched out on the davenport in the living room. Olga was sitting quietly in a chair across the room. For a moment there was silence. Then Olga said, " There is a tall girl, blue-eyed, blonde, smiling, standing beside you. She says to tell you that she is Lynn, and that you must stop grieving. You did not fail her. You were unable to heal her body, but you healed her spirit. Strange "—here Olga paused—" now she is bending over, kissing you on the forehead. She says, ' Tell him I'm returning his kiss.' "

My friend, the minister, jumped to his feet. " How could

you have known that? No living person could know it. A few days before Lynn died, she had a sinking spell. Just the two of us were in the hospital room. As she lay there with only her head sticking out of the iron lung, I bent over and kissed her forehead." For the first time in days, there was joy on the minister's face.

Still another Washington friend of mine, Jane, also possesses this gift and has frequently had similar experiences when she was least expecting them. Jane was named for an aunt who was a beautiful blonde. When the aunt was in her thirties, she developed diabetes.

In that late summer long ago, Aunt Jane came to visit in the family home. It soon became apparent that she was a very sick woman. This seemed the more tragic because Aunt Jane was to have been married in the fall.

For convenience, the sick woman's bed was moved to a first-floor parlour. This was the era of heavy damask portières and draperies, of dresses with taffeta petticoats.

One day the family physician decided to give an injection of glucose because the invalid was rapidly sinking into a coma. As he worked over the patient in the parlour-bedroom, he asked young Jane to hold a light for him. An ether anaesthetic was being used, and its odour permeated the rooms hangings. It was weeks before the smell of ether disappeared.

Later the aunt died. Two weeks after her funeral, the family wanted to take some flowers to her grave. But the teenage Jane and Stella, a friend, decided to stay at home. The two girls were left alone, sitting in rocking chairs on the front porch.

Suddenly both girls heard the rustle of taffeta petticoats in the front hall. Jane, nearest the door, ran to the screen door. There she saw her Aunt Jane starting up the stairs, wearing a black dress, looking chipper, very flesh and blood, not at all ghostlike.

Involuntarily the girl called out, " Aunt Jane! It's you! What do you want?"

There was no answer. The woman continued on up the stairs, her petticoats rustling with every step. Then as she got within three steps of the landing, she turned her head slightly, so that Jane saw her face clearly. Then she disappeared.

In telling me of this incident, my friend commented, "At the time, I couldn't see any reason for the experience. Then I remembered that my aunt had willed me a lovely garnet ring, and the ring was missing. At first, I thought perhaps she had come back to show us the ring's hiding place. But we never recovered it.

"Then for ten years after that, at intervals, a strong odour of ether would reappear in the parlour—but only for me—not for other members of the family.

"What has bothered me most about this and a whole procession of like experiences is that I can't see any reason for them in the Christian scheme of things. I don't seek them. In fact, I'm impatient with them. Yet they keep coming to me. What good purpose do they serve?"

Yet it would not occur to us to ask, "What good purpose does physical sight serve?" We see the faces, the smiles, the gestures of our friends; the wagging tail of a dog; the tapestry of leaves against a darkening sky. We see—and it is enough.

Just so, there are those who seem to be able to see just as naturally into the world of the spirit that lies all about us. The early church may well have had members with this gift. Is it possible that the Apostle Paul was speaking of it when he referred to the gift of "discerning of spirits" (1 CORINTHIANS 12:10)?

In spite of that, the church has frowned on any probing of life after death. Her traditional position has been that Christ told us what He wanted us to know about the life to come and that, because that world of spirit is real, excursions into it can be dangerous if they are not centred in Christ.

A friend of mine who is a physician with a large practice in Richmond, Virginia, had an experience that was exactly that—Christ-centred. It is one of the most astonishing stories I have ever heard. Had I got the story secondhand, I might have doubted its validity. But knowing my physician-friend as well as I do, I cannot.

"As a doctor," he said, in telling me the story, "I have learned that there is more to human beings than their bodies. But I'd know it anyway because of an extraordinary experience I had when I was nineteen."

This experience revolutionized the basis of the young man's life. Moreover, there are parts of the incident that he feels he cannot yet reveal to anyone.

Even as a little boy, George had wanted to be a doctor. By nineteen he had completed his pre-med work.

Then came World War II. November 1943 found him a private in the Army, stationed at Camp Barkeley near Abilene, Texas.

But the Army needed doctors. So George, still a private, was given the glad news that he was being transferred to the Army's Specialized Training Programme to complete his medical training. What was even better fortune, on December 20 he was to be sent back to his home town—Richmond—to the Medical College of Virginia.

Nine days before he was due to leave Camp Barkeley, the boy became ill with pneumonia. After a week in the Army Hospital, he was much better. In fact on the night of December 19, he and a friend left the recuperation ward to go to a picture show. They got back to the ward about nine o'clock.

Five hours later, at 2 a.m., George had a relapse. When the ward boy took his temperature, it was 106.5. Hastily the boy summoned a nurse and the O. D.

They saw that the patient was too ill to walk, but insisted that they should try to X-ray his chest. "Do you think you could stand just long enough for us to get one film?"

His face flushed with fever, his eyes a little glazed, George nodded that he thought he could. The last thing he remembered was the humming of the X-ray machine. Then he crumpled into an unconscious heap on the floor.

Later he was told what happened from the viewpoint of the hospital staff. . . . He was carried to a bed in a new ward section—not back to the recuperation ward.

He remained desperately ill and unconscious for two days. The hospital routine specified that the ward boys were to make four rounds each night for checks. At three o'clock on the morning of December 22, when the ward boy got to George's bed, he was shocked at his appearance. He looked—dead. A closer scrutiny revealed that there seemed to be no pulse, no respiration.

The boy ran for the captain, the O. D. in charge. After the captain had examined the patient, he straightened up—sighed—"Blood pressure at zero, no pulse, no respiration, body temperature falling rapidly. I'm sorry—"

The ward boy standing on the other side of the bed was shocked. "But it can't have happened that suddenly. He was so young—"

The doctor left. A few minutes later, the ward boy sought him out again. "I'm sorry to bother you, sir, but that private—I can't get him off my mind—Shouldn't we make one try to do something, sir? Maybe adrenalin—or something?"

The O. D. looked at the youngster with compassion in his eyes. He saw that the ward boy was shaken. "All right, I'll go and examine him once more. Prepare a large hypo with adrenalin and bring it along in case I decide to use it."

Once again George was examined. Once again the O. D. sighed. "It's no use. He's gone."

"Please, sir. Let's use the hypo anyway."

Without saying a word, the O. D. plunged the needle directly into the heart muscle. . . .

While all this was going on, George was having quite a different set of experiences. As the X-ray was being taken, he had been preoccupied with just one thing . . . the next day he was to leave for Richmond and medical school.

That would be the fulfilment of a lifetime dream. What if he couldn't go? What if—because of the delay—someone else would get his place in the Specialized Training Programme?

He remembers sitting on the edge of his hospital bed thinking, " I've got to get out of here—but fast."

As he got to his feet, he glanced back at the bed. What he saw was shocking. Someone who looked like himself was still lying there. He had seen a few dead people in his life, and this one looked—dead. It was himself all right. He recognized his familiar class ring on the left hand of the one on the bed.

He started toward the door. A ward boy was coming in. George thought that they were going to collide. He tried to step aside, only to find that the ward boy did not see him. He walked right through him.

George didn't understand it. He went out into the corridor and wandered around, trying to figure things out.

Nobody who passed him seemed to see him. He felt totally unable to communicate with anyone alive. This separation from his fellow human beings caused him an acute anguish of loneliness.

Then he looked down at his hands. If he was to be a doctor, he would need his hands. But he couldn't touch things. Material objects—substances—did not seem solid any more. He tested this out by leaning against the guy wire of a telephone pole. His hand went right through the wire.

That decided it. No man in this fix could become a doctor. He decided to go back, find his body, and somehow make connection with it again.

He retraced his steps along the hospital corridor. But his body had been moved. The soldier went in and out of one hospital corridor after another. Finally he found it in an isolation ward. His class ring was still on the left hand. But what a ridiculous situation. How did one get back in one's own body?

" Then," George said in relating the incident to me,

" suddenly I was no longer alone. Someone stood there. I knew that it was Christ, though my chief impression was of light—dazzling, blinding light.

" He asked, ' What have you done with your life?'

" ' Well—I—got to be an Eagle Scout.'

" ' This glorified you.' There was a long pause.

" ' I tried to help some boys and girls in high school.'

" He said, ' What have you done to tell them about Me?'

" I changed the subject. ' I'm too young to die.'

" Very kindly the One immersed in light said, ' Nobody is too young to die.'

" A lot more passed between us," George says. " I've never felt free to tell anyone the rest of it. I saw how selfish my life had been, and that Christ held me personally responsible for how I had wasted my time on earth. I made up my mind right then that, if by some miracle, He would let me live on earth a while longer, I would do better in the future.

" The miracle happened. Suddenly I found myself back in the family housing of flesh. With my right hand I touched the class ring and turned it round and round—and marvelled. A little later I discovered that four days had passed. It was the morning of the twenty-fourth of December."

George was in the hospital until the third of January. His weight had gone down from 178 to 135 pounds. During his last week there, the head nurse, knowing how curious he was about what had happened to him, let him see his chart. Everything was recorded—the 106.5 temperature, the collapse, the two examinations, the injection of adrenalin into the heart muscle.

" It's true," the nurse said, " all true. There was no sign of life at all. I saw you examined."

" I don't know what others will think of all this," the prominent physician says today. " Let them explain it as they please, put their own connotation on it. I only know that it remains the most vivid experience of my life. From that day on, I have not been the same person."

Peter Marshall's father had died when his son was four, and ever afterward Peter eagerly sought information about him. In addition, anything about that other life " behind the curtain," as he called it, fascinated him.

When Peter was eighteen, before he emigrated to America, he and two friends went one night to visit a man who had what the Scots call " second sight." That evening the man claimed that he could receive messages through table-rapping. There were various messages, including one said to be from a man who had lived in France 200 years before. He told his name (Peter always remembered it; I do not), some facts about his life, where he was buried.

Then the table rapped out the name " Peter Marshall." Some facts followed which jibed with what Peter knew of his father's early life . . . the date of his marriage to Peter's mother in Switzerland; the full names and certain facts about long-dead relatives. Then came this message for Peter : " You must never again toy with spiritualism. For you, it is very dangerous." That was all.

Peter took that as authoritative and obeyed it to the letter —not because he was certain that the message really had come from his father, but because an instinct told him that the warning was authentic. Though to the end of his life he found the subject compelling, thereafter he never went outside the framework of the Christian church to investigate it.

Within that framework, Peter arrived at an absolute assurance of immortality. Where others might hope it was true, he knew it was true. Often, by the simple, matter-of-fact way in which he spoke of the next life, he was able to transmit his assurance to other people.

One day at the Willard Hotel in Washington, during a luncheon talk to a national convention of music teachers, Dr Marshall tossed this in. . . . " I love music and have always wanted to study it. But I've never had the opportunity, the money, nor the time. In my next existence, I look forward to the study of music as one of the satisfactions I'm going to have."

One woman present that day later wrote to tell me what Peter's comment had meant to her:

There was such confidence in his assurance, that for me it bridged the gap between this life and the next. Never before had I felt that reality. . . .

On the tape that recorded Dr Marshall's last pastoral prayer and last Sunday morning sermon two days before his death, were these words.

Father, we join our prayers in asking Thy help for those, who bereaved, still feel lonely. They have not even yet found the joy of Thy Resurrection and the sense of the presence of those they love who are with Thee.

Grant that those who have loved and lost may feel their loved ones near; may somehow be persuaded that they still live, that they are happy, that they still love us as we love them.

May such assurances come to all the hearts that need them today. . . .

Then, after Peter's death, I found among his papers a copy of a letter he had written to the young widow of a physician in Atlanta. It contained these paragraphs:

Doubtless, many times before, the doctor had left you and the children to answer a call, and he may have been detained longer than you expected. You, as a doctor's wife, had known what it was to be left alone at all hours of the day and night.

This time the doctor went in answer to a call—the

last call which we must all obey, but this time he is not coming back—at least not in the way he used to do. That he will come back is a deep conviction of my own faith.

I believe that those who have died are with us still in different form and communicate with us in different ways. It takes time and also the grace of God and a simple Christian faith to feel the presence of our beloved departed, but that in itself is a comfort and consolation that will fill up the vacuum left in your life. . . .

It was one sentence in this letter plus one clause in the Apostles' Creed that sent me on the second part of my search. The sentence was . . . "I believe that those who have died are with us still in a different form and communicate with us in different ways. . . ." I wondered . . . what ways? How? And the clause in the Apostles' Creed was . . . "I believe in . . . the communion of saints. . . ."

The minister of a church where I sometimes worshipped always ended his pastoral prayer by thanking God for the communion of saints. One Sunday I lingered after the benediction to ask him just what he meant by the communion of saints.

Immediately he lapsed into traditional theological jargon. . . . "We are told that we are surrounded by a great cloud of witnesses. Of course, you know that in New Testament parlance, any member of Christ's Body, the church, is called a ' saint,'—not just ' good ' people in an earthly sense. Therefore, the communion of the saints refers to the interaction, the fellowship, between the Church Militant—the saints here on earth—and the Church Triumphant—the saints already in the next life."

That did not satisfy me. . . . "Yes, but what kind of inter-action? What kind of fellowship? And how can someone like me have fellowship like that?"

At that point, the minister's answers became shadowy,

vague. At last he confessed that I was asking questions beyond him. "Perhaps," he admitted, "because death has not brushed me personally," I admired him for his honesty.

Then I started searching on my own. I knew that the Apostles' Creed in its present form dates back to the fourth century. What experiences of the early church had crystallized into that clause about the communion of saints? Did Christians then know something about personal contact across the dividing line of death that we do not know today?

The first fact I uncovered was that, from the establishment of the church after Pentecost to the Protestant Reformation in the sixteenth century, prayer for and with the dead had been universally practised by Christendom. This followed naturally from two bedrock beliefs of the Apostolic Church: (1) that of immortality, that Christ—through His resurrection, to which the earliest Christians claimed to be eye-witnesses— had for ever conquered death; and (2) that the unity of the church—the Body of Christ—was such that death could not dismember it.

The prayers of the first Christians for the dead were not mere petitions that the departed be delivered from some state of eternal punishment. To them, prayer was as natural as breathing. It was the life of the spirit; it was their life line with the Risen Lord. He had taught them that they were "members one of another" of an organic fellowship; that His riches in glory were their individual and corporate heritage; that they should confidently and joyously present their needs to Him.

Therefore, they prayed for all sorts of things: for the forgiveness of sins and the breaking of sinful habit patterns; for strength in temptation; for the healing of sickness and disease; for specific directions from God; for their enemies; for those still outside the Christian fellowship, that they might find the joy of the faith.

They lived in days of upheaval with death all around them. Often members of their families or friends, who had been an integral part of their prayer fellowship, would be there one day, and the next day would be thrown to lions in the arena or bound to stakes on one of the roads outside Rome to become blazing human torches. In the midst of such terror, they were able to keep their sanity only because they were so sure that the pain of dying was brief, that death was only an incident in continuing life. To them it was unthinkable that the incident of death should sever their communion with each other and with the living Christ.

The epitaphs of the martyrs under the Emperors Nero, Domitian, Trajan, Hadrian, Antoninus Pius, and Marcus Aurelius in the catacombs of Rome dramatize the hazardous life of the first-century Christians. . . .

> IN CHRIST IN THE TIME OF THE EMPEROR ADRIAN, MARIUS,
> A YOUNG MILITARY OFFICER, WHO LIVED LONG ENOUGH
> AS HE SHED HIS BLOOD FOR CHRIST, AND DIED IN PEACE.
> HIS FRIENDS SET THIS UP. . . .

Another reads. . . .

> IN CHRIST ALEXANDER IS NOT DEAD, BUT LIVES ABOVE
> THE STARS, AND HIS BODY RESTS IN THIS TOMB. HE
> ENDED HIS LIFE UNDER THE EMPEROR ANTONINE. . . .
> FOR WHILE ON HIS KNEES, AND ABOUT TO SACRIFICE
> UNTO THE TRUE GOD, HE WAS LED AWAY TO HIS EXECU-
> TION.

Some like Alexander may have been snatched into martyr-dom so suddenly that there was not time to finish the "sacrifice unto the true God," no time for any last confession or any tender words of parting to family and friends. What then?

Did someone else, perhaps the one who cared enough to make the inscription, then undertake a last confession for Alexander? Though it seems reasonable to suppose so because of the closeness of the fellowship, still the New

Testament is sketchy on this practice. We have only one
clue, given us by Paul. He was writing about immortality.
. . .

> If Christ did not rise, your faith is futile, you are
> still in your sins. More than that: those who have slept
> the sleep of death in Christ have perished after all. . . .
> But it is not so! Christ did rise from the dead . . . Other-
> wise, if there is no such thing as a resurrection, what is
> the meaning of people getting baptized on behalf of their
> dead? If dead men do not rise at all, why do people get
> baptized on their behalf?
>
> (MOFFATT; I CORINTHIANS 15)

Here, in a chapter whose whole thesis is immortality, Paul
mentions a common practice of the Apostolic Church—that
of being baptized on behalf of the dead.

Apparently events were moving so swiftly that sometimes
one like Marius, the young military officer, may have taken
all but the last step into the faith—that of baptism—only
to be cruelly wrested from his Christian friends. In such
a case, a friend would be baptized on behalf of the martyred
person. Paul does not argue about this; he takes it for
granted.

Other evidence of a strong belief in the fellowship of
prayer is given us in the earliest liturgies surviving, those
from the first part of the third century. From the Liturgy
of St James comes . . .

> We implore of Thee, O Almighty Lord, to unite us
> without delay to the company of the first-born, who are
> written in heaven.
>
> We remember them so that they also may remember
> us before Thee, and may communicate with us in this
> spiritual sacrifice for the preservation of those who live,
> for the consolation of all who are in trouble, and for
> the repose of the faithful departed, our fathers, brethren,

and rulers, by the grace and through the mercies of Thy only Son. . . .

And from the Liturgy of St Ignacius . . .

Because of Thy great goodness, O Lord, receive peacefully and calmly the spirits and souls of Thy servants and worshippers who out of this present life have departed to Thee. . . .

Because of Thy great love to mankind, grant them that life that knows not old age; give them the good things that pass not away, and the joys which are endless. May they obtain mercy through Thy clemency, and rest through Thy mercy. Hide them under the shadow of Thy wings. . . .

The writings of the earliest church fathers who came after the apostles—such as Tertullian and Cyprian—also bear unanimous testimony that the fellowship of prayer with those in the next life was taken for granted. Then in Augustine's *Confessions* we have his prayer for his mother Monica, written after her death.

In the Anglo-Saxon church the communion of the saints seems to have taken three forms—prayer; a special, tenderly beautiful Eucharist for the dead; and the giving of alms on behalf of the dead, much as we today give a memorial gift to a favourite charity.

According to descriptions that have come down to us of social gatherings, when the loving cup—originally a symbol of goodwill and Christian charity—went round, a prayer for the dead was always included in the ceremony. Some of these prayers are engraved around the rims of the loving cups and can be seen today in museums in the British Isles. The thought was that the living should remember the dead in the midst of happy times and on special anniversaries.

Then through the Middle Ages came the corruption of what had been pure and loving practices, a corruption that finally brought about the Protestant Reformation. Were the abuses widespread? Or did a flagrant spark here and there kindle a great fire? The distance of the years makes it difficult to tell.

One Dominican monk who helped to kindle the flame of righteous indignation in Martin Luther's heart was John Tetzel, the son of a goldsmith in Leipzig. He had been put in charge of indulgences by Albert, Archbishop of Mainz. For a fee, Tetzel claimed to be able to forgive any sin—for the living or the dead.

In England the reign of Henry VIII was a hideous procession of corrupt practices. The Reformation was almost inevitable.

At first, there were those within the church who tried to sift out the bad, keep the good. For example, in 1536, the Ten Articles appeared. The last of the Ten dealt with the abuses that had crept into the Apostolic doctrine of the communion of the saints. . . .

. . . for as much as due order of charity requireth . . . and all these ancient documents clearly show that it is a very good and charitable deed to pray for the souls departed, for as much also as such usage as has continued in the church . . . even from the beginning, we will . . . that no man ought to be grieved with the continuance of the same. . . .

Wherefore it is much necessary that such abuses be clearly put away, which under the name of purgatory has been advanced, as to make men believe that through the bishop of Rome's pardon, souls might be clearly delivered out of purgatory and all the pains of death . . . and other like abuses.

Conciliatory men tried to retain the practice of praying "for the souls departed," but their voices were drowned in the rising emotional tide of the Reformation. At the crest of the tide, frenzied mobs wrecked cathedrals and abbeys, destroying priceless, medieval stained-glass windows and irreplaceable art treasures. In Scotland, I have stood in the shells of some of those wrecked abbeys, the empty bones of the windows, like patterns of fragile old lace, so exquisite that only patient, dedicated hands could have chiselled their cobweblike traceries.

It is not too surprising that the wrecking mood resulted in some strange decisions. From the Protestant point of view the reformers were justified in their zeal for purifying the church. But they were emotion-blind, and much good was thrown out with the bad. Men had begun to worship art treasures instead of the living Christ, so many churches were stripped bare. Some of the ceremonies, including the masses and music, had become an end in themselves. So in many Reformed churches, no musical instruments were permitted, only tuning forks; nothing but psalms could be sung.

And what of the communion of the saints? It had been corrupted by indulgences. So the Reformed church taught that there was no need for any fellowship of prayer with and for the dead. The inference was that to pray for the dead was a sin.

Yet at least two vestiges of the communion of the saints escaped the wrecking. In the *Book of Common Prayer* are still remnants of this universal practice of the early church. In the service of Holy Communion are these words:

And we also bless thy Holy Name for all thy servants departed this life in thy faith and fear; beseeching thee to grant them continual growth in thy love and service, and to give us grace so to follow their good examples, that with them we may be partakers of thy heavenly kingdom. . . .

And in the service for the burial of the dead are a number of such prayers, among them:

O God, whose mercies cannot be numbered; accept our prayers on behalf of the soul of thy servant departed, and grant him an entrance into the land of light and joy, in the fellowship of thy saints, through Jesus Christ our Lord. AMEN.

Then there is that one clause in the Creed—" I believe in . . . the communion of saints "—that somehow survived the Reformation. It comes down to us like a few bars of a half-remembered melody.

When I first became aware of it, I could not escape the feeling that it should mean something special. In my own need for comfort and assurance, I kept groping for something that seemed to be missing in the church's teaching in our day.

We stand at an open grave. It seems that our memories, hopes and dreams—a part of us—are being buried there. In our anguish, the church says to us, 'There is no death. Christ has for ever conquered it. Believe that your husband (or wife or brother or child) is not in that grave. You will get all the comfort you need for accepting that.'

Then the sorrowing leave the cemetery and go back to an empty house. Desperately the mind tries to fathom those soaring words, " There is no death." Then where is the one whose body was left in the grave? And how —in the daily round of life—do the rest of us live out our belief in immortality?

Even children wonder about it. A certain little boy always named each member of his family in his bedtime prayers and asked God to bless and to take care of each one.

The child's father had long been ill. On the night he died, an aunt was hearing the boy's prayers. The child started to include his father as usual. But the aunt interrupted, " You mustn't pray for your father any more. He is with God now and doesn't need our prayers."

She meant well. But many years later, the man, recalling the incident, said, " The effect of her words was like a curtain coming down, or a heavy door being shut between me and my father. He was behind that door, for ever lost to me. Yet the minister who had called at our home had taken me on his knee and told me that my father was still alive and that he still loved me. And my childish mind reasoned that I certainly loved him as I always had. So why couldn't I ask God to bless him?"

Why indeed? Is that heresy? I don't think so.

For a time after death invaded my life, this feeling of something missing in the church's credo about immortality went no further than an intellectual conviction. Then came a personal crisis, a big one, one I was not equipped to handle. It was a problem involving my husband and his work, too complex and painful to write about even now.

One day in a prayer tinged with desperation, my petition took a strange turn, surprising even to me. . . . " O God, You've asked me to accept by faith the fact that Peter is still alive. I've tried, but it isn't real to me. But if he is, then he will be as concerned as I about that problem.

" I don't know how this works—but if it's possible, then I ask that Peter join me in this prayer asking for Your specific help. And I ask that he and I together claim that wonderful promise (ROMANS 8 : 28) that You will take this messy situation and bring real good out of it—not just for us, but for Your Kingdom."

From one point of view, such an untraditional prayer made me feel like a fool. Yet if ever there was a desperate effort to act out a belief in immortality, that was it.

Within two months the crisis passed. One door closed; another opened. The good appeared. It was significant beyond imagining. The crisis led directly to the writing of *A Man Called Peter*.

Had this fellowship of the spirit across the barrier between life and death been real? I was not sure. I only knew that never before had I experienced such a far-reaching answer to prayer.

It made me wonder even more about that clause of the

Creed whose meaning had been all but lost. On earth, human fellowship always involves the inner person, the spirit. Then what about after death? Either there is simply oblivion, or else the spirit that is the real person lives on in conscious awareness. If the latter, then the only possible communion across the barrier is through spirit. And for the Christian, the most potent vehicle of spirit—as well as the safest—is prayer.

About that time, an old friend told me of two of his experiences. This man had been a teacher of English in a small college. " In observing my students through the years," he told me, " I always saw some with more sensitivity, more creativity, than others. One might expect that. But when I probed into the lives of the most creative ones to find out what made them tick, I discovered that almost always someone near to them had died.

" I can't prove this. But it's as if death had opened doors to life. As if those who had gone on into the next life were able to bestow added capacities, added awareness, added creativity."

" That's too big a thought for me," I told him frankly. " I'm sceptical. But what was the second experience?"

" That came after the death of my mother. Always I had wanted to write. Up to that time, I had tried to be content with teaching my students to write. Then after mother's death, suddenly things began happening in my life. The prayers that were my deepest desires were answered, as if my mother was somehow able to open the way for me."

" And the result?"

He paused and smiled. " In thirty years I've had fifteen books published."

Since then I have learned of several others who have done some experimenting of their own with the communion of the saints. Most of them do not talk about it readily; if they did, they wouldn't dream of calling it by any such high-flown theological term.

One of these—a well-known minister—lost his father

not long ago. The father also had been a minister, the founder of twelve churches, a man with a vital mind and an agile sense of humour. Always father and son had relished pitting mind against mind, batting ideas back and forth.

" Since my father's death," the minister told me, " there have been times when I've been aware of this same process. That is, I toss an idea out. Presently a counter-idea is tossed back with the stamp of my father's personality on it, with his characteristic twist of humour. This isn't anything I've consciously sought. Yet it's happened a good many times."

Another person, Helen Chappell White, the wife of a retired university president, began searching out of her deep need when her elder son, a bomber navigator, was shot down over the Baltic Sea in 1944. It was a young chaplain who supplied the first clue. The sorrowing mother had admitted to him that neither God nor prayer was real to her any more.

" Then talk to your boy," the chaplain advised her. " Ask him to help you find and know God. He's closer to God now than you and I are—he'll lead you to Him."[1]

The mother felt that nothing could be lost by trying. She began by setting aside a few minutes in her bedroom each morning, relaxing her body, quieting her mind, silently affirming her faith in the promise that her son was alive.

She has had no startling experiences. " I don't think that it is for ' signs and wonders ' that this companionship across the line is permitted or should be cultivated," she wrote to me. But she has found more precious things— healing for her grief; a feeling of daily companionship with her boy; and like the minister, at times a tossing of ideas back and forth amounting almost to conversation. " There's a solid, steadily growing core of utter reality in this spiritual companionship," she says. " Often just a kind of happy sharing. . . . I should not care to live at all without it any more; the past would hurt, and the future terrify me."

[1] White, Helen Chappell, *With Wings As Eagles*, p. 198, Rinehart & Company, Inc., New York, 1953.

One of my correspondents, a widower from Kansas City, the one who had insisted upon being so honest, had asked:

> I cannot believe in personal immortality. . . . You seem to believe it. . . . Can you offer the rest of us any proof?

And my answer had been . . . no, not final proof as the scientist means proof, not yet in our day. When I sought that proof, I found that the best reasoning of the finest minds, plus all the piling up of evidential testimony, can take us only part of the way.

The work of Dr J. B. Rhine of Duke University has taken at least the first tentative steps towards proving extra-sensory perception, telepathy, and clairvoyance, and thus that there is something more to life than the material.

But until science can finally prove life after death beyond evidential experiences, we are backed up against faith. For anything relating to the spirit, the irreversible order is faith first, then knowledge. That is because faith has a way of slicing through prejudicial and intellectual barriers and opening the eyes of the spirit.

I am a child of the scientific age and do not find this order easy to accept. Yet the order is a fact.

Christ has told us. . . .

> Whosoever liveth and believeth in me shall never die.
> Believest thou this?   (JOHN 11:26)

Not only did He tell us, but to prove immortality He rose from the dead, and over a period of forty days appeared and reappeared to more than five hundred witnesses.

All that is without the bounds of my experience. Yet if I disbelieve what Christ said about immortality, then I have no right to credit anything else He said or did. And I have experienced too much to believe that He was a fraud.

Moreover, though I do not understand the resurrection

with my mind, the proof to me lies in what believing it did for those first Christians. Men do not have their characters reversed, bisect history, make an impact on generations to come, because of something they have imagined.

So there came the moment in my search when I had to get down on my knees to get through the low door of faith; I had to accept immortality on faith because Christ has assured us that it is true. I knew that if any proof were to come to me, it would have to follow, not precede, that acceptance.

I am not a mystic nor do I have any psychic gifts. I have no experiences to report that could not have happened to anyone. That night on Cape Cod, during the first summer after Peter's death, I had been told that if I would believe in Peter's presence when I needed him, the feeling and the proof would come later. Exactly that has happened. A strengthened faith has replaced the feeling of irremediable loss through death. My crisis prayers have been answered in an extraordinary way. There has been a steady stream of help, directions from without.

There has come the restoration of perspective on life; the knowledge that our world is connected with joy and hope to another; that we who refuse to explore its spiritual and physical boundaries with zest and a sense of adventure, who will not lift our eyes to its far horizons, cheat only ourselves.

CHAPTER 12

Adventure in Hollywood

It was August in California—one of those days when low clouds were playing hide and seek with the sun. Three people in the Buick on highway 101 were travelling from Oceanside to Los Angeles—two teenage boys and a Negro woman, the family cook.

Lamar, the older boy, was at the wheel. His fourteen-year-old brother, John, was in the front seat beside him, and Hattie, the cook, was in the back.

Suddenly in the midst of lively conversation, a fruit-truck trailer was hurtling towards them. There was the screaming, grinding crash of metal on metal. Then men shouting and running, the sound of sirens. . . .

The *Los Angeles Evening Herald and Express* reported the next day:

FILM PRODUCER'S SON FIGHTS FOR LIFE AS CRASH
KILLS BROTHER

One son of film producer Lamar Trotti fought for his life today while his brother and the family maid were dead of injuries received in a head-on auto-truck collision yesterday at San Clemente. Lamar Trotti, Jr, 18, and the Negro maid Hattie Johnson, 50, were killed instantly. John Trotti, 14, suffering a spine fracture and other injuries, was taken to St Joseph's Hospital in Santa Ana.

The younger boy was operated on and he was given transfusions early today. . . .

The boys' parents took it hard. Lamar Trotti's friends at Twentieth Century-Fox studios, who knew that he had suffered a heart attack two years before, watched him battle his grief, struggle to piece his life together.

A clergyman friend, Dr Albert Harris from Macon, Georgia, sent him a book that he thought might help.

Mr Trotti wrote his friend to thank him:

Dear Dr Harris:

I am . . . taking a six months' leave of absence in the hope that in that time I will be able to adjust myself to all the things that happened to me when Lamar died.

This is a prelude to saying that as soon as I get to the beach, where we are spending the summer, I will very carefully read *A Man Called Peter*. . . . Frankly, that may be just what I need to do. . . .

Lamar Trotti evaluated any book in terms of potential movie material. He began to make notes on *A Man Called Peter*. Though this man had come into the motion-picture industry by an unusual route, he was where he belonged. He saw all life in terms of drama.

He was a native of Atlanta, Georgia, a former newspaper-man. Then he had had a stint of writing and directing publicity for the Motion Pictures Producers and Distributors Association in New York. Intrigued by the problems peculiar to the writing of screen plays, he had himself written fifteen.

In 1942 he had turned producer. Such successful movies as " Wilson," " The Ox-Bow Incident," " Cheaper by the Dozen," " Razor's Edge," " Captain from Castile," " My Blue Heaven," " Alexander's Ragtime Band," and " Guadalcanal Diary," had brought him to the top of his profession.

Several things about the Peter Marshall story intrigued Mr Trotti. Much of it had an Atlanta setting. That struck a responsive chord. Then there was the strong emphasis on immortality. For example, the Sunday of Pearl Harbour Day Dr Marshall had preached at the Naval Academy in Annapolis, and had talked about death—and life. What a stirring scene that would make! Since his son's death,

Lamar Trotti had come to know how deep and widespread the need was for reassurance, for strengthening on this point.

But Mr Trotti was not to be the one to use these notes. Suddenly on August 28, 1952, two years after his son's death, a second heart attack struck. That one carried him away.

Lamar Trotti's notes passed into the hands of one of his fellow producers at Fox—Samuel G. Engel. They were to play their own part in the movie "A Man Called Peter."

The wire delivered to me aboard the westbound *Chief* read:

WOULD YOU PLEASE ARRANGE TO GET OFF TRAIN AT PASADENA STATION AT 7.55 A.M. STUDIO CAR WILL MEET YOU THERE. THIS IS A SMALL STATION AND IT WILL BE EASIER TO RECOGNIZE YOU AND TO HANDLE YOUR LUGGAGE THAN AT THE LOS ANGELES STATION. REGARDS.

> JOHN ADAMS
> TRANSPORTATION DIVISION
> TWENTIETH CENTURY FOX STUDIOS

The hand holding the telegram trembled a little. There had been some surprising adventures since Peter's death; surely this was the strangest.

The procession of palm trees flying past the train windows told me that I was not only in California but was nearing my destination. Thoughts chased themselves through my mind: Here I am—all alone . . . I don't know anyone at the Fox studios . . . I've never set foot on a movie lot. . . . Who do I think I am, making this sally into Hollywood? And along with these realizations came an upsurge of emotion quite like stage fright. Suddenly the palms of my hands were moist; my stomach was doing a series of flipflops.

For a moment just before the *Chief* came to a gentle stop in the Pasadena station, I felt like someone standing in the wing of a theatre, waiting for her cue to go on stage.

What does an actress experience during those moments of waiting? I thought I knew . . . mounting tension, a wary uneasiness interlaced with fear, a strange lifting of the senses in an effort to catch the mood and measure the receptivity of the people out beyond the footlights.

My stage fright lasted only until the action began. Mr Adams, the studio representative who had come to meet me, was young and easy-going. Meeting and squiring assorted actors and actresses, authors and publicity people, was obviously just part of the day's work—nothing to get excited about.

" The studio car is right over there, Mrs Marshall. We've made reservations for you at the Beverly Hills Hotel. I'll take you there first. Then we'll go on to the studio later this morning to meet your producer, Sam Engel."

We were scarcely settled in the studio limousine before I made my first faux pas. " My former college room-mate lives in California now," I said. " She's anxious for me to visit her—lives in Menlo Park. Mr Adams, maybe you could tell me—how long would it take to run over there?"

The man looked at me in tolerant amusement. " Well—you see, actually—Menlo Park is some five hundred miles away. It's a suburb of San Francisco, not Los Angeles. You could make it to San Francisco overnight on the train. About two hours by air." And his eyes seemed to be trying to take the measure of the woman who had written *A Man Called Peter*, but who didn't know the difference between Los Angeles and San Francisco.

The room to which I was shown in the luxurious Beverly Hills Hotel was an immense one with wide windows and a balcony overlooking a swimming pool—quite in keeping with my preconceived ideas of Hollywood glamour. The bedroom was decorated in shades of pinky taupes—subtle understatements of femininity. It had thick carpeting; French Provincial furniture in light fruitwood; heavy hammered-satin bedspreads and draperies; many mirrors; and an oversized vanity table in the bath-dressing room, its mirror surrounded by fluorescent lights—obviously for women who took their make-up seriously.

And when I opened the top bureau drawer, an exquisite fragrance floated out. Immediately it set my imagination working. Had the last occupant of this room been a famous actress? I thought not. Just a beautiful woman whose costly, personally blended perfume had lingered behind her.

But I had to pull my thoughts back to the business at hand. Soon I would be walking into the inner sanctum of the Fox studios. I recalled the events that had brought me to this moment. . . .

It was in the late fall of 1952 that I had first heard from a certain producer at Twentieth Century-Fox who was interested in *A Man Called Peter*. Hollywood's attention had been directed to the book because it had then been on the best-seller list for more than fifty consecutive weeks, and that fall had reached the top.

Even so, I had been told by my publisher's agent on the West Coast that the professional movie makers were sceptical that this particular book could be made into a successful movie. After all, the element of conflict—the catalyst for drama—was mostly missing from the Peter Marshall story. True, there was sweeping across the nation such a revival of interest in religion that some analysts were unabashedly calling it " a spiritual awakening." But Hollywood remained sceptical. The truth was that previous motion pictures about the lives of ministers, even the most popular like " One Foot in Heaven " and " Stars in My Crown," were not the most successful financial ventures.

Moreover, in the fall of 1952 the studios were cautious about buying book rights. The nation's mounting interest in television had Hollywood's collective teeth chattering. Obviously this was not gambling weather—especially for a religious book. No other studio was bidding against Fox for *A Man Called Peter*.

All of this added up to the fact that the overtures made

to me for an option on the book were not financially allur-
ing. Still, the men at Fox seemed reasonably eager to have
the option and kept pressing me by wire and phone for a
decision.

During those days I wrote my thoughts down to try to
clarify them:

> I am not interested in the money that has been offered
> me if the option is eventually picked up. . . .
> Nor am I interested in more publicity. I have more than
> I can handle now, or have any taste for.
> The one thing I *am* interested in is what the movie
> could mean in constructive help to thousands of Ameri-
> cans, perhaps to the nation as a whole. This is the
> possibility I want to explore. . . .

On the other hand, I knew that turning a book over to
the movie men is always a calculated risk. If they Holly-
woodized the Peter Marshall story and ruined it, I could
forget about its being a constructive help to anyone.

While I pondered all this, Louella Parsons in her column
for November 25 let out the news that Fox was negotiating
for the book—only she made it appear that it was all
settled:

> *A Man Called Peter*, the life of the late Peter Marshall,
> chaplain of the U.S. Senate, has been bought by 20th
> Century-Fox. . . . Sam Engel who will produce the
> story, has chosen Richard Burton, the British actor, to
> play Peter, while Jean Peters will be seen as Catherine
> (Mrs Marshall). . . .

Immediately I began to receive a flood of mail. . . .

> Can any good come out of Hollywood? I've got my
> fingers crossed. . . . Please don't allow it to become too
> Hollywoodish . . . Who in the world could ever play

Peter Marshall . . .? My family and I have enjoyed this story so much that we feel that it is too sacred to be imitated or substituted. . . .

I don't want you to be disappointed in your project. . . . Mrs Marshall, let me give you some good advice. You speak right up " in meetin' " out there in Hollywood. . . .

I could understand why my friends were so uneasy. They seemed to feel that Hollywood's forte was the physical and the material. Would the movie industry have the sensitivity to handle material dealing with the human spirit?

Such was my questioning also. I knew that in this as in all situations, there were imponderables. Obviously something more than my best judgment was needed. So—very simply— I asked God to tell me what my decision should be.

There came the day when I knew the answer; it came as a strong and unmistakable feeling. I was to keep the door open to the possibility of a movie. Therefore, I gave Fox the option in the faith that if God did not want this movie made, the option would never be picked up or the legal negotiations would bog down; if He did want it, then it would be His project just as the book had been. He would then see to the final result.

I had agreed to this first trip to Hollywood as a private scouting expedition. I was not there to be dined, fêted, and soft-soaped, but to examine the situation for myself, to observe and to be observed. The big question was . . . could Mr Engel and I work together to translate *A Man Called Peter* into a fine screenplay? If so, I felt that something would have to be added to what I had always been told was Hollywood's usual attitude towards authors : " We'll treat you like a queen for a few days and then get you out of our hair as quickly as possible." If this was really true, then I felt that a special effort would have to be made to achieve rapport between the producer, the script writer, and me.

By eleven that morning I had been whisked down Beverly Drive to the Santa Monica Bay Boulevard entrance to the studio. The watchman at the double gate recognized the driver of the studio car and signalled us through. We drove down a narrow road lined with warehouses filled with props —all manner of doors, thousands of window frames, columns, mantles and architectural gewgaws—past well-kept flower beds to the Administration building.

Mr Engel was a middle-aged man with dark hair and black horn-rimmed spectacles. His setting was a suite of offices in early American style, decorated in greens and tawny beiges. Behind a large desk was a bookcase filled with leather-bound copies of the screenplays of movies Mr Engel had produced— " Come to the Stable," " Follow the Sun," " Sitting Pretty," " Frogmen," and many others. That first day's meeting held surprises on both sides. There was curiosity in the producer's eyes. Was it that I didn't quite fit his preconceived mould of the minister's widow?

And marvellously, within hours after I had first set foot on the Fox lot, my question about Hollywood's handling of spiritual material was answered in an unusual way. I had brought with me some of the tape recordings of Peter's sermons made the last year of his life. Mr Engel was eager to hear Peter Marshall's voice. Immediately he ordered a tape recorder brought to his office. He shut the door, selected " The Rock That Moved," and settled himself in his swivel chair.

Soon the musical voice with the familiar Scottish burr filled the office. Mr Engel seemed absorbed and chuckled frequently during the colourful description of the St Andrews Society dinner with which the sermon opened. . . .

My, what memories came back, as the drumsticks twirled above the drum, and the kettledrums rolled . . . and our feet tapped out the time to *Cock o' the North,*
The Forty-Second
and *Hieland Laddie.*

In memory I saw a battalion of the Gordon Highlanders,
swinging down from Edinburgh Castle to Princes Street
when I was last in Scotland—the pipes skirling
and the kilts swinging,
with the pride that only Scotsmen fully know.

I thought of home . . . and long ago. . . .
We sang the old songs . . . and many an eye was
misty. . . .

But then, after this light beginning, Peter plunged directly
into the heart of his message . . .

Memories . . . they come surging back into the heart to
make it clean again . . . or to accuse it.

Yes . . . to some it is music . . . or a song.
      To others it is a picture or the face of a friend,
but to Simon Peter it was the crowing of a cock.

He had seen the last flickering torch disappear round the
turn of the path that wound down hill.
Only once in a while could the lights of the procession
be seen through the trees—like giant fireflies. . . .

There swept over Peter the realization that his Master
had at least been captured and was marching away to die.
The icy fear that gripped—[1]

Suddenly Mr Engel flicked off the machine. "My wife Ruth
is coming to join us for lunch. I'd like her to hear this.
Suppose we wait. We can hear the rest later."

I was surprised, uneasy. He had seemed so impressed by
the sermon. But the three of us had a pleasant lunch in the
studio commissary, and I forgot my disappointment.

[1] Marshall, Peter, *Mr Jones, Meet the Master*, pp. 89-90, London,
Peter Davies Ltd., 1954.

On the way back I got glimpses of the sets from movies I had seen—the bridge for " My Cousin Rachel ! " was pointed out to me ; a cobblestoned French village that looked familiar ; the gigantic tank used for " The Titanic " ; some sets from " Daddy Long Legs." But all of the sets were deserted ; nothing was shooting. The lot was like a ghost town. As we walked down the long corridors of the Administration building, I noticed that many of the executive offices were empty. I asked why.

" I've been here a long time," Mr Engel said. " I've never seen production at such a low ebb."

" Why? How do you account for that?"

" TV," he said simply. " Something's got to break soon or this industry's a goner. The wide screen could be one answer. By the way, your picture may be the first one made in Cinemascope."

Back in the producer's office, once more the recorder was turned on. Clearly Mr Engel was engrossed all over again. Yet as the voice with the burr began building the drama of Simon Peter's denial to its climax, once more Mr Engel jumped up and flicked off the recorder.

" I've a friend here in the studio, David Brown, who really ought to hear this. If you two don't mind . . . I think I'll wait. He may be able to join us later this afternoon."

But the same procedure was followed with the friend. He too heard only a portion of the sermon. By then I knew something strange was going on. Peter Marshall's voice and message held a fascination for Sam Engel. Like a moth to a flame, he came back to it again and again. But there was something else—some agony in it. I thought I knew. The bedrock reality, the incisiveness of the message underneath the music of the words was creating fear, spiritual tension, pain.

Later I learned that after dinner, when the lot was deserted except for the night watchman, Mr Engel had closeted himself in his locked office and had listened to the end of " The Rock That Moved."

The same Jesus who called Simon is calling you.
The same Jesus who saved Simon can save you.
The same mighty hand will hold you up.
The denials that you have made were made by Simon.
Yet he was restored; so may you be restored.
    Christ changed Simon into Peter,
      the sinner into the saint.

He can change your life, if you are willing![2]

After that, the producer was all enthusiasm for the tapes.
He had copies made for himself—one set for his home, one
for his office. For weeks to come, he would insist on playing
them for anyone who would listen.

This episode was a key to the character and personality of
the movie producer. Sam Engel had been born into the stream
of a rich and authentic religious heritage. His grandfather
had been an orthodox Jewish rabbi. One of the childhood
memories that had impressed him deeply was that of his
grandfather dropping a warm Lincoln penny into his hand
on the days when he had successfully completed his Hebrew
lesson. "An angel from heaven sent this," the venerable
old man would say. "If you'll believe in God and learn His
holy Torah, you'll be blessed a millionfold."

There was in Sam Engel a sensitivity to spiritual matters
that could only have been the fruit of such a heritage. He
longed to leave the world a better place than he had found
it. Religion drew him. Yet in this materialistic world, particularly in Hollywood, his religious heritage sometimes ran
head-on into other values. Giving the spiritual real priority
might jeopardize those other values. That he knew.

The next morning Mr Engel showed me his personal copy
of *A Man Called Peter*. It was dog-eared, copiously marked
with red pencil.

"I want you to see something else. Did you ever hear of
Lamar Trotti?"

[2] Marshall, Peter, *Mr Jones, Meet the Master*, p. 86, London, Fontana, 1964.

" Yes—yes I have."

" Well, these are his notes on your book in his own hand-writing. Mrs Trotti sent them to me after his death."

" What made him that interested in the book—enough to make notes, I mean?"

" He needed a lift himself." Then I learned from Mr Engel the story of Lamar Trotti's last days—the death of his son in the automobile accident, his terrible grief, and finally his own death from a heart attack.

Mr Engel leaned back in his swivel chair, his eyes on the ceiling. " Funny thing . . . far too many men around here dying of heart attacks . . . frightening. . . . When death comes to my friends, I try so hard to think of something—uh—really helpful—comforting—to say to those left."

" It *is* hard."

" Sure—sure is. That's one thing about your book. Peter had a real message about death. Everybody needs it. If we didn't do anything else in this movie but give help like that, it would be worth everything."

That afternoon I met the girl who had been assigned to work on the screenplay. She brought along a step sheet for " A Man Called Peter " bound between blue covers.

Mr Engel knew that I'd never before seen a step sheet. " This is the first go-round in writing a screenplay," he explained. " To take a book and make it into a motion picture, we have to see the story as a sequence of scenes. A step sheet is just what it says—the scenes step by step, in progression, numbered. Now let's go over it."

1. Establish Agnes Scott College for women, Decatur, Georgia—southern atmosphere of the campus, etc.
2. Tennis courts at college. Catherine and another girl playing doubles with two young men. . . .
3. Dissolve to exterior of Westminster Church as Catherine and friend approach bulletin board. It announces Dr Marshall's sermon " Praying Is Dangerous Business ".

4. As Catherine and her friend enter the church. . . .

That was fine, except that in step 10 we suddenly took off into pure fiction. A coloured boy named Phillip Humes was introduced. He was supposed to be the son of the church janitor in Atlanta. His story was to run all through the movie, ending with his death in the Pacific in World War II.

I objected. The subsequent discussion between Sam, the writer, and me revealed a sharp difference of opinion. To the producer and the script-writer, fiction was as good as truth, provided it was plausible.

My viewpoint was that truth was often more exciting than fiction, sometimes had more dramatic possibilities. Moreover, I felt that the film would wield its greatest impact only if the movie audiences knew that they were seeing what had really happened. The dilemma was not resolved that day. It was to haunt us.

Before I left for Washington, Mr Engel offered, if Fox picked up the option, to give me the position of technical adviser to the script. That meant that he trusted me enough to let me be a party to all decisions about the screenplay. I would be included in further conferences. But it did not mean that he would be obligated to accept my suggestions.

He and I parted good friends. He was so hopeful that the option would be picked up that he instructed the script-writer to proceed with a first-draft continuity taken from an expanded step sheet. In time I would hear from Fox's lawyers about the option.

Back in the East, I made some inquiries to find a lawyer who had had some experience with motion-picture contracts. Knowing my lack of business know-how and how difficult it was for me to make sense of the legal terminology in any contract, this seemed only common sense.

It was not until August 12 that I learned that Twentieth Century-Fox had decided to exercise their option. A contract followed by mail. I knew nothing about contracts, but that one seemed hardly fair. My impression was that it was a trial balloon sent up to see just how gullible I was. For instance, they asked for all drama rights to *A Man Called Peter*, including television rights stretching ten years into the future. Later I found that these were standard clauses in most movie contracts.

My lawyer took nine months to negotiate the changes that we considered important. He tried hard to get final veto rights in case anything turned up in the movie script to which I objected. We did not win that. But I did get veto power over anything libellous or detrimental to the character of Peter Marshall. In the end, the contract was at least reasonable, though the buying price was what it had been from the beginning.

In the meantime, the script-writer's first-draft continuity had been sent me. It was conscientious work but had more fiction in it than truth. For example, I was supposed to be shocked out of tuberculosis back into health by seeing an automobile accident from my bedroom window. This was not only fiction but scarcely plausible fiction!

Increasingly, though I liked the girl personally, I began to feel that she did not understand the basis of the Peter Marshall story and therefore was on the wrong assignment. Should I, I wondered, share that conviction with Mr Engel?

I decided against it; that would be overstepping my bounds. The producer knew his scenario writers under contract—their interests and capabilities. Frequently during those weeks he telephoned me. Since he seemed quite happy with the writer chosen, I kept quiet about how I felt.

I did, however, pray about it. The essence of my prayer was, " Oh, God, if this is the writer for this job, then fine. If not, then will You please get that point across to Sam Engel? I leave the matter in Your hands."

About ten days later an airmail special delivery came:

Dear Catherine:

After much deliberation I have come to the conclusion

that the script-writer on the job for "A Man Called Peter" is not the one for the project. . . .

I have for the past two weeks discussed "Peter" with another woman writer whose work I am familiar with and respect. She is an extremely capable craftsman and is highly enthusiastic about undertaking the job.

Already I have had several conferences with her and we have made excellent progress. It is my hope to have a step sheet of the new line-up ready by the time of your next visit here.

I hope that this change I am making won't cause you any anxiety, and that you will be pleased with the new writer when you meet her.

With every good wish.

　　　　　　　　　　　　　　　　　　　　　　　Sam

P.S. Incidentally, the new writer feels very strongly the need to stick pretty close to the biographical facts contained in your book. I know this will please you.

Far from causing me any anxiety, I was so elated I almost took off in all directions. Rarely had I received such a prompt, incisive, and specific answer to prayer. This was the reassurance I needed that the movie really was God's project, and that He was quite capable of handling all complications.

My next Hollywood trip was set for November 10. I had been asked to stay for at least a month of daily script conferences. These would be crucial, policy making. My growing feeling for the movie and my emotional investment in the final result can be judged by a letter I wrote Sam Engel about that time:

To be sure, moving, inspirational entertainment is not discounted. But, Sam, I long for this particular movie to be far more than that. And I think you do too. I long for this picture to show movie audiences all over America what God can do for modern men and women, and so to change lives and set feet on the right track.

Now I know that what I'm asking for is virtually a documentary film—one that's true to the facts, not of a book but of life—only handled with all the artistry of fiction. That would not be an easy scenario to write. I know that. I think I understand some of the difficulties. But I'm convinced that it could be done, and that it would make movie history. . . .

What I did not share with Mr Engel was any mention of a spiritual problem involved. It might have seemed irrelevant to him; to me, it was basic. . . . Peter and I had had evidence in our lives that God can guide modern men and women. But God has also given us freedom of choice. He won't violate that. He can certainly direct those who want Him to direct. But can He guide those who aren't aware of any need for His help and don't seek it?

I was trying to be realistic. It seemed probable that some of those in the movie industry who would be making " A Man Called Peter " would fall into the category of those who sought no help from God. What then? Is prayer for other people effective only if those for whom we pray are dedicated men of God?

About that time I was reading parts of the Old Testament. Certain things impressed me as never before—the God-centred view of history—God standing in the shadows keeping vigil through the long centuries of civilization's slow upward progress; the Bible's unwhitewashed heroes, presented as sinners like all men; the lusty sex, unabashedly set forth, taken for granted as a part of life; the continual raprap of the ancient writers' insistence on the Almightiness of God.

This last gave me pause. Those early writers really believed that there were no limits to God's power. No problem about man's freedom of will bothered them. For example, out of jealousy and anger, Joseph's brothers sold him into slavery in Egypt. Yet God's hand was above all, overruling, so that later, as the "ruler over all the land of Egypt," Joseph could say . . .

> . . . be not grieved, nor angry with yourselves, that ye sold me hither. . . . It was not you that sent me hither, but God. . . .
>
> (GENESIS 45 : 5, 8)

In the same way, God overruled the Pharoah of the bondage.

> He removeth kings and setteth up kings. . . .
>
> (DANIEL 2 : 21)

Like a gold thread this reiteration of the Omnipotence of God runs through all Scripture. . . . A man's heart

> is in the hand of the Lord, as the rivers of water;
> he turneth it whithersoever he will.   (PROVERBS 21 : 1)

Either God lives—or He doesn't. Either He has real power —or it is all delusion. If God could overrule Joseph's brothers and assorted Pharaohs and kings, then He could manage modern rulers—and Hollywood. At least, I thought, now I have a good chance to find out.

But the Bible also insists that we have to ask for God's help in order to get it. That is the point of petitionary prayer. And the asking seems to have more power when many join their petitions in agreement on "what they shall ask."

It was out of that background that I decided to write to each of those who had sent me letters after reading *A Man Called Peter* to ask for their specific prayer about the movie project. I told neither my publisher nor Mr Engel that I was doing this. . . .

November 1, 1953

Dear Friend:

I remember with gratitude the most thoughtful letter which you wrote me sometime ago, in which you shared with me how God spoke to your own life through Peter Marshall's story and sermons.

Now I want to ask a personal favour of you. Twentieth Century-Fox plans to make a movie of *A Man Called Peter*. This movie could speak to the heart of America. It could mean a great deal to our time and generation —using this modern movie medium.

I can visualize movie audiences—made up of whole families—alternatively laughing and shedding a few tears as they relive certain episodes of *A Man Called Peter* on the screen, as they see God Himself shining through one man's life. I can see vast audiences streaming out of the theatres on to the sidewalks of a hundred thousand Main Streets, entertained, uplifted, inspired, with the thought singing through many a mind. . . . " If God could solve Peter Marshall's problems, maybe He can solve mine—and my nation's. I'm going to give Him a chance. . . ."

I can see the scenario writer, the producer—Mr Samuel G. Engel—the director, the entire cast given by God inspiration and ability quite beyond all natural talent.

But all this can happen only if this whole project is literally floated on a gigantic wave of prayer. It is precisely because I well know what a difference prayer can make, that I am writing this letter to you and 1800 other choice friends, requesting your specific prayer about the movie " A Man Called Peter."

The next two months will see many crucial decisions made. The scenario is not yet completed. The movie has not been cast. The director has not been chosen. I leave for Hollywood on November 10 to make what suggestions I can. . . .

Usually most people pay little attention to a form letter. Yet this one drew an amazing response. I heard from almost everyone who received it. Most of the replies were written in longhand. It was evident that my request for prayer was being taken as seriously as I had hoped. . . .

From Toronto, Ohio:

Your fine circular letter just come. I am so grateful to be one of the many hundreds who will be praying with you about the filming of *A Man Called Peter*.

Both you and he already belong to America. I think of you as " Catherine " . . .

From Cincinnati:

Your letter came just an hour ago. I found it on returning home from my day's work in a steel shop. . . . I am nobody special. Lady, I'm just an uneducated steel worker, 38 years at this trade. . . .

I was never one who could express myself in prayer. But I've searched my mind. . . . With God's help, Lady, nothing can fail. . . .

From Winona Lake, Indiana:

I prize highly your request for my prayers that " A Man Called Peter " may be directed by our wonderful Lord Himself . . . I hope I'll be able to get out and see the picture when it's ready. At seventy-one I was stricken with my second coronary. . . .

From Tyler, Texas:

Your letter was very welcome. I'll not only pray, I'll ask my prayer group to. . . . My husband and I have talked it over and we think Clark Gable would be perfect for the part of Peter. . . .

From Springfield, Pennsylvania:

Our first reaction to your letter was one of immediate opposition, fearing that Hollywood would insist upon injecting its polish into the biography of a man who was far more concerned with inner composure than with exterior appearances. Unless we do Hollywood and the movie industry a grave injustice, Mrs Marshall, their motive for making a movie of Peter's life would be almost purely monetary; your motive, on the other hand, was spiritual. The fact that your biography has been a financial success was incidental. . . .

At the same time our hearts and our common sense suggested that you yourself would not accept any situation that would compromise the sanctity of Peter's life. . . . Thus our prayers have not been for the production of the movie, but for your guidance. . . .

From a businessman in Dayton, Ohio:

How can my prayers for your movie project be of any help when God does not seem to listen to my prayers for myself? But at least I can try. . . .

While I was away, Peter John stayed in Washington with friends who had two children themselves. This kind couple moved their whole family into our home and kept house for Peter.

This time Twentieth Century-Fox provided me with a three-room apartment on Wilshire Boulevard, close to Westwood Village, within six minutes' driving time of the studio. The living room, with its two walls of windows, opened on a swimming pool. Flowers had been placed in the apartment as a greeting from Sam Engel and his wife.

As I unpacked that evening, my thoughts were on the first script conference set for the next morning. An idea kept plucking at my mind . . . ' That conference should open with a prayer asking God's blessing on the work. You're the one to suggest it. You've asked other people to pray. Now it's your turn.'

I tried to brush the thought aside. The last thing I wanted was to seem like a religious eccentric to Mr Engel. Nor did I want him to think I was suggesting such a thing for effect.

I went on hanging up dresses and putting lingerie in the drawers. The thought returned.

It was easy to think up excuses. . . . What if I did suggest that we start the conference with prayer, and word got out? People in Hollywood are publicity conscious. They might think the whole thing a publicity stunt.

I dismissed the matter and deposited my toothbrush and some toiletries in the bathroom. The idea came back. It stuck like flypaper. I had a sinking feeling that the minute before that conference began in the morning, I would have an opportunity I'd never have again. And if I passed it up, I might be failing not just myself, but Christ. I had trouble going to sleep that night.

At ten the next morning three of us joined Mr Engel in his office—Eleanore Griffin, the script-writer, a Catholic; a secretary who was a Mormon; and I, a Presbyterian. Mr Engel was, of course, of the Jewish faith. Apparently the Lord had something cosmic in mind.

I was seated in a wing chair before Mr Engel's desk. Miss Griffin was sitting on the davenport, scanning the material abandoned by the other writer. The secretary was poised to take notes. The moment I had anticipated had arrived. My mouth was as dry as cotton. The words would surely stick in my throat.

" Sam, I've something to ask you."

" Sure, Catherine, shoot."

" Well, you know how I told you that every morning while I was writing *A Man Called Peter*, before I began, I said a quick little prayer and asked God to write that book through me. Seems maybe He did, judging by the

results. . . . We've got a big job ahead of us. We'll never
do it right on our own hook. Would you think me goofy if
I suggested that we pause for just a minute and ask for
God's help?"

For half a minute no one said anything. Time hung in
space. The brown eyes batted once behind the spectacles
and then looked straight at me. There was no embarrassment
in them. A sober look flicked across the mobile features.
Then . . . "I'd love that, Catherine! Will you do it?"

The prayer was short, informal, and to the point. When
I had finished, I found Eleanore Griffin's eyes glued to my
face. For a minute there was a hush in the room. Then
the shop-talk began.

The goal of the ten-to-five conferences every day was to
hammer out the story line. Our biggest problem was that
of selectivity. Most motion pictures run only an hour and
a half to an hour and forty-five minutes. How could we
effectively portray a man's life in so short a time? What
should be put in, what leave out?

I soon saw that there was a difference between fictionaliz-
ing for its own sake and the legitimate modification of facts
necessary to translate a book into a screenplay. There would
have to be some time compression, some shifting of the
sequence of events, some changing of details. For example,
in real life Peter and I had spent our honeymoon in New
York, not on Cape Cod; in the script there was the necessity
of introducing Cape Cod early in the story. In real life
Peter John was born on January 25, 1940, not in December
of 1941. Yet this time shift simplified the Annapolis
sequence in the movie, and so on and on. Changes of this
sort did not bother me, because they did no violence to the
spirit of the truth.

We talked the story out—scene by scene. Some sessions
were exciting. Mind sparked mind. Inspiration flowed.
Ideas piled up. At such times, Sam would pace the room,
gesturing, spitting words like bullets. Whenever he was
forced to pause for breath, Eleanore and I would leap into

the breach. Sometimes Sam would throw off his coat and walk up and down, plucking at his braces as if they were fiddle strings. Often he would get carried away, try to dramatize a scene, taking all the parts himself. He might drop to one knee, change his voice to falsetto . . . "This is Catherine speaking—" swing his arms, sit on the desk, take his glasses on and off, drink glass after glass of water, shoot questions at me.

Often these questions would go beyond what I had written in *A Man Called Peter*. Sam was using the book as a jumping-off place. Sometimes they would be as penetrating as psycho-analysis. He probed motive and thought, seeking to get beneath the surface. He wanted to know my emotions under given circumstances . . . "Think back, Catherine. How did you feel at the moment the doctor called? See this scene. What should the actress feel?"

For me the probing days were wearying days. I was talking about myself; yet I wasn't. Soon it seemed natural to say "Catherine" rather than "I." . . . "Well, if Peter leaves without proposing, and Catherine goes to her dorm room, weeping—don't you think—?"

Over and over, Sam appeared to be amazed at this objectivity. "I don't know how you do it. You've made an amazing recovery from Peter's death—or you couldn't. Besides, most authors battle for their stuff like tigers, consider every word straight from Sinai."

Eleanore and Sam turned to me for all theology, for anything pertaining to hymnology, for information about the Protestant church and a minister's life. At various times they asked me to explain deacons, elders, the Presbytery, the General Assembly, preludes and postulates, a minister's call, what a manse is, an every-member canvass, the whys and why-nots of the ministerial collar, the Geneva gown, etc.

One morning, Sam leaned back in his chair and said, "Catherine, there's something I've just got to ask you—"

"Of course—"

"You know that formal dinner the church gave you and Peter right after you went to Washington?"

"Yes, in a private room of the Mayflower Hotel."

"Well, tell me . . . didn't they serve any liquor at all? None at all?"

"No, Sam, they didn't."

"Well, I'll be—! Sorry!" And he said nothing more, just clucking his tongue.

At another time, Eleanore asked, "Catherine, I'm curious about something. How much salary did Peter make?"

"A very good one, as ministers' salaries go. At the time of his death, 11,500 dollars. That would be plus some fees and honoraria."

"But that's not possible—"

Sam interrupted, "A man like Peter—11,500 dollars! Why, in any other job under the sun he could have pulled down—"

"But Sam, the average minister gets something like 3,000 dollars a year. And don't forget that he has the expense of three years of postgraduate work on top of college."

That news about Peter's salary proved to be quite a bombshell. Obviously, Sam and Eleanore were oriented to the salary scales of the entertainment world. Nothing else I might have said could have so convinced them of the authenticity of Peter's call to the ministry and of his sincerity.

I soon learned the jargon of script-writing and enjoyed flinging it around—montage . . . establishing shot . . . narration . . . fade in . . . fade out . . . dissolve to . . . echo chamber . . . reverse shot . . . cut to . . . a tag. Always there was a secretary to take notes, but I took some for myself—in between doodling. I became a master doodler. One day it would be geometric designs; another day elaborate flowers. One morning I designed five new flags.

But sometimes it was as if we were walking barefoot on hot cinders when the story line seemed to be veering in a wrong direction. There was the time when Sam toyed with the idea of injecting an incident about a frustrated woman taking sleeping pills. We had been talking about the dilemmas and temptations suffered by most professional men through designing women. Mr Engel wanted to crystallize this problem in Peter's life through a fictional vignette. . . . Several scenes would reveal a woman's scheming to get close to her minister. Her plans would fail. Then she would take an overdose of sleeping pills and be rescued just in time.

" Sam, we'd be on dangerous ground," Eleanore objected. " People won't bother to separate truth from fiction. They'd always think ' where there's smoke, there's fire.' "

I agreed with Eleanore. But Sam had dreamed up so many nice details for the vignette that he was loath to drop it. " Let's think about it," he suggested.

The second day he was still in favour of using it. Nothing Eleanore or I could say moved him. It looked as if the poor woman and her sleeping pills might be in the screenplay for keeps.

Yet on the third day Sam announced, " About that sleeping pill incident—something tells me ' no ' on that. It won't really add anything. We can do better. Let's just forget it."

This process was repeated at several crucial points. Soon I learned to rely on it. Sam made his own decisions from the inside—sometimes wavered—but in the end, made them right.

Increasingly, Eleanore became aware of the process too, believed in it, leaned on it. " This is the greatest experience of my life," she would say to me privately. " We're sure getting help from some place. Golly, you'll never know how glad I am I didn't miss this assignment! "

On several mornings she would ask that we begin with prayer. " Other people don't need to know about it. Anyhow, who gives a hang what they think? The prayer does make a difference."

As the conferences went on, Sam became eager to include actual sermon material in the script. " You wouldn't make the Jolson story without songs," he would say. " And Peter Marshall was first, last, and always a preacher. Preaching was the music of his life. All right then, can you tell his story without letting him preach?"

" Right." Eleanore and I nodded.

" But, of course, you realize," he paused, frowning, " —this is daring. It's never been done. It will be a trail blazer. And another thing—I want one of those sermons to deal with immortality. Maybe some of 'Go Down Death.' That's terribly important. I couldn't let Lamar Trotti down on that."

My visit to Hollywood wasn't all work. The studio loaned me a car—a big unwieldy Lincoln. On holidays or days when we couldn't work, week-ends, and after hours, I played. There was a week-end at Laguna Beach, a drive to the Old Mission at San Juan Capistrano, a meal at Knott's Berry Farm, a visit to friends in the San Fernando Valley, a morning spent wandering through the Farmer's Market. I soaked up sunshine, drank gallons of fresh orange juice, ate fruits flown in from Hawaii, and bought an evening dress at Bullock's, Westwood, that was so right for me that it quickly became my favourite.

I spent a delightful evening with Margaret Lee Runbeck, the author, and drove out to Monrovia to see Starr and Marie Daily. At Ciro's one evening George Burns and Gracie Allen were at an adjoining table (I concluded that Gracie's pictures don't do her justice), and Cary Grant was just across the room. There was a dinner party in the home of Dennis Morgan, the actor, and an evening with the Hollywood Christian Group, where I met Dale and Roy Rogers and Jane Russell.

Hollywood is a place of strange contrasts. One day Queen Frederica and King Paul of Greece came to see the Twentieth Century-Fox studios. That morning I watched Marilyn Monroe and Debra Paget jockey—female fashion—for top position in the receiving line, and that same evening attended a formal dinner given for me by Dr Edgar J. Goodspeed, the Bible scholar and translator. Such is the fascinating variety of personalities in the Los Angeles area!

At a Literary Celebrities Luncheon in Pasadena, I sat next to James Hilton, the author of *Lost Horizon* and *Goodbye, Mr Chips*, and had a memorable conversation with him.

" I saw the movie ' Lost Horizon ' in London in 1937," I told him. " I'll never forget certain scenes—particularly that one in the pass where the beautiful girl turns into a hideous old woman. Mr Hilton, where or how did the idea for Shangri-La come to you?"

In his eyes was reverie. " Funny thing that you should ask that. The idea came to me as a little boy. Ever since, it's been a part of my life. You know, I think the idea matured in me as I grew up."

There were certain fleeting impressions . . . that Hollywood's glitter is that of tinsel—not diamonds; that in this area must surely be the world's greatest concentration of roses, Cadillacs, sports cars, and mink stoles. Where materialism is rampant, people judge and catalogue one another according to life's trappings. Thus a rush business is done renting mink stoles, capes, and coats for important dates or interviews.

In the midst of this materialism is great loneliness. Popularity as the stars know it doesn't preclude desperate aloneness. To most of the motion-picture executives, the stars are not people, but commodities, worth such and such on the box-office market. To the fans, the stars are idols. Even idols can have wistful eyes.

Yet loneliness as a Hollywood disease is not limited to the stars. It's all-pervading presence was dramatized for me by an organization called " Listeners, Inc." For a fee, one could purchase an hour's time in which to pour one's self out. The conferee was there only to listen. He was obligated to offer neither advice nor comment. Such a business could prosper only in a city where friendship does not.

There in the movie capital is the greatest spiritual hunger

and thirst I've ever felt anywhere. People hunt greedily, hunt everywhere, for some meaning to life, some answer, some structure. Alcoholics Anonymous, and more recently, Divorcees Anonymous, thrive. In addition, the religious fringe groups and pseudo-religions draw crowds in Los Angeles— along with the established churches—as nowhere else in the nation. A Science of Mind Church fills the Fox Wilshire Theatre each Sunday morning. Yet God's name is scarcely mentioned at all there, or if so, half apologetically, it seemed to me. A Church of All Religions tries to live up to its name by encompassing every faith and creed.

Yet Christianity flourishes, too. A church like the First Presbyterian Church of Hollywood pulsates with vitality. Dr Raymond Lindquist's preaching and Dr Charles Hirt's music draw overflow crowds for three services each Sunday —alert, expectant, open-hearted congregations. Genuine conversions, changed lives, cures from alcoholism, crowds of enthusiastic teen-agers and young married couples are not at all unusual.

The script conferences were finally over. We had not covered all the story, but Christmas was approaching. Wilshire Boulevard had blossomed into an avenue of pink boudoir-looking Christmas trees! Besides we were being pushed for an early deadline. Since Eleanore Griffin would be starting over with the screenplay, it was necessary to drop the conferences and let her start on the first-draft continuity. She would send me pages for criticism as she went.

I left Hollywood grateful for one of the most stimulating experiences of my life, with many wonderful new friends, and armed with lists of material to send Eleanor:

Excerpts from my college journals;
A copy of the Senate prayers;
A copy of the sermon that Peter had been preaching when he had his first heart attack;

A list of favourite Scottish songs;
Copies of Peter's sermons printed in the
    Congressional Record;
Several sermons on young people and marriage; etc.

I got back to Washington in time to celebrate Christmas with my son.

CHAPTER 13

"The Lord God Omnipotent Reigneth"

Many people think of the camera work as the hard work of movie making. Actually with most pictures the shooting takes from one to three months; the preparation of the screenplay many times as long. With "A Man Called Peter," the shooting took two months, the screenplay, one year and nine months.

One of the reasons for such a long-drawn-out process is that the script writer has so many people to please. Other forms of the arts can be solitary work—poetry, the short story, the novel, painting, sculpture, certain kinds of music. But making a movie requires teamwork to end all teamwork.

When I left Hollywood, Eleanore Griffin had nothing but several hundred pages of typed notes from our three-way conferences. Her first step was to turn out a rough writer's working script from those notes. After that, the screenplay went through four drafts, covering ten months of continuous work on Eleanore's part, and hundreds of suggestions from Mr Engel and me.

The first draft was some fifty pages too long. Thereafter each revision was directed toward cutting and tightening. I kept protesting the cutting in my letters to Mr Engel:

Dear Sam:

It is good news indeed that Mr Zanuck likes the First Draft Continuity. However, I cringe, hold my breath, and keep my shoelaces crossed at his saying that "drastic cuts must be made." In my wildest dreams I can't imagine where.

Let us hope—and hope—and hope some more that he will not want us to drop out most of the sermon material.

I predict that's what the movie audiences are going to
eat up. . . .

Having just seen " Gone with the Wind " again—three
hours and forty minutes of it—I am impressed all over
by the scope a longer screenplay allows for character
development, and how it gets over the hurdle of the
choppiness of many movies.

How can real artistry be poured into the mould of a
set number of pages? Should all other values be sacrificed to length? Is no compromise possible? . . .

And Mr Engel answered:

Good news! I have gotten Mr Zanuck's comments.
Like you, I had kept my fingers crossed, fearing that
he might suggest deleting, or at least drastically cutting
the sermons; the Youth Rally; and some of the religious
content. Happily that is not the case. . . .

Over and over again, I have had to debate with myself
as to what values are to be retained, and where to take
a legitimate, dramatic license by omitting some of the
facts. Mind you, I said " omitting "—not distorting.
And more and more I have become convinced that
Peter's continuing ministry must not be sacrificed to
so-called documentary facts or chronological developments. . . .

Length was not the only problem. As the months went
on, my suggestions crystallized in several specific directions.
I battled (1) putting too much emphasis on the love story;
(2) presenting a distorted picture of the Protestant ministry
by, for example, giving it too much glamour; (3) putting
Peter up on a pedestal where he merely snapped his fingers
and God's directions came clear and all his prayers were
immediately answered. This last would have been discouraging to the movie audiences, and above all, unrealistic.
Prayer had never been that easy for Peter. He had often felt

inadequate, had had seasons of agonising over his inability to get through to God.

Mr Engel was always patient in considering my point of view. In the beginning of our work together, he had said, "Catherine, this project has to be founded on mutual trust. I know you've had some warnings from people who have had dismal experiences in Hollywood. That doesn't lay much of a foundation for trust. But you've got to believe in my good will, because it's a fact."

It was a fact. Whenever Sam Engel and I failed to understand each other, it wasn't for lack of trying.

In the spring of 1954 the producer decided that he and Miss Griffin should come East. We needed more of the three-way conferences; he wanted to scout out shooting sites in Washington and Atlanta, and he felt that it would help Eleanore to see the places she was writing about and to talk with people who had known Peter.

It was up to me to bring together Eleanore and the people who could help her. Accordingly, the first event was a small dinner party at my home. That evening Eleanore and Sam had two reactions which they made no effort to conceal. . . . They were amazed at how modestly I lived in Washington; once again they appeared surprised with the discovery that people could be so gay and have so much fun without the lift of liquor.

On subsequent days a group of men—including some of the officers of our church—gathered for a luncheon with them in a private dining room in a Washington hotel. Then some thirty young people spent an evening with Miss Griffin. She asked penetrating questions. They answered them all and reminisced about Peter with humour and gusto.

The mornings we devoted to script conferences, the afternoons to seeing the sites connected with the story. Then suddenly Sam announced one morning that he was giving up the Atlanta trip and would be starting back to California the next day.

"It isn't really necessary," he said, "to see the Georgia

sites. We can do just as well making our own sets for the Agnes Scott campus and Peter's two Georgia churches."

This, I felt, was bad news. "A Man Called Peter" was recent history. Why build sets when the real spots were available? Far too many people would know the difference. Eleanore and I were convinced, even without discussing it, that the picture would suffer without those authentic scenes. I also knew that seeing Peter's first little church in Covington, meeting some of the folks who had known him there, and feeling for themselves the flavour of a Southern woman's college, would bring Eleanore and Sam—and therefore the movie—that much closer to the realities of Peter's life.

We pleaded, but Sam was adamant. Finally we could say nothing more. The atmosphere was a little grim as we parted for the day.

Eleanore's months of reading Peter Marshall's sermons and working on the screenplay had given her a growing conviction that prayer does change things, that it is the appointed way of co-operation between man and God. That afternoon she leaped into the breach in a way that shamed me. Secretly she wired a mutual friend of ours, Haywood P. Sconce, a minister in Oregon. "Just pray," she asked, "that Mr Engel will do—even without knowing it—what God wants him to do about the Atlanta trip." A reassuring wire came back.

That evening Sam telephoned me . . . "I've been thinking. Maybe I was wrong. There isn't any real pressure about my getting back to the studio this week. Eleanore says she could be ready to leave for Atlanta tomorrow. Can you?"

Could I . . .! The visits to Atlanta and Covington turned out to be as crucial as we had thought. To this day I can't quite imagine what the movie would have been without them.

Miss Griffin and Mr Engel saw the Westminster Presbyterian Church and Stone Mountain in Atlanta, the Agnes Scott campus and Columbia Seminary in Decatur, and the church in Covington. The result was that, when the cameras started grinding in late September, the scenes in these places were shot on location.

But what charmed Eleanore and Sam most were the people they met. This was the first taste either of them had ever had of the warm-hearted hospitality of Christian folk in the Deep South. In Covington, they met the men who had known Peter Marshall fresh out of seminary when his Scottish burr was still thick, his hair always tousled, and his knowledge of life in the United States meagre. The doors of the Stephenson home where he had roomed, and the Gardner home where he had boarded, were opened wide to the visitors. At Agnes Scott they were included in a faculty dinner, and Sam, basking in the atmosphere, rose and delighted the group with a spirited analysis of what really goes on behind the scenes in movie making and of what he planned for the fall when the cast and camera crews moved on to the campus.

The three of us also had several days of script conferences, trying to hammer out more story line. A secretarial agency recorded the talks and later delivered a copy of the notes to each of us, 312 pages of them. It looked like a court transcript.

I had often toyed with the idea that this same procedure might be one way for a writer to learn how to handle dialogue —that is, secretly record actual conversation, transcribe it to paper, and study the result. But after seeing the scrambled gobbledygook of conversations, I was far from sure that the would-be writer would learn much. A look at almost any page was a humbling experience, enough to make a person decide never to open his mouth again . . .!

MR ENGEL: That's right, when he speaks there—but, you know, that's all very good, but I'm just thinking now, also, -how-how-how this gal can work for us, whatever we'll call her, Miss Pemberton, or—
MISS GRIFFIN: Miss Pemberton will be her name. I'll make a note. . . .

MR ENGEL : But, but. . . .

MRS MARSHALL : Did you ever study tombstones for names?

MR ENGEL : (Apparently ignoring me) But supposing— supposing that—you see—here's how—here's how Peter became beholden to her. Just supposing he needs very badly certain things, song books, or hymn books, or things that—that the board hasn't appropriated money for, and. . . .

MISS GRIFFIN : Or she pays for the choir director.

MR ENGEL : Ummmm, Ummmm— Well, I think— You see, anything that he wants to institute, and. . . .

MRS MARSHALL : Yeah, I understand that. I also have a question though. And I'm just trying to save y'all trouble, you understand. Now—

MISS GRIFFIN : Fine, yeah.

MRS MASHALL : And he could get that cocker spaniel look on his face like he used to, you know—

MR ENGEL : Now Peter can feel—that she's a good soul, after all—

MISS GRIFFIN : Silly, but a good egg. That kind of thing.

MR ENGEL : That kind of thing. Well, on the other hand, Catherine, dog-gone, well, that's fine, if she wants to buy little books or Bibles or whatever.

MISS GRIFFIN : Catherine just has to be eliminated.

MRS MARSHALL : Uh huh. Why honeychill! I don't object to being eliminated. . . .

Already my days were punctuated with communications by wire and phone from production people at the studio. The director of research wanted to know :

1. What kind of a car Peter Marshall drove in Washington.
2. What type of suits he wore for everyday.

3. Did he wear a business suit in the Senate or a Geneva gown?
4. Did he have a clan tartan?

The studio was unable to get clearance on *The Case of the Perfumed Mouse* mentioned in my book. Did I have any suggestion? They could not find the music of " Oh, You Beautiful Doll." Could I help? The wardrobe department wanted to know what kind of a wrist watch I would have worn during college days. The thoroughness with which the movie people went after these details was amazing.

It never occurred to me that after the picture went into production, this interchange would not continue. There had been so much of it! So far, I had surely been needed; I thought I would be needed to the end. I was to find out differently.

My first intimation of this was in relation to casting. I was not consulted. That was easy to accept, because I had had no experience with it and was not sufficiently well acquainted with available talent anyway. Events were to prove that no help from me was necessary; a better Hand than mine was directing casting as well as a lot of other things.

One of the modern translations of the New Testament speaks of everything fitting " into a pattern for good "[1] for those who love and acknowledge God. The New Testament writer was not just stringing words together. This is the " how " of God's omnipotence—an awe-inspiring fact.

Sometimes it works like a play set on a cosmic stage. People of whom we've never heard are added to the cast. They may be summoned from across the world. Sometimes there are time lags between the scenes, but always the characters are at the bidding of the Master Director. The right props appear at the right time. The hand fits the glove. The chessmen are moved with precision. Every piece of the jigsaw puzzle finds its place. . . .

[1] Phillips, J. B., *Letters to Young Churches*, p. 19, The Macmillan Company Inc., New York, 1951, Romans 8:28.

A case in point was the casting of the male lead in the movie " A Man Called Peter " and the part that one of the props—some tape recordings—played in that casting. The first scene was set in the winter of 1948. . . .

It was twenty minutes to eleven on a Sunday morning. The two men in the dimly lit kitchen at the New York Avenue Presbyterian Church in Washington were working swiftly, saying little. Finally one of them, Jack Ingram, spoke. . . . " That just about does it. The wiring's been tricky. Of course the podium would be over the kitchen! "

The other, Charles Chapman, shrugged. " And what a spot! It doesn't take much imagination to see Abraham Lincoln right over there—by that antiquated stove maybe—delivering a postscript to the Gettysburg address."

Mr Ingram smiled. . . . " Well, anyway, I'm glad we got the trustees' okay on setting up the equipment. Did I tell you I won this the hard way? "

" How d'you mean? "

" I had lunch with Peter on Thursday. When I asked about tape-recording his sermons, he laughed in my face. Pooh-poohed me."

" How did you persuade him? "

" Out of nowhere I had an idea. . . . The shut-ins and old people. Record the sermons, then take the tapes to them. Peter finally agreed on that basis. What a guy! "

S. Jack Ingram was and is in the aviation engine business in Dallas, Texas. He had come to Washington in 1942. Until a few months before, he had not been inside a church for years. Then his wife, Pat, had persuaded him to go and hear Dr Peter Marshall. That did it! From then on, he tried never to miss a Sunday morning service.

That winter he had sought out Dr Marshall, and the two men had become friends. " I never knew," Jack had told Peter, " that Christianity could be such fun. I'm happier than I've been in years. It's like getting a good meal every Sunday. But I don't want to keep such exciting preaching to myself.

Would you be willing—if I bought some tape-recording equipment myself—?"

What Jack Ingram could not have guessed was the precision of his timing. The sermons that he had methodically recorded Sunday after Sunday turned out to be those of the last year of Peter Marshall's life. On January 23, he sat in the kitchen over his controls and captured " The Sin of Silence " on tape. On Tuesday morning he got the news that the voice from the pulpit was still.

The next scene took place four years later in Hollywood. A movie producer was being interviewed by Celestine Sibley of the *Atlanta Constitution*. She had come to talk about the proposed film on the life of Peter Marshall.

" Mr Engel, you probably know that Atlanta has always claimed Peter Marshall. Atlantans are all agog over the movie. What everybody wants to know is—who's going to play Peter?"

" I wish I knew. One thing sure. It's going to have to be a Britisher. I've said that from the beginning. Nobody else can handle the King's English as Marshall did.—But before we talk about casting, there's something I want you to hear—"

Miss Sibley later reported in her column:

Mr Engel had a tape recorder by his desk and as I settled down he turned it on, and the rich, deep voice with its pleasant Scots burr poured into the room. . . .

" You see," said Mr Engel, turning off the machine, " the voice is magnificent—and it's going to take an English actor to play the role. I'd like Richard Burton, but nobody knows how long he'll be tied up on ' The Robe '. And then he has an engagement with the Abbey Theatre in Ireland. And of course, there's Laurence Olivier. . . ."

Whether or not Olivier who has been playing Shakespeare with his wife, Vivien Leigh, would be interested, is something Fox is now trying to find out. . . .

" We'd thought of Richard Todd (of the ' Hasty Heart ' and ' Robin Hood '), Mr Engel added—

The girl standing in the doorway of the house in Pinkneys Green was small, blonde. " Anything interesting in the mail?"

Her husband, Richard Todd, waved a letter at her. " Oh —so, so. A letter from America—Beverly Hills."

" One of the studios?"

" Fox. It's a formal query as to my being available—"

" For what?"

" Something I never heard of. ' A Man Called Peter.' "

" Well—are you—available?"

" Don't think so. I've more interesting things to do right here."

Five days later a copy of *A Man Called Peter* arrived by air parcel post. The actor read the book, but felt that he was not physically suited to the rôle. Peter Marshall had been of above-average height, broad-shouldered, originally a blond whose hair had darkened. Todd was inches shorter, a brunet.

Mr Todd was also secretly afraid of what approach Hollywood might make to the story. He talked it over with his wife. " If they were to pull out the integrity and put all the emphasis on the love story—as they're likely to do, the picture would be a dud." Therefore he insisted that he would not even consider the rôle without seeing the finished script.

The script was at that time far from finished, but Mr Engel sent the latest draft. Richard Todd was not impressed. The treatment seemed too long, unwieldy. He wrote Sam Engel, turning the part down and suggesting two other British actors who he felt could do it better than he. That, he thought, ended that.

But the studio persisted. Two weeks went by. One day a flat package arrived from Beverly Hills. It was a copy of one of Jack Ingram's tapes—" Were You There?"—a sermon on the crucifixion.

Later by transatlantic telephone Dick Todd told Mr Engel, "I've played it over and over. Each time I'm more stirred. What an inspired word painter that man was. And what a sense of timing! The material is any actor's dream."

"You'll do it then?"

There was a pause. Then the voice with the clipped British accent said hesitantly, "I still can't commit myself. There's one more test I'd like to make. I wonder—may I have your permission to deliver part of one of the sermons over here and have the scene put on film?"

"Certainly. By all means. And we can use it as we would a screen test."

One evening at six, after a hard day's work in the studio, Mr Todd rounded up some forty people. Deliberately, he picked an odd assortment. There were technicians, wardrobe and make-up people, some of the camera crew, several old-time character actors. In the front row was a hard-bitten blonde off the street, with her boy-friend on her arm. None of the group knew why they were there or what was coming.

Dick Todd mounted a makeshift pulpit and looked out over his hastily gathered congregation. What he wanted was not only a screen test but a reaction from human beings. If Peter Marshall's sermon material could move this group, it would move anybody!

The words poured out over the Elstree sound stage. For eight minutes Todd spoke. When he had finished, the blonde in the front row was in tears. So were several others. An electrician came down off his perch and gripped the actor's hand. "You must do that picture. I never heard of it. But you must do it."

Dick Todd cabled the Fox studios that he would take the rôle.

It was from Mr Engel that I got the news:

Dear Catherine:

By the time you receive this, Richard Todd will have

been signed. He made a great, very great test for us! Everyone who has seen it was thrilled! Mr Zanuck sent me a note saying, " I was simply mesmerized. I couldn't believe this was something on film." Todd's diction, accent, and delivery strikingly resemble Peter's. . . .

It would be very nice indeed if you would drop Mr Todd a note. I enclose his address. . . .

Everything is going forward splendidly.

All the best,

Sam

I did write Mr Todd. In his reply he mentioned the now famous tapes :

Pinkneys Green
Maidenhead
Berks.

My dear Mrs Marshall :

I was very pleased and very touched by your letter, and indeed by your kind thought in writing to me at all. . . .

I feel great humility and diffidence about my choice for this rôle. I am still very conscious of the fact that in appearance I cannot be as close as I would wish to the ideal person to personify Peter Marshall. . . .

I look forward very much indeed to meeting you while I am in America. . . . In the meantime, I would appreciate very much indeed any pointers which you could give me to help me with my characterization. If you have any other recordings, might I borrow them from you for a time during the initial part of the progress on the film . . .?

In the meantime, again very many thanks for your kindness, and my sincere hope that our film will match up to the excellence of your book and to your memories.

Yours sincerely,
Richard Todd

What Mr Todd had in mind in asking to hear the other recordings was not a forced imitation of Dr Marshall's accent and delivery. Todd's ideal characterization went much deeper.

"Each man is unique," he was later to say to me. "I'm not Peter Marshall. But I can saturate myself with the timbre of the man's voice, with the sparkle of his personality, with the inner essence, until something of the man's spirit shines through. It's the difference between a photograph and a painting. If I try to imitate rather than create an impression, my characterization will fail."

I was impressed by his sound and intelligent approach. In order to achieve it, the British actor made several uses of the tapes. "I'm trying an experiment," he explained to me. "I listen to Peter Marshall's voice for a while just before falling asleep. That way, perhaps an impression will be made on my subconscious mind that will come out later in depth-dimension portrayal."

And when the time came for shooting, Mr Todd was to order a tape recorder brought to his dressing-room. Often he would listen to a portion of a sermon between takes.

Mr Engel was relieved to have the male lead settled. The matter of the director had also been decided. Henry Koster, who had directed many successful movies, including "Désirée" and "The Robe," had been chosen. As for Catherine, Mr Engel had never been too concerned about who was to play the part. He felt that a number of the younger actresses could do it adequately. Shooting was scheduled to start in September. July was drawing to a close —and still no Catherine.

Finally in late August, Eleanore wrote me that Eva Marie Saint and Elizabeth Taylor were being considered for the rôle of Catherine. ". . . Wouldn't you like to be played by the most beautiful girl in the world . . .?"

I replied that I found it hard to understand the ways of the movie studios. I was appalled by the fact that the feminine lead had still not been chosen. Surely the September 20 starting date had been postponed. As for Elizabeth Taylor, she was, I feared, too beautiful—so beautiful that it might obscure the rôle itself.

After that, other actresses were considered—Jean Simmons, Dorothy McGuire, Donna Reed, and Jean Peters, who had recently starred in " Three Coins in the Fountain."

From the beginning, it had been Miss Peters whom the gossip columnists and movie magazines had reported as having captured the part. Many of these rumours were reported as fact months before the studio had ever begun casting. This time, however, the rumours, no matter how premature, proved prophetic. Miss Peters was offered the rôle. Six days before shooting started, she accepted it.

Covington and Atlanta enjoyed their contact with the movie personnel. The day that the stars arrived, the *Atlanta Journal* ran headlines :

MOVIE CAMERAS WHIRRING AT NORRIS

Filming of Catherine Marshall's book *A Man Called Peter* began Friday morning on the shores of Norris Lake in DeKalb County following the arrival of Jean Peters and Richard Todd Thursday night. . . .

In Covington, hundreds of citizens dressed in the fashions of the 1930s acted as extras for the crowd scenes in the church, while most of the rest of the town watched. The *Journal* reported :

FILM FOLK CREATE UPROAR AT SCOTT

The usual quiet and serene campus of Agnes Scott College Saturday was in an uproar.

Stars Richard Todd and Jean Peters arrived early with the supervisor of the second unit, James D. Clark, and a small army of technicians and paraphernalia to begin filming campus sequences.

Following in their wake were some seventy-five extras (most of them Agnes Scott students) and dozens of fans wanting autographs. . . .

For three days all academic work was practically at a standstill. The professors were very patient. How else could they deal with 500 starry-eyed, movie-struck girls?

Then, by September 28, the campus shots were completed. The old cars had been driven off. The last camera had been loaded into the last truck. In the middle of the quadrangle stood one of the freshmen who had been used as an extra, gazing mournfully after the camera truck as it disappeared round the bend of the road. At that moment, the dean of women walked by. She saw the wistfulness written on the girl's face, the slim shoulders sagging. She heard the girl sigh, "And *now* what is there to live for?"

As soon as I had heard that Jean Peters was to play Catherine, I had written her, welcoming her to the cast. Probably the note went astray. At any rate there was no reply. I sent another note to her Atlanta hotel, saying that I hoped to meet her when the cast moved on to Washington.

The cast arrived in town, but Miss Peters was not with them. Mr Eckhardt, the unit manager, explained that the star had for urgent personal reasons gone back to Hollywood. A stand-in was to be used for the Washington scenes.

Dick Todd telephoned me, came to dinner, and spent the evening talking out his rôle. Though I had been told about his height, I was not prepared to find him as short a man as he is. Already I knew how the studio planned to handle this—lifts in his shoes and carefully angled camera shots.

His personality and attitude delighted me. He was refreshingly candid and clear-eyed about himself. . . . "We cinema people aren't always realistic about ourselves. I try hard to be. I'm not brilliant, far from it. Therefore, in handling my rôles, I have to do some plodding—just plain hard work."

It was also obvious that Mr Todd was taking his Peter Marshall rôle seriously. There was no false sentimentality. He had a deep respect for the person he was portraying—for Peter's vitality as a man, as well as for his gentleness and spiritual sensitivity.

He was also concerned about fine points. For example, he had begged from his London studio a skimpy, poorly-cut suit which he felt would be just right for the immigrant Peter to wear for the shipboard scenes.

The British actor studied all the photographs of my husband in my possession; he questioned me carefully about Peter's pulpit gestures and mannerisms. By the time the evening was over, I had a secure feeling that Peter's part was in the right hands.

During the company's stay in Washington, I was impressed with how hard the crew had to work to make relatively small scenes.

Sometimes for a scene that had to be shot in semi-darkness, like the one in which Peter, newly arrived in Washington, takes Catherine to see his church at midnight—shooting had to start as early as five-thirty in the morning. Since make-up took an hour and a half, this meant that Dick Todd and Marion McDonough—Miss Peters' stand-in—had to roll out of bed at 3.30 a.m.

Another Washington scene was a sidewalk shot of a line of people waiting on a rainy day to get into a church service. A local modelling agency was tapped for extras. The girls, feeling that this was their big chance, knocked themselves out with fresh hair-dos, make-up, and their prettiest clothes. But they were photographed with umbrellas hiding their faces, their backs to the cameras!

Actually, the historic old building in which Peter Marshall had preached had been torn down soon after his death and another church built on the site. The new building was enough like the old so that the exterior could be used for the movie. For the interior, a studio set had to be built in Hollywood, carefully copied from photographs taken on the last day of the old church's life.

Nor could the actual manse be used. It had by then been sold, and the new owner had made extensive changes. Therefore, a house of about the same architecture near Capitol Hill was chosen. There, with the Capitol dome in the background, more of the flavour of Washington could be packed into less film footage.

One morning I visited the Capitol Hill set. Huge trucks and vans were parked across the street from the " Manse." The car that Dick Todd was to drive stood in front of the house. Clouds obscured the sun. Mr Todd, Miss McDonough, and the camera crew were standing by, waiting for the sun to break through. It never did, so work was postponed until the next day. It turned out that the clouds that day cheated me of the one chance I might have had to see a bit of my movie being shot.

During the watching that day, Mr Eckhardt had asked me to pose for some pictures with Mr Todd. Naïvely I had agreed. Naïvely, because I should have asked how the pictures were to be used.

The Fox publicity people sent that particular picture to newspapers all over the nation. Usually the caption read:

On Hollywood set—Mrs Marshall, technical director, with Richard Todd, who portrays her husband in the picture " A Man Called Peter."

This was misleading. It was true that I was technical adviser to the script, but not to the movie. There is a vast difference. As events turned out, I never saw a single scene shot, and I was not in Hollywood while any of the filming was going on.

I knew that if the men at Fox wanted me on the sets, they would not hesitate to say so. But I did not want to force the issue. I also knew that they would be receptive to suggestions from me only if they really wanted those suggestions.

No such invitation ever came, so I stayed in Washington. For me it was a difficult time. I was too intimately bound up with the movie project to tell myself that it didn't matter how it turned out. Already I had given it two years of my time and thought. My heart was with the work going on in Hollywood. Try as I might, I couldn't extricate myself from it.

Only one recourse was left—prayer. Faith was needed. That's what God was asking of me.

I had thought that I had to keep my fingers on the progress of the movie venture. Sheer presumption probably! At any rate, denied that, I must somehow muster enough faith to believe that God could take over on the sets of "A Man Called Peter." I concentrated on that, remembering those hundreds of memorable letters promising prayer from my friends.

Though my faith may have been small, it was deposited in the right Source. It was rewarded. But there was a price to be paid. The price was a lien on my pride. Later, much later, I learned some of the things that happened on the sets.

One evening at the close of a day's work in one of the churches, Dick Todd surprised everyone by making a special request. . . . "Would it be possible for me to be left alone for a while here tomorrow before we start shooting? I'd like to practise my sermon, really get into the spirit of it."

The director, Henry Koster, had had much experience with the temperamental quirks of movie stars. He wondered if Todd's request was temperament. If so, at least it was a new kind.

Aloud he said, "Okay. It will hold things up a bit. But I'm game. How long do you want by yourself?"

"At least an hour and a half."

"All right. Then the rest of you won't report back here until ten tomorrow morning."

The next day a policeman on duty at one of the gates asked for time off to hear Todd preach. Wardrobe people, electricians, and mechanics quietly made their way to the church set. Afterwards, one of the mechanics described what happened. . . . " You should've seen the crowd listenin'. Practically everybody on the lot was there—from the lowliest mechanic like me to the directors and producers—everybody. You could've heard a pin drop. There was a kind of hush in the air. Then when Mr Todd finished, and the director yelled ' Cut,' all of us started applaudin' . . . I'll tell you somethin' else too. This is downright peculiar . . . I haven't heard a single cuss word on that set. Man, that's somethin'!"

Mr Koster, the director, said it in another way during an interview, " There was a happy co-operative feeling on the set of ' A Man Called Peter '—something so rare that —well—. Anyway, it's the happiest picture I've ever been connected with."

He went on to supply details. " It was like an aura around the picture. Everything good happened. We would go out on location. The rain would come down. Time was important. We would decide to get ready to shoot, anyway. When we were ready, the rain would stop, the sun would come out. . . . We hired two special people for the cast. They turned out to be all wrong. Sam Engel and I talked it over, trying to decide the best way to get rid of them. First, one resigned voluntarily. Then the other.

" I'm not superstitious, nor would I dare call these incidents divine intervention for our benefit. But things like that happened over and over. It gave me an odd feeling about the picture. Take that break we got at Annapolis, for instance."

Mr Koster was referring to a scene in which Richard Todd, after preaching at the Naval Academy, had to leave the chapel and stride across the grounds toward his car. Just as the actor got halfway to the car, the doors of the building behind him burst open and all the midshipmen came pouring out. The movie crew had not dared to inconvenience the Academy by requesting anything like that. As it was, the uniformed cadets in the background added the perfect touch.

That same day another incident occurred, this time inside the chapel where Dr Marshall's Pearl Harbour Day sermon was to be filmed. Twelve hundred midshipmen were in the pews. In the finished film, this scene turned out to be the longest single take in the history of the Fox studios. Mr Todd was before the camera without a break for eight and a half minutes.

Everyone thought it unwise to put the cadets through that much. Therefore, Dick Todd was to start the sermon, let the cameras pick up shots of the chapel with close-ups of the men's faces as they listened.

James—fourth chapter—fourteenth verse: "For what is your life? It is even a vapour that appeareth for a little time and then vanisheth away."

What a queer thing for James to say. . . .

Then the actor would do only the concluding sentences the rest would be shot in Hollywood. . . .

That life that shall never end . . . shall be the journey's end for the heart and all its hopes. It shall be the end of the rainbow for the child-explorers of God. We have His promise for that. . . .

But that was underestimating both the sermon and the cadets. The midshipmen became so interested in the content of the sermon that they started clamouring for more. Mr Todd gave them the eight and a half minutes' worth. Then they called for the rest. In the end, Dick Todd had to preach the whole sermon before they would let him go.

These were small incidents. A more important one was something that happened to Marjorie Rambeau. "A small miracle," she called it. Miss Rambeau is a veteran actress with fifty-seven years of stage and screen experience. Still a beautiful woman, in "A Man Called Peter" she took the part of the fictitious character, Miss Fowler.

At twilight on a winter's afternoon in February, 1945, the actress and her sister Thelma were in an automobile accident. The sister was killed. Nine days later Miss Rambeau regained consciousness. She had been cruelly hurt—her right shoulder broken, fifty-six stitches in her head, her right leg opened to the bone, thigh to knee, the left hip socket crushed.

Three months later, she left the hospital, a cripple, confined to a wheel chair. After five years of constant pain, a corrective operation was performed, then a second. Her left leg was still three inches shorter than her right. The pain in the hip socket was gone, but there was muscular pain. Any undue strain or tiredness produced muscular spasms that could only be relieved by inter-muscular injections. The doctors gave Miss Rambeau no hope of ever walking without her crutches.

Then Mr Engel summoned her to the Fox studios. "You'd be perfect for the part of Miss Fowler. Can you walk without crutches?"

"I'm sorry to say—no. But do you remember 'Torch Song' with Joan Crawford?"

"Yes, of course."

"Well, you may remember that I did my entire part seated on a sofa. The best I can manage is a step or two with a cane for an entrance or an exit. But I'd like to have this part. I must have been one of the first to read the book. It came at a time when it meant so much to me. . . ."

Miss Rambeau left that afternoon with the script under her arm.

Production had been in progress for two weeks when the actress was called for her scenes. Special arrangements had been made, so that no walking would be required. She was to be photographed sitting in a church pew, then standing at the front of the church, leaning on her gold-headed cane.

The director asked for silence. Richard Todd started
preaching. . . .

> Surely, He had power to lift from the dust
> of disease the flowers whose stems had been crushed
> or withered in the mildews of human misery!
> As this thought burned itself into her mind her faith
> was curiously stirred as it wrestled in the birth-throes
> of a great resolve.
>
> It was daring—fantastic, perhaps.
> Her heart thumped
> but it was worth trying.
>   It could only fail
>   and she was no stranger to failure. . . .
>
> *She touched Him in faith—in desperate believing
> faith and He stopped!*
> The touch of one anonymous woman in a crowd
> halted the Lord of glory. *That is the glorious truth
> of this incident. She touched Him. So can we. . . .*[2]

Suddenly, sitting there listening to Peter Marshall's words
the actress said to herself, "Marjorie, you do believe. Put
yourself in God's hands. You *can* walk down that aisle.'
The extras—acting the part of the congregation—stood up
and started toward the front of the church. Marjorie got
to her feet. No one paid any attention at first. But when
she started walking down the aisle without her crutches,
there was a concerted gasp.
Miss Rambeau motioned for silence; the rehearsal could
not be interrupted. She walked the entire length of the aisle,
100 feet of it. As she reached the chancel, a stage-hand,
unable to believe his eyes, came running forward with a

[2] Marshall, Peter, *Mr Jones, Meet the Master*, pp. 179, 182. London,
Fontana, 1964.

stool. He was so agitated that he almost knocked her over with it.

Marjorie's husband, Francis A. Grudger, a retired vice-president of the E. I. du Pont de Nemours Company, was on the set and saw the incident. Practically holding his breath during her long trek, he had expected his wife to fall at any moment. By the time she reached the end of the aisle he was at her side, begging her to get off her feet immediately.

She refused. She had done it once. She would do it again —and again—for as many rehearsals as were necessary.

Her husband watched in agony. In vain, he pleaded with her to stop. He was sure that she would pay for her foolhardiness with hours of agonizing pain that night. Finally, unable to bear the sight any longer, he turned on his heel and left the set.

That night Miss Rambeau was tired, but there was no pain. Her maid prepared a hypodermic and put it on her nightstand.

" Mr Grudger said to have it ready just in case, madam."

" In case of what?" the actress asked. " There isn't any pain. I feel nothing but good healthy tiredness."

After the movie was released, the actress wrote to tell me about it. . . .

A miracle did happen to me while making the picture. A blessing from you and yours and our Saviour. I discarded my crutches one day after listening with my heart —not my ears—to one of Peter's sermons. To the utter amazement of everyone in the cast, I walked. God took over. I have never gone back to my crutches. There is no need.

Forgive this long letter. But I did so want you to know about it.

Gratefully,
Marjorie Rambeau

Of course, at the time I knew nothing at all of all this.

Back in Washington, I could only wait and wonder and hope. My first intimation of how the picture had turned out came in a note from Eleanore Griffin. It was a copy of a memo sent to everyone on the lot—a memo originally to Mr Darryl Zanuck by Harry Brand, the head of publicity and exploitation:

> I just looked at a rough cut of " A Man Called Peter " and was held spellbound, and came out exalted. . . .
>
> This picture can't help but be a memorable achievement, and, because it is so unusual, you should be highly lauded for your courage in having it produced.
>
> I will write to New York to convey this information. . . .

Eleanore's accompanying note said, " This is just an echo of the feeling on the lot. There was never so much surprise and enthusiasm over a picture. . . ."

This was wonderful news but I still had mental reservations. After all, Mr Brand's memo had been for his boss's consumption.

Then on January 24, eighty clergymen, Catholic, Jewish, and Protestant, saw the same rough-cut version in a special showing on the Twentieth Century-Fox lot. No musical score had yet been dubbed in.

Later that day I had a telegram from Dr Louis Evans, the former pastor of the Hollywood Presbyterian Church:

> WE SAW THE PREVIEW AND FELT WE HAD BEEN LIFTED BY THE ARMS OF A GREAT SWELLING SEA OF COURAGE AND FAITH. HAVE NO FEARS, AND IT WILL BLESS MILLIONS. GOD BLESS THE TEAM THAT MADE IT POSSIBLE.

I had enthusiastic comments from others who were present that day. While I was relieved at the good news, still

I wanted to see for myself. But I had to wait another five weeks. By then, the picture was set in concrete; no more changes could be made. Already fifteen minutes' worth of the rough-cut version had hit the cutting-room floor.

Finally I was invited to a special meeting in the New York offices of Twentieth Century-Fox. I asked my long-time friend, A. D. Fuller, to go with me. On March 7, as we flew to New York, I kept wondering what I would say to Sam Engel, if the picture was not what I hoped. I was not willing to be a hypocrite. In any case, he knew me too well for me to deceive him.

The private theatre on the fifth floor of the old Fox office building turned out to be an ornate baroque setting. There was only a handful of us in a room meant to seat several hundred. Several representatives from my publishing house were among those invited. On one side of me sat A. D.; on the other, my editor, Ed Aswell. In the row in front and across the aisle were a dozen or so Fox executives who had not yet seen the movie.

Only a few days before, Hedda Hopper had reported to the nation that "A Man Called Peter" was emotion-packed, a "six handkerchief picture." This had alarmed me. What if it were maudlin emotion, overdone, in poor taste?

On the other hand, if it was well done, I might break down completely. For that reason, I had been hoping that my first viewing might be private, with only my family and a few friends present.

The situation on March 7 was scarcely that. The publicity men there seemed as much interested in my reactions as in the picture. Knowing that, I was tense. I did not realize how tense until later that day. Every nerve was stretching taut; every emotion dammed up behind a wall of resolution; every hope steeled against disappointment.

The lights went off; the musical score came on. The name of the book that had become a part of my life flashed before me, set on a deep blue background. It was a peculiar feeling seeing my own name there in gold letters on the wide screen. The moment toward which I had worked and prayed was upon me.

The deep slashes of the cutting-room shears were immediately apparent—at least to me. Some memorable scenes had been sacrificed to length. We were catapulted all the way from Peter digging ditches in New Jersey to his graduation from Seminary.

Then came Dick Todd's first sermon material. . . .

There are men and women in the world today who say that God orders their lives—guides them in making decisions, answers their prayers, provides for their needs —in ways that are often strange and unexpected. That is the testimony of my own experience. And there are many here who can make the same statement. But if you, yourself, have not had that experience in your life, do not be too quick to jump to the conclusion that we who say these things are daft—mad. . . .

I couldn't believe what I was hearing! The voice was authentic. The message rang true. The words were vibrant with power. The spirit of the man I knew so well was there, coming through, spilling over, glowingly alive again. From that moment, I knew that whatever small faults the picture had, it was all right. The miracle I and hundreds of others had prayed for had happened.

When the lights came on, most of the rough-hewn Fox executives had their handkerchiefs out wiping their eyes. I had not wept; I was still much too tense. It was not until I saw the picture for the second time under quite different circumstances that my tears flowed too. Later I found out that the men that day were dismayed that I had not cried. They feared that my lack of obvious emotion meant that the picture was not a success.

In Hollywood Sam Engel was awaiting my reaction. On the way back to Washington, I carefully composed a wire to him:

THIS MORNING AT FOX'S NEW YORK OFFICE I SAW
A MAN CALLED PETER. . . . PETER'S SPIRIT AND PER-
SONALITY COME THROUGH WITH COMPLETE INTEGRITY.
EVEN THE MOST EMOTIONAL SCENES HAVE THE
RESTRAINT OF REAL ARTISTRY. MAY THE PICTURE
BECOME A MILESTONE BOTH IN MOTION PICTURE HISTORY
AND IN THE SPIRITUAL LIFE OF THE NATION.

I could not forget my fan-mail friends. Surely they
deserved the next word. . . .

In November, 1953, I sent a letter to many of my
friends asking for specific prayer in connection with the
making of *A Man Called Peter* into a motion picture.

Sixteen months have passed since then. The movie
is finished and in most cities will be released shortly
before Easter. I wanted to wait until I had seen the
finished product to report back to you. . . .

Out of this experience, I have learned one of the
greatest lessons of my life. The lesson is that our
God is still an Omnipotent God.

In the two years " A Man Called Peter " was in process,
I went through some very bad moments. At times, those
concerned were on the verge of very wrong decisions.
My faith often wavered and faltered. . . . I was Technical
Adviser for the screenplay. But from the moment that
shooting started, I was not Technical Adviser for the
movie itself. I saw none of it shot.

Yet God's Hand was on the project, so He did not need
mine. He still reigns in His World! In response to
prayer, He can still rule and overrule; can still have
His way with His creatures—even in Hollywood. It
has been an awe-inspiring and humbling experience to
have seen this worked out step by step. The Lord God
Omnipotent still reigns . . . !

" All That Glitters . . ."

At the Byrd Theatre in Richmond, Virginia, the special preview showing of " A Man Called Peter " was just over. I had not been able to attend because of radio and press interviews in New York, but Peter John was there with my mother.

In the theatre lobby, a newspaper woman elbowed her way through the crowd toward a tall blond boy. " I understand that you are Peter Marshall's son. How did you like the picture?"

" Okay—very good."

" How true to the facts is it? Do you have any critiscisms?"

" Well—maybe—our Cape Cod cottage is bigger and nicer than the one in the movie—"

When the article came out the next day, March 25, in the *Richmond Times-Dispatch*, it reported . . .

> They gave their unqualified approval to the picture, although Peter John stated that the Cape Cod cottage in the film is larger and more elaborate than the one he and his parents occupied during summer vacations. . . .

Peter was furious. This was his first brush with publicity, and he felt that he had been grievously misquoted on an important point. The cottage had always been his favourite place. " The one in the movie was just a box," he railed. " If ours was smaller than that, it would be a *dog* house."

" You'll have to get used to being misquoted," I laughed at him out of a little recent experience. " It happens all the time."

My trip to New York included six press interviews, three

radio broadcasts, newsreel pictures in Mr Spyros Skouras's office, the recording of a speech greeting for the Glasgow opening and one for Japan.

The newspaper people were consistently gracious with me. I found them easy to talk to, perhaps because I have never been on the defensive with the press. Always my viewpoint has been that reporters have a job to do, and that I want to give them the best possible interview.

However, my baptism of fire was still to come. On my last day in New York, reporters from a national weekly news magazine contacted me. My time was filled, but they were insistent. Finally it was arranged that they would interview me on the way to La Guardia Airport. Two brisk and businesslike women reporters were sent for the job.

After some preliminary questions, one of the women said, "We'd better be frank with you, Mrs Marshall. We're here for one purpose above all others. We have emphatic instructions from the top brass to uncover the facts about your finances. There are some people who think that you've made a good thing out of the book—and now the movie—who question your motives—"

The other woman added, "Of course, it's entirely up to you how you'll answer. You can give us the usual blunt 'no comment' and tell us it's none of our business. But in that case, we'll dig up the facts anywhere we can get them, and you'll have to take the consequences. Or you can square with us."

I could feel the blood rushing to my face. It sounded like an inquisition. This type of approach made the rest of my interviews seem like milk toast. Despite my annoyance, I tried to think fast.

Suddenly I knew that frankness and putting myself, along with the facts, at the mercy of the reporters was the only intelligent course. Some of the things they would want to know undoubtedly were none of their business, but I knew that the minute I clammed up, I risked their hostility.

"Look," I said. "I have nothing to hide. Suppose I

state the facts, and then leave to your discretion what you'll print. I ask only that you stay within the bounds of good taste. But first, as to the sale of the movie rights, I don't even know whether or not I have the right—so far as Fox is concerned—to reveal the figure."

Both reporters laughed. "Don't worry about that. We've already dug that up. Not exactly whopping—$30,000. But do you get any percentage of box-office receipts in addition?"

"No—none—$30,000—period. And I'm sure you know that my publisher, lawyer, agent, and Uncle Sam got hunks of that. I tried to take an even smaller amount plus the percentage plan, because I believed in the movie. But my lawyer couldn't swing it."

An exceedingly frank talk followed. My openness seemed to win the women. Still I scanned the next issue of the magazine with some misgivings.

Their report used most of a page. It was restrained and sympathetic. . . .

From her Washington, D.C., home this week a . . . woman headed for New York to see a movie. Seven years ago, Catherine Marshall was the mistress of the manse and the happy wife of Dr Peter Marshall, pastor of the New York Avenue Presbyterian Church in Washington and Chaplain of the U.S. Senate. This week she was to attend the premiere—simultaneously presented in Glasgow—of " A Man Called Peter," the film version of her best-selling biography of her late husband. . . .

For one thing, she receives between 150 and 200 letters a month and has had to hire a full-time secretary. She has made no great fortune from her writings (the movie rights, for example, sold for only $30,000) and while she is comfortably situated, she cooks all the meals and employs only a part-time maid. . . .

The simultaneous premieres to which the magazine referred were to be on the night of March 31, 1955, at Roxy's in

New York and at La Scala in Glasgow, Scotland. The Roxy opening was to be for the joint benefit of the Highland Fund (for the economic and social development of the Scottish Highlands, of which Lord Malcolm Douglas-Hamilton was chairman) and for the Caledonian Hospital in Brooklyn.

Jean Peters had sent word that she could not attend either premiere; therefore I had agreed to appear with Richard Todd at Roxy's. I had no idea what this " appearance " was to entail.

On the day before the premiere I flew to New York for an appearance on Garry Moore's *I've Got a Secret*. The rest of the family was to follow later. The trip up was rough. In the midst of what the airlines call " turbulence," a voice came over the intercom . . . " Message for Mrs Morrell, on landing at La Guardia, will she please remain on the plane until all other passengers are off, and deplane last?"

Since the name " Mrs Morrell " meant nothing to me, I paid no attention. The sign " Fasten Seat Belts " was on all the way, so there was no chance to freshen up. Before we landed, I didn't even bother to powder my nose. Feeling very casual about the whole thing, I started to get off with the rest of the passengers.

It was raining, and there was a cold whipping wind. Suddenly through the sound of the wind and the rain, I heard the unmistakable wail of a bagpipe. Then I saw a group of people coming toward the plane, several of them dressed in kilts, with the bagpiper in their midst. As soon as they spied me coming down the plane steps with the rest of the passengers, the group began frantically waving me back.

An airlines official standing at the bottom of the steps asked, " Are you Catherine Marshall?"

" Yes, I am."

" Would you please go back into the plane and wait until everyone else is off? We tried to send a message to that effect but apparently it got garbled."

So that was it! Docilely, I retreated and sat down, wondering what was coming. Finally even the pilot and the navigator left the plane. Then I timidly started down the steps for the second time.

The lone piper took a deep breath, started up again. He was succeeding in making an incredible amount of noise for one man. Two photographers yelled above the noise of the wind and the rain, " Hold it." So with the pipes screaming in my left ear and the blowing rain pelting down, I waited while two girls dressed in kilts rushed forward to thrust a huge wet bouquet of roses into my arms. On the other side of me stood a man whom I did not know. He turned out to be Lord Malcolm Douglas-Hamilton, straight from Scotland to represent his Highland Fund.

Meanwhile, any feminine pride in appearance left to me was being borne away on the screeching wind. Wisps of my hair were blowing across my eyes. The ribbon ties at the neck of my blouse were standing straight out. On my nose were glistening raindrops. Looking more like a drowned rat by the minute, I managed a sickly smile.

The publicity stunt over, I was taken to the Warwick Hotel, where Fox had reserved a suite of rooms. Several messages were waiting, including one informing me casually that Roxy's was sold out for the next night—6,000 people; that I was to appear on the stage with Richard Todd and would be asked to say a " few words "; that Fox had a standing arrangement with a certain furrier; and that I was to be given the loan of any fur I wished to wear to the premiere.

The next morning, half wondering if someone was having a little joke at my expense, I took a cab around to the fur salon—one of New York's oldest and most famous houses. Since I had a full schedule, including an appointment at the hairdressers, I planned to take only thirty minutes to select the wrap.

A frock-coated gentleman met me at the elevator and led the way through a deeply carpeted foyer to a room with gilt French furniture and many mirrors. There he introduced me to two salesladies.

They looked me over carefully, while pretending not to look at all. " Tell us—your gown for tonight—describe it," one of them said.

" It's white-lace, simple lines, a moulded, off-the-shoulder bodice, floor length, very full skirt."

" White—mm—hmn— Well, dear, first of all, do you have any particular type of wrap in mind?"

" I don't think I'd like one of the fluffy furs—like white fox. I thought it might be fun to try white ermine first."

" All right then, ermine—perhaps also white mink. We'll have some modelled for you—"

Two models appeared wearing the most gorgeous furs I had ever seen. Quickly I decided that the white mink left ermine far behind. My exclamations of delight drew other members of the establishment into the room.

Soon one of the men standing watching said, " You say that you have to appear on the stage at the Roxy tonight? Then this has to be right. And we really can't do it correctly without seeing your gown. Why not let us send a messenger around to your hotel for the dress?"

I couldn't imagine their wanting to go to that much trouble, but I agreed, and gave them the information about my room number and where the dress was hanging. Then we sat down in the gilt chairs to wait. Eagerly they asked me about the book—how long had I taken to write it?—and the movie—what was it like to see yourself portrayed on the screen. When finally the messenger arrived with my white lace over his arm, we were good friends. Now they insisted that I model the dress and furs.

We started all over. There seemed to be no other customers that morning, so the entire staff stood around making comments. After much discussion, the consensus of opinion was that none of the white furs would do. They were too creamy against the chalk white of the dress. Then too, pictures—newsreel and stills—were to be taken. Contrast was needed.

Wrap followed wrap . . . ranch mink and Emba blue

mutation mink. "Not the right shades for the dress. Try something darker." A hooded stole of autumn-haze mutation mink . . . "Style not right for her, not young enough—"

Then one of the men interrupted, "We haven't yet tried sable. Try a tiny wrap in Russian sable."

So the sables were brought in, deep-skinned, glossy, precious. I slipped into a waist-length jacket with a stand-away collar. It felt just right. But then, curiously, I looked at the price tag—and gasped.

One of the men clapped his hands. "That's *it*! Beautiful! Perfect!"

"It really is," a woman said more cautiously. "Very youthful. And just right with the dress."

So it was decided. Someone took away the little fur and my dress to box them. Four people escorted me to the elevator! "It was such a delight to meet you. Have a wonderful night—a real Cinderella night. We'll send a messenger for the jacket in the morning."

Haltingly, I tried to thank them, still scarcely believing what I had just experienced. . . . All that enthusiasm, warmth, interest, and outgoingness in the City of New York . . . three hours of it . . . when the furriers knew that nothing more than the loan of a wrap was involved. . . . Who could have believed it?

Peter John had asked for time off from school for the premiere. Mother and Father had also been easy to persuade, but I had some trouble with the rest of my family. From both my sister Em and my sister-in-law Mary, I received almost identical replies, "We'd love to go, but since the last several years have been given over to babies instead of social life, we haven't anything to wear."

Then some of their neighbours and friends began insisting, "You just have to go. It would be a shame to miss it. Don't let clothes stop you. We'll lend you anything we have."

Their offerings poured in—evening dresses, fur wraps,

evening purses, gloves and costume jewellery. The two girls relaxed and took it in their stride.

After days of trying on and swapping, Mary ended up with a dress of my secretary's, a neighbour's fur coat, and some of her sister's jewellery.

Em finally decided on a dress and wrap of mine, a neighbour's jewellery, and a pair of Mother's gloves.

Compared to this, the men had no problem. They simply rented tuxedos, though we had some trouble in finding one for Peter John with long enough sleeves. And Father, being rather stout in the middle, had to have careful tucks taken in his cummerbund so that it didn't stand up straight just above his stomach like a kangeroo's pouch.

With this odd assortment of possessions, my family arrived at the Warwick Hotel about noon on the day of the premiere. Then there was enacted a little drama for which the Warwick personnel were ill prepared.

Before the rest of the party was out of the two cabs, Father had charged into the hotel lobby and up to the desk. His deep-throated ministerial voice rang loud and clear, " I'm John A. Wood. Mrs Marshall is my daughter, and we want to check in."

" Yes, sir. Do you have reservations, Mr Wood?"

" Yes, we do. Someone from Twentieth Century-Fox made them. I don't know whose name they're under."

The clerk looked puzzled. Then as if resigned to the hazards of his occupation, he said patiently, " Wood? Let me check, sir— We have nothing under the name of Wood. What did you say the other name was?"

Dad boomed, " Mrs Marshall, Mrs Peter Marshall."

By that time everyone in the Warwick knew that someone by the name of Marshall had arrived. After several more exchanges, four keys were finally produced. Father appropriated them and, with the air of a conquering hero, led his little army to the wrong rooms on the wrong floors.

After another half hour of stewing, Mother and Father

were installed in 1407; Em and Harlow in 1203; Mary and Bob in 1411. But the luggage was still mixed up. The total effect of the hour's manoeuvre had the hotel management so confused that they were leaving Father and his luggage strictly alone.

Still Father was not satisfied. He felt that the hotel would want to know which couple now had which room. Once again he galloped up to the harried desk clerk.

" Young man, I want to report a change in the Marshall party's rooms."

" Yes, sir, if you don't like your rooms, perhaps we can arrange—"

" They're fine. It's just that we moved my daughter and her husband into room 1203, when you had reserved 1407 for them. Mrs Wood and I are now in—"

" Now I don't quite get all that. Aren't your daughter and her son in a suite on the seventh floor?"

" Yes—no—you misunderstand me. I have another daughter, Mrs Hoskins. She and her husband are now in 1203, and—"

" Mr Wood, let's start all over. There's something I don't quite—"

That session didn't end the matter. Each time during the next twenty-four hours that Father walked through the lobby, he and the desk clerk had a work-out at getting the record straight.

The havoc Father wrought with the Warwick's bookkeeping system was clearly reflected in the final bill. It read simply: " Marshall party. Rooms for two nights—$96.42."

That evening we had ringside seats from which to observe the showmanship that goes into a movie premiere. Three limousines were to be sent around to the hotel at seven-thirty. Every detail had been planned—which member of the family was to sit in which car, the route, the moment at which we would arrive at Roxy's.

The three long, black limousines proceeded slowly. As

soon as we turned into Seventh Avenue, we could see the searchlights and hear a bagpipe band. For the last three blocks, the cars had to inch their way because of the crowds. At ten minutes to eight we double-parked around the corner from Roxy's to wait until the exact moment we were due to arrive. At three minutes to eight we drew up before the theatre. Cordons of police were holding the people back in order to keep a cleared space on the sidewalk. Both the outer and inner lobbies were decorated with tartan and heather, and there were scores of photographers and radio interviewers with portable microphones.

A Fox man took me by the elbow and tugged me from place to place through the closely packed crowd—to be introduced to this person—" to say a few words, please " into that microphone.

I was as interested in watching the celebrities arrive as everyone else. I couldn't help wondering how much pressure had been put on some of them to be present in order to have " names " there—Jayne Meadows and her sister Audrey, Gloria Swanson, Monica Lewis, Rudy Vallee, William Reid—the royal chief of the Scottish clans in the United States and Canada—Lord and Lady Douglas-Hamilton, Mr Skouras, the president of Twentieth Century-Fox, and his wife, Mr and Mrs Richard Todd. Once I almost lost my tall son when he lingered behind to stare at Terry Moore.

By eight-thirty the hullabaloo was over, and we were shown to our seats. The theatre lights went out; the stage lights went on. Richard Todd, now wearing a pointed goatee for the filming of " Sir Walter Raleigh," came to escort me to the stage. Others joined us there—William Maclair, the executive director of Roxy's; Lord Douglas-Hamilton; and some representatives from the Caledonian Hospital.

Standing there on the stage, I had an impression only of light—light—light—from the blinding footlights. When my time came to step up to the microphone, my heart was beating wildly. There was the feeling of being stranded, engulfed in white incandescent heat. I was groping through a blazing sea of light to make contact with an audience whose faces were out there somewhere, but were lost to me.

I spoke of the fact that almost three years of dreaming and hoping, of resolution and hard work, of teamwork unparalleled in my experience, had gone into the picture; of the debt that I owed to Mr Engel, Mr Koster, Jean Peters, Richard Todd, and many more. . . .

Then it was time for the movie. Throughout that particular showing I had every antenna out, alert to audience reaction. Very soon I became aware of the sophistication of the New Yorkers. They laughed at some of the wrong places and did not laugh when they were supposed to. The thought crossed my mind that perhaps this wasn't a " big city " movie. Later this impression was verified by the fact that the picture was not the success in New York that it was in smaller cities and towns.

I had seen the movie but once before. For this second viewing, I relaxed enough to let myself be swept into it. I wept at times; yet had little sense of reality that I had lived out the rôle I was now seeing on the screen. I had trouble identifying myself with Jean Peters, even though this was a girl with my hair-do and a gesture or two typical of me. Todd's rôle was a little more real to me. In one scene—the first one in which he did some preaching—I could hear Peter. Then in a scene lasting a few seconds—portraying Peter in an oxygen tent after his heart attack—I could see my husband. For me these were two completely authentic moments.

Still, when the lights came on, I must have been in quite a fog because I struggled for several minutes to get my arms into the sleeves of the borrowed sable jacket. Finally I discovered that I had been trying to put it on upside down.

The rest of my family came down to earth more quickly. Back at the hotel, Peter John said that premieres always made him hungry, and couldn't we please get something to eat?

So at almost midnight, the eight of us trooped into the

nearest drugstore—tuxedoes, trailing dresses and all. We perched on stools at the counter while Peter John nibbled on a three-decker club sandwich and gulped down a double vanilla malted. I had considerable trouble hanging on to a soda with one hand and the sable jacket with the other, while trying to keep the voluminous skirts of my white lace dress off the floor.

Meanwhile the talk flew back and forth as we shared our varied impressions of the evening. . . . " Who was that distinguished-looking couple sitting behind you, Catherine? They seemed to know you." . . . " I like Dick Todd with a goatee." . . . " Jean Peters was at her best in the Youth Rally scene. She's just as cute as a bug's ear. . . ."

Finally curiosity got the better of one of the soda-fountain boys. " Look, this is none of my business," he blurted out, " but are you people refugees from a night club? Or where in t'thunder have you been?"

The trip back to Washington the day after the premiere was in sharp contrast to the trumped-up fanfare of my arrival at La Guardia. The rest of my family was returning by train, so I joined them. By nine the next morning, Cinderella had shed the sables and had sent them back by bonded messenger. Ten o'clock found her in her own clothes, sitting on her suitcase in Pennsylvania station, waiting patiently for the ten-thirty train to be called—not a photographer nor a Fox man in sight.

I sat there reading William K. Zinsser's account of the premiere and his critique of the movie in the *New York Herald Tribune* . . .

. . . there is no reason why it shouldn't please all the people who like the book and several million more . . . told simply . . . acted well . . . refreshingly free of the sticky piety that mars so many Hollywood ventures into the spiritual life. . . .

So far so good. One reviewer on our side. But already

I was wondering how the nation as a whole would receive this movie.

The first reports were disheartening, and as it turned out, misleading In Los Angeles the picture opened at Grauman's Chinese Theatre. A week after the New York premiere, I received a note from Eleanore Griffin:

> Dearest Catherine:
>   Just a stricken note. For all the wonderful reviews, "Peter" is flopping at the box office. This just can't happen. You prayed for it to be a wonderful picture—so pray that people will go to see it. Love,
>
>   Eleanore

No, it just couldn't happen. Though it would mean nothing to me financially, I naturally had hoped that the picture would be a real success at the box office. This alone would prove something about American tastes to the Hollywood movie makers that I longed to see proved: that spiritual help related directly to people's real problems would draw movie audiences as strongly as Hollywood's two favourite magnets—escaped entertainment and unabashed sex

A few days later came another note from the script writer:

> Dear Catherine:
>   Sam just called to tell me that AMCP is turning into a smash. Simply fabulous—and from word-of-mouth advertising. I am so happy. I hope you heard Bing Crosby interrupt his radio programme to rave about "A Man," probably the nicest thing that has happened. Love,
>
>   Eleanore

The reviews of which Eleanore spoke were consistently good—with a single exception I read scores of them, and so far as I know, only *Time* magazine's was adverse:

. . . And yet, for all its big talk about God, Peter
Marshall's story as it emerges on the screen has depress-
ingly little to say about religion. On the evidence given
in the film, the man was more to be praised for his
social than for his spiritual qualities. The film, much
more strongly than the book, gives the impression that
Peter Marshall was a great salesman, who sold Christianity
the way another man might sell frontage in an exclusive
suburb. And his death at 46, which is apparently intended
to move one like the death of a martyr, has instead
a kind of sorry unimportance on the screen, as if Connecticut, and not Heaven, had been his destination.

This acid account brought me some curious little experiences. Several people (who apparently still believed everything they read in print) wrote me, saying that they had
read *Time*'s comments and were bitterly disappointed that
I had thus betrayed Peter Marshall. They had no intention
of going near this picture.

In my reply, I pointed out that there was at least food
for thought in the fact that *Time*'s reaction seemed to be
a minority report—in fact a minority of one. I was surprised that they were willing to judge and condemn something on secondhand evidence. I suggested merely that they
see the movie and let it stand or fall on its own merits.

To a person, each correspondent went to see the picture,
loved it, wrote to tell me so, and to apologize for the tone of
the letter he had written earlier.

A letter from Mr Engel summarized for me how the
picture was doing . . .

Dear Catherine:

In this country and Canada it is a solid hit everywhere.
. . . Word-of-mouth is so good that invariably the returns
are greater the second week than the first. Typical of
this capability to build on itself is this cable which Mr

Skouras received the other day from Ernest Turnbull, our Fox representative in Australia . . .

" ' Man Called Peter ' has established remarkable performance by breaking all time non-holiday first week record. Stop. Second week exceeded first week. Stop. Third week exceeded second, and fourth week exceeded all previous three weeks. Stop. . . ."

Unfortunately and inexplicably, the picture is turning out to be financially disappointing in Scotland and England. In the latter case, it got a bad break. It was released during the London newspaper strike. Consequently movie-goers never saw the reviews, which were excellent. In the British Isles, moviegoers pay much more attention to critics than they do in the United States. . . . However, the picture's ability to generate good word-of-mouth opinion may indicate that there was a more serious reason why it hasn't done as well there. . . .

Whatever the reason for the growing interest in the picture, I felt sure it was not due to the ads run by Twentieth Century-Fox. About this time I was contacted frequently by Fox's advertising department, who were eager for me to make public appearances. During one of our telephone conversations, I requested that they let me see some of their advertising copy. They sent me a package of sample blurbs, but not until after they had been released to national periodicals and newspapers. To say that I was shocked at some of them and felt that they were misleading is to put it mildly. . . . " Their love surges with exaltation from the first second to the last sigh. . . ." " It could only have been written by the woman who loved him. . . ." " Let yourself glow with ' A Man Called Peter.' " They might have been blurbs for any torrid love story.

Life magazine, in its issue of April 4, gave a five-page spread to the picture but was caustic in its comments on Fox's advertising:

Now " A Man Called Peter " is to be released in a sentimental though credibly artistic form, as a movie
which will certainly be even more successful. It will
owe no thanks, however, to some ads by 20th Century-
Fox (" He was a lovin' kind of guy. . . ." " He was
God's kind of guy ") that set something of a record
for plain bad taste and skirted close to blasphemy.

Soon it became apparent what was happening. The picture,
like the book, was not reaching its greatest success in the
large cities. But when it hit grass-roots America, and when
the word-of-mouth reaction began spreading, then everywhere
theatre managers had to hold it over. To the surprise of most
of the movie industry in that year of 1955, " A Man Called
Peter " was to chalk up Fox's largest box-office take.

The movie won a new group of friends that my book had
not seriously touched—the teen-agers. Across the nation,
they flocked to see " A Man Called Peter." They went
and went again—three times, four times, seven times. The
record—so far as I know—is twelve times.

The picture seemed to call forth all their latent idealism,
their longing for someone to put on a pedestal. It launched
their own private dreaming, and sometimes swung the dreaming into surprising action.

Their letters piled into the Fox studios asking for copies
of Jean Peters' Youth Rally speech. . . .

I've seen the movie four times. But I want to know and
keep every word of Jean Peters' speech—especially that
part about learning from a man what it means to be a
woman. Will you please send me a copy of that
talk . . .?

They wrote to me—exuberant, bubbling over, telling me
about themselves, asking me for this and that, especially
for a picture of Peter Marshall, expecting an answer in the

next mail. Always Peter had won the teen-agers in life; now he had his favourite audience back. . . .

Pottstown, Penn

Dear Mrs Marshall:

I will be 15 on November 3. I have just come back from seeing " A Man Called Peter " for the seventh time. . . . I think that sermon Peter gave at Annapolis was the best he ever gave. Could you send me a copy of it so that I could memorize it?

Also, would you please send me a picture of Dr Marshall—wallet size will be fine—for my very own.

Yours truly,

(with a cramped finger)

South Wales, N.Y.

Dear Mrs Marshall:

I am 14 and away at boarding school. Recently I have seen the movie " A Man Called Peter " and after that I read the book. I have greatly admired Peter and the way he was close to God. . . .

On Monday night, December 2, I received a call from home saying that my father had had a heart attack. I immediately became panicky. Then I remembered what you did when Peter had a heart attack. So I prayed the way you did. Then my being scared left, and I felt a peace of mind that was so welcome. . . .

I am writing you this letter, because you are the one who taught me this through your stirring book *A Man Called Peter*.

Thank you for everything.

Love, your friend and admirer,

Des Plaines, Ill.

Dear Mrs Marshall:

I'm 14 years old, and last summer I saw the movie " A Man Called Peter." Since then, I have read the book four times, and the story seems more wonderful to me each time. . . .

It would be impossible to tell anyone how Peter has changed my life, but God knows. . . .

Now my one ambition is to enjoy life as Peter did, to have his faith, to know God as he did, and to serve God as he did. Then I know I'll be happy. . . .

Very sincerely yours,

And from a somewhat older boy . . .

Anderson, S.C.

My dear Mrs Marshall:

I realize the contents of this letter will be startling. . . . I work for a newspaper. I'm the assistant sports editor. . . . I had planned some day to be a teacher-coach, that is, until last April. . . .

Then one night in April, I was alone. It was 8.45. Something within seemed to say "Go and see 'A Man Called Peter'." I did.

Then came the scene where young P. M. was walking across the moors in a fog. Suddenly I felt as if there was nothing in the theatre but a Voice and me. "So, it's You, God. So it's You." The words pounded in my heart. It frightened me.

Afterwards I drove out to the lakeside, seeking some sort of answer. It's a long story, but I want to tell it step by step. . . .

Well, the net result is that I've found my real vocation. I'm going to be a minister. I'm to enter Columbia Seminary in the fall. It's strange and wonderful and all because I went to see a movie. . . .

May I ask you this one favour? Will you pray for me as you did for Peter Marshall?

Sincerely,

The ultimate touchstone of the movie's success for me did not lie in the realm of money, but in human values.

When I had written that prayer letter to my correspondents even as the movie was being conceived, I had dreamed of "vast audiences streaming on to the sidewalks of a hundred thousand Main Streets, entertained, uplifted, inspired, with the thought singing through many a mind . . . 'If God could solve Peter Marshall's problems, maybe He can solve mine—and my nation's. I'm going to give Him a chance. . . .'"

And Mr Engel, the movie producer, had dreamed of "A Man Called Peter" helping especially with those universal problems that prod all men into uneasiness—death—grief—immortality.

He and I had dreamed more accurately than we knew. Ultimately our dreams had been clothed in reality, had lived and breathed. The true stories that came to me spoke for themselves. Those dreams had walked straight into human hearts. . . .

At the Miracle Theatre in Miami, the special preview showing of the picture was just over. A dozen men, most of them strangers to one another, were in the men's room.

"I'd heard only vaguely of this guy Marshall," one man said to another. "How old was he when he died?"

His companion seemed to be thinking about something else . . . "I don't know—pretty young."

A tall man in the corner said, "He was forty-six."

Someone else commented, "Those Senate prayers were sure pungent—most unusual. But that one scene, where Peter was shown praying in the Senate, was curiously chopped up—"

Several agreed. The tall man said, "I have it straight from the horse's mouth— One of the chief problems of making this movie was with length. That chopped-up feeling was the fault of the cutting room."

Another man said, "You know, I'm a naturalized American.

That scene towards the end—when the Marshall family was
walking the little cocker—what was his name—with the
Capitol dome in the background—that was beautiful. Something about that scene got me. I felt a great surge of gratitude
for being an American—"

No one spoke for a minute. Then the tall man in the
corner said laconically, " The cocker's name is Jeff."

As one man, the group turned to the tall one. " Hey,
how do you know so much about it?"

" I'm Bob Ingraham. I gave Jeff to the Marshalls. I'm
their neighbour on Cape Cod."

A tight little knot of interested men gathered round. The
questions flew. Time passed; Mr Ingraham was an interesting talker.

Outside in the theatre lobby a score of impatient wives
stood cooling their heels, wondering what on earth was
going on behind the sacrosanct door marked " Men." . . .

The letter was postmarked "Lynchburg, Virginia." " This
is a true story," the young woman named Violet wrote. " You
should know about it. . . ."

" A Man Called Peter," which had been held over for
some time, was in its last few days in Lynchburg. All
week I had tried to get my mother and father to go.
But each time they had said that it just didn't suit that
day.

Then early Saturday morning I was tidying up, vacuum-
ing. Something seemed to insist: " Try again today."

Mama said, " I'll ask Father. But I know he won't
go on a Saturday."

" But tell him that it's the last day."

When Mama returned to the telephone, she seemed
surprised. " Father said he'd try to go. He'll deliver his
eggs before noon."

So the three of us went to the 2.30 show. Afterwards

as Papa let me out at my front door, he said, " I like that movie more than any I've ever seen—especially the way Peter Marshall spoke of dying."

Well, Catherine Marshall, at eight o'clock that night, Papa was watching the Jackie Gleason Show. He had his shoes kicked off, his feet up on the big ottoman, his bride of fifty years by his side. And suddenly, he just closed his eyes and joined Peter Marshall. As simple as that.

I wouldn't trade that Saturday afternoon for all the money in the world. I just thought you'd be grateful to know the contribution you and Peter Marshall made to the last day of my father's life. . . .

In late October and early November, 1955, seven Russian journalists visited the United States. A public relations man whom I know was asked by the State Department to be one of those to squire the visitors around the nation.

One Saturday afternoon, November 12, he telephoned me. "We're just back from our tour," he explained. " It's been quite an experience! I've a favour to ask of you. It will take a little explaining though—"

"I can't imagine— Go ahead—"

"Well, when we were in Hollywood, the seven editors were shown three movies. Each of the three major studios was asked to choose one as being representative of the industry. They were Harvey, An American in Paris, and A Man Called Peter. Did you know that?"

"No—I certainly didn't."

"Your movie was translated for them as they saw it— even the sermon material. When the translator finished, he was in tears, and so were several of the Russians."

"But aren't they usually pretty emotional?"

" On the contrary, that was the first time all the way across the country that I'd seen them really touched. Well, after that, they couldn't seem to get that picture off their minds. They kept bringing it up, kept asking me questions. When we got to Phoenix on our way back, one day out of a clear sky, one of the men said almost defiantly, ' I don't think that Catherine Marshall exists.' I said, ' Sure, she exists. I know her. Would you like to meet her?' "

After a little pause he went on, " You see, they were intrigued—very curious as to whether the story you wrote could really be true. Well, then I had a brainwave—'I go to a certain church in Washington,' I told him. 'If I could clear it with the State Department and arrange it with Mrs Marshall, would you like to meet her there and attend a typical American church service?' "

" I think I know what's coming—" I said.

" Probably you do— The State Department has given its blessing, though they seemed a trifle astonished. Would you be willing to meet us at my church tomorrow?"

The next day I was at the church at a quarter to eleven. Five of the seven Russians were there, together with my friend and one interpreter. The Russians were big, energetic-looking men who seemed a little uncomfortable in city clothes.

The introductions were garnished with much bowing and scraping. One of the Russians, Boris Izakov of *International Life*, spoke English.

Mr Izakov asked, " Was the movie made right after the book?"

" Yes, it was."

" When we were seeing it, we had the feeling that these were real people, and that this was the real America."

Then it was time for the church service. The theme of the minister's sermon that Sunday was Christian love, the necessity of our forgiving other people, no exceptions allowed. I kept thinking what a strange thesis this idea of Christian love must seem to the Russians. I wondered how much of the service and the sermon they could grasp through the interpreter. But perhaps the Spirit of God was interpreting at a depth that no translator could.

After the service, the Russians questioned me further about the movie. Then one of them asked, " How old is your son?" And before I could answer, "Would you like to see pictures of my family?"

Several of the men began pulling pictures out of their wallets, and proceeded to tell me the precise ages of their children. "We leave for home tomorrow. Soon we shall be seeing our wives and children."

Mr Izakov made a point of telling me, "Nikolai Gribachev here has—like you—written a book that has been made into a movie."

"I'm so interested. What kind of a book?"

"It's—well—like a Jack London story. . . ." He changed the subject quickly. "We must go now. We have to be on a television show. Mrs Marshall, I'm an atheist, but I enjoyed coming here today. Attending this church has helped me to understand the American people better."

There was more bowing over my hand. . . . "Thank you, thank you. . . ." Then one man, looking at me, said, "Mrs Marshall, you have lovely big blue eyes."

That's the only piece of Communist propaganda I ever enjoyed.

Preachers have traditionally been fond of telling the rest of us that fame and money do not bring happiness. Most of us only half believe this. Secretly we would be more than willing to try a little of the fame and security on for size.

Yet I know now that the preachers are right. I found out the hard way. For in the backwash of the movie of "A Man Called Peter" there was plenty of publicity. A portion of my life had been dramatized for all the world to see. My name had been on theatre marquees from coast to coast. No escape was possible—up the back stairs or anywhere.

At first, it had been exhilarating to watch the ashes of grief turn into the fairy gold of success. There had been adventure in walking through doors that opened before me; satisfaction in knowing that I could earn my way when it was necessary; excitement in seeing how high the tower of success could be built. Still I tried never to forget whose Hand had unlocked the doors, whose direction and help had made possible the success.

Then in time my sense of mission was followed by a feeling of futility. The fame turned back to ashes; the glitter was not all gold. How can I explain what happened?

Success in our world panders to the human ego. In effect, the world says, " A laurel wreath for you! Your human powers have accomplished thus and so!" And the world's voice all but drowns out another Voice, that of a quiet Figure standing in the shadows saying, " Without Me ye can do nothing."

We are helpless without the God who made us and whose Spirit animates us. Yet the cult of self-sufficiency is not yet dead. It beats daily at our eardrums. It encourages selfishness. It devaluates working for the joy of working instead of for the reward of money; it scorns living to serve other people.

I was well aware of the conflict of the voices. I knew that happiness flees when self takes the centre of the stage. There was a period when I prayed daily, " Oh God, don't let me take any credit for the success of these books. Keep me simple, keep me humble, keep my vision clear."

Yet—did the ashes in my mouth mean that somehow I had taken my eyes off that quiet Figure in the shadows and focused them on myself? Perhaps. Admittedly, it's hard to be clear-eyed about oneself.

Perhaps on the plus side of the ledger was my negative reaction to publicity. This was a good sign. A little of it I had found heady wine; more than a little I found cloying.

This principle of moderation I had learned early through an unforgettable childhood lesson. In Mississippi, we had lived in a manse adjoining the church. On Communion Sundays, at the close of the service, the silver trays with their tiny glasses of grape juice—some empty, some untouched— were always left on our back porch until the glasses could be washed.

At age four, grape juice was my favourite beverage. One Sunday, disregarding the sacred use for which that particular grape juice was intended, I methodically drained glass after glass, dozens of them. My stomach promptly rebelled; I was a very sick little girl.

Since I belonged to a teasing family, it took the rest of my childhood for me to live down my indulgence. For years thereafter an uncle called me his " grape-juice girl."

At the beginning of my venture into the world of writing, I thought publicity as enjoyable as once I had thought grape juice. Then in the end, there was too much of it for my taste, and something in me violently rebelled.

Part of the rebellion was my reaction to those who tended to idealize me. With the release of the movie, Peter Marshall had become something of a legend, his memory placed on a pedestal. It was as if the public then insisted that I should share the pedestal.

In time, so much of this living in my husband's light became a problem to me. One era of my life was over— whether I liked it or not. Circumstances were forcing me to build a new life of my own. Yet I was haunted by the question . . . how could I find myself as a woman or as a writer, in order to make that new life—so long as so many people insisted on seeing me solely as Mrs Peter Marshall?

I shall not soon forget an incident at a World Day of Prayer service where I had been asked to speak. A large crowd had gathered. Just before the service, as I tried to push my way through the crowd into the church, suddenly I felt someone tugging at my arm. I turned around questioningly and saw a nicely dressed woman just behind me. Very seriously she said, " Mrs Marshall, I hope I didn't bruise your arm. I just wanted to be able to tell my friends that I had touched Peter Marshall's wife."

It was her lack of humour rather than her idealism that disturbed me. For weeks her words haunted me. Touch me? Why? She had meant it only in kindness. Perhaps she had thought that I would be flattered.

Yet idealizing can soon become idolizing, and no human being should idolize another. We open ourselves to inevitable disillusionment when we do. And we do the object of our idolizing an injustice, for pedestal-sitting can be a lonely business.

It is especially lonely when there is no one with whom to share what the world calls "success." A businessman whose wife had died expressed this to me in several poignant sentences. . . .

> Since Jean died, my business has suddenly flourished and is now successful beyond my greatest hopes. . . . Yet I would gladly give up the success, if I could have Jean again.
>
> What fun is it to get big orders when you have no one waiting at home to hear about them? What does money mean to me when I have no one I love on whom to spend it? In fact, my success now only highlights my loneliness. . . .

I understood only too well what this widower meant. No matter how full and friendly the outside world may be, the house stands quiet, the evenings empty. But there are additional complications for a woman caught in the same situation. The conflict in me that had been born that day of the autograph tea for *Mr Jones, Meet the Master* had built to a climax about the time of the movie.

Many women in our time know the same conflict, both those who have sought careers and those who have had careers thrust on them by necessity. The crux of the problem is . . . can a woman replace love with accomplishment, marriage with a career, or even combine a career with marriage, and find her life entirely satisfying?

Men usually accept at face value the estimate of themselves that society accords them because of the work they've done. Not so most women. Our values are usually rooted in relationships to others, not in personal accomplishment. As wives, we have not lived our own lives. We have lived through a man. As wives we must accept—grudgingly or delightedly—the place in society that our husband's work has won. The same is true of us as mothers. To one degree or another we live through our children.

But our most sensitive awareness of ourselves as persons has come through our relationship with one man. Soon after we met him, we found that in his presence we were aware of our femininity as never before—our dependence; our passivity; the way our emotions ruled our reason; our delight in people rather than in abstract ideas; our compassion; our preoccupation with the minutiae of living— a flower arrangement for a party, the next meeting of the PTA, the selection of new draperies for the living room, a missing button on a shirt.

With a new awareness, we understood that men and women were meant to be different. We revelled in our differentness.

Then life dealt us a blow; 7,595,000 of us in the United States have lost our husbands through death. Economic need has forced many of us to earn our own living. We who had known completeness only in our relationship with a man who loved us, were now asked to be complete within ourselves. In order to survive, we have had to do a hundred things we had never done before—handle money, sell and buy property, keep a man's working hours, try to be both father and mother to our children.

We managed all this by summoning up latent masculine qualities we did not know we possessed—the necessity of accepting responsibility, aggressiveness, competitiveness, drive, a partial submerging of feeling in favour of reason.

Even as this happened, we found treasured values slipping away. In the business world, we saw differences between the sexes blurred in a way we had not known in marriage. With the blurring, life lost something precious.

It made us stop and think, " What am I now—since my husband's death? Have I got off the track? Am I still a woman?" And that led inevitably to the questions asked by every widow: "What was I then—in marriage? What is a woman supposed to be?"

The attitude of our men friends made us question our new position even more sharply. For we found that even as they lauded us for carrying on so bravely as widows, they did not personally like the changes they saw in us. They did not like women whose heads ruled their emotions, or aggressive women, or competitive women.

The dilemma went even deeper. A woman's need is to be loved for herself, not for any accomplishment. A true woman finds her reassurance, her reason for living, by looking into the eyes of a man who loves her. And when that is withdrawn from her—well—then what? She may achieve something that society recognizes as fine, only to find herself unable to accept society's new estimate of her.

Perhaps in my case this conflict was one reason for an agonizing period of profound self-doubt. I had performed a certain mission. The world said that it had helped many. But as a woman I was not impressed with any accomplishment of mine. As a woman I felt drained, empty.

I stood looking back over the way I had travelled since Peter's death and knew that my personal answer to whether or not a woman can replace marriage with a career and find it satisfying was—no, definitely not. The career left the woman still wanting to be—only a woman.

CHAPTER 15

Dreams Do Come True

I was sitting at the kitchen table preparing the vegetables for dinner. Since we had our usual quota of guests at Waverley, there was quite a pile of potatoes to be peeled, peas to be shelled. From where I sat, I could look through the windows into the back garden. Phlox, zinnias, and petunias were in bloom. A bird, with much fluttering of feathers, was giving himself a vigorous scrubbing in the bird-bath. Even as I watched, a rabbit slipped under the picket fence and practised small jumps across the grass.

It was a lazy afternoon and the potato peeling was relaxing. All at once a new idea appeared as if out of nowhere, full-blown in my mind. There had been no knocking for admittance; the idea dropped into my mind—kerplunk! Where are your father and mother going to live when your father retires from the ministry?

My mind roamed back over their lives. . . . How they had met at the Ebenezer Mission School in the Great Smoky Mountains of Tennessee. . . . Then, six pastorates in five states. . . . I thought of how they had lived in a procession of manses supplied by different churches. . . . Of how Father, who had always liked using tools and building things, was always making improvements in each successive house. . . . Of how Mother had planted and planted in each yard—and then always had to go off and leave her flowers.

I remembered the way they had given themselves so unstintingly to their church and to the community wherever they had been . . . Father with his love for people and his easy outgoingness . . . Mother in her more restrained way counselling with many a young person, quietly encouraging a teen-ager's ambition to go to college or to find the right spot of service or the right person to marry.

314

And now that retirement was upon my parents—what? Immediately the idea came: Why not find a small farm within easy driving distance of Washington? Then let them dispense the hospitality to their city children and grandchildren. They would love that.

I sat there turning the new thought over and over as one would stare at a shining pebble. Entrancing, yes—but wasn't it impractical? Dad is scarcely the farmer type, I thought.

I decided not to mention the idea to anyone until it had been given the test of time. If this were just my own unsupported idea, it would evaporate as quickly as it had come. But if it was authentic, then it would persist.

Far from evaporating, the dream about the farm haunted me all summer. Many times during those weeks I pondered the intriguing fact that everything in the world starts with an idea of a picture in someone's mind. Some man, thousands of years ago, conceived the idea of a wheel. At that moment, the history of transportation entered a new phase. But the wheel had to be a picture in that unknown man's mind before it could be projected into wood. In the same way, the Wright brothers had to have an idea about heavier-than-air craft before they could translate that idea into wood, steel, canvas, and wire.

The architect has to have a blueprint; the dressmaker, a pattern. Even the cosmos—the Genesis account tells us —was an idea in the mind of God, before order could be created out of chaos, light out of darkness. . . .

It's because everything does start with an idea that dreaming, visualizing, is important. In fact it can be a way of prayer —a very effective way. When the farm idea persisted, I began to wonder if it might not be more than just a lovely daydream, the real thing—a God-inspired dream.

Not long before his death, Peter had given some thought to the problem of Dad's retirement, but had reached no solution. It was a problem, because ministers' salaries are notoriously meagre, leaving little leeway for savings. And since church

pensions were a relatively recent innovation, my father's
would be small.

Finally I decided to give the farm-retirement plan the
next test by mentioning it casually to Mother and Dad
I picked a leisurely moment just as we were finishing lunch
one day. The family was around the umbrella table in the
side yard, sipping the last of our iced tea and enjoying the
sparkling sea air.

"You know, Dad," I began, "how Peter always thought
maybe you and Mother would live here when you retired."

Father pushed back his chair. "I know. But it's too far
away from the rest of the family. We'd never see enough of
our grandchildren—"

"Well, I have another idea—" Then I told them. To
my surprise they were immediately enthusiastic. My father
stood up, his husky six-foot frame belying his years. He ran
a hand through his full head of white hair, excitement in
his every move. Behind glasses, Mother's blue eyes sparkled.
And just so, the idea took root. From the outset, it seemed
to transform their retirement from a dismal "must" at the
end of life to an exciting adventure with all the flavour of
a new beginning.

I had thought of the plan as primarily for my parents. But
as with any of God's plans, it benefited all who touched it.
It gave me a lot of satisfaction to be able to return in this
way some of the love that they had always lavished on me.
It also proved to be one of my last steps out of grief. The
bereaved must find new and creative patterns for the rebuilding
of their lives. For me the farm represented an important part
of that new pattern.

The Leesburg real-estate agent was a patient man. He had
shown me a new ranch-type house set in an open field. . . .
"It's a lovely house—but too new—no trees—no shade. . . ."
He had me inspect a renovated house, a hundred years
old. . . . "Great charm—but there are six grandchildren in

the family now . . . not enough room." Next I was taken to see a large stone house set on a hillside. . . . " Large enough, but much too expensive—couldn't touch it."

A year and a half had gone by since that afternoon at Waverley. We had investigated every area within sixty miles of Washington. It was the rolling, fertile countryside of Loudoun County, Virginia, ringed by the mountains of the Blue Ridge, that each member of our family found most appealing.

On the way back to Leesburg, we drove through a small settlement. Waving one arm out of the car window, the realtor explained: " This is the village of Lincoln, population 101, used to be called Goose Creek—settled by the Quakers about 1735. There—over there—is the Friends Meeting House."

All at once around the bend of the road, a white house set back in tall boxwood and rhododendron came into view.

" What about this place?" I asked.

The real-estate man slowed the car to a crawl. " Beautiful, all right. Well known in this section—been in the same family almost a century. Used to belong to the Hoges. He was a Quaker minister—now owned by Hoge's nephew, a Baltimore physician. I don't think it's for sale, though." With that the realtor speeded up and seemed to dismiss the subject.

Out of the back window of the car, I was still staring. The sign said " Evergreen Farm." Several of the tallest evergreens I had ever seen gave support to the name. At that moment something clicked in my mind. I had the strange feeling that the next step in the implementation of my dream had just come into view.

But then reality settled in like a heavy cloud. The grounds were like a living fairyland—surely completely out of my reach financially. And anyway the place wasn't even for sale.

But during the next few weeks, I was to realize all over again that God's dreams are usually more wonderful than

ours. The problem for most of us is how to stretch ourselve
enough to accept His munifience.

Ten months later in a lawyer's office in Leesburg, I—
mentally pinching myself to be sure it was true—was signin
in triplicate the papers that made me the mortgage-happy
mistress of " Evergreen."

The farmhouse had stood unoccupied for over ten year
except for brief visits from the owner. It was only becaus
the house and the farm generally needed so much work tha
I was able to buy it.

There was still eight months to go before my father'
retirement; I had until then to get the house ready. As
minimum, we were going to have to install a heating plant
all new plumbing, a new kitchen, bathrooms, overhaul the
water system, put closets in each room, redecorate th
interior.

The main part of the house had been built in 1816 by
Yardley Taylor, a Quaker. Yardley, like most of the Friends
built his house according to a standard plan approved by
William Penn himself—walls of fieldstone, a foot-and-a-hal.
thick, with little binding. The masons of that day built
dry wall, filling the wide hollow space with tightly packed
stones and sand. Only after the house was finished did the
point up the walls with lime and mud. The thick walls wer
designed to keep out the cold of winter and the heat o
summer. Always there was a large basement, low ceilings
massive hand-hewn beams, deep window sills. The plan
was such that rooms could be added as the family increased

Penn, in a tract published in London in 1684, minutel
described his standard plan:

> To build then, a house of thirty foot long and thirteen
> broad, with a partition near the middle and another to
> divide one end of the House into two small rooms . . .

The two small rooms immediately to the left of the from

door, were originally bedrooms. At Evergreen, they had
later been used as a parlour and sitting room. Another
Quaker architectural device heated the rooms—two fireplaces
built back to back, at an angle in a V shape, with a single
chimney flue serving both. Throwing the two rooms together
would make the spacious living room that the house needed.
But that would necessitate the major task of rebuilding most
of the chimney.

William Penn's standard house plan, London, 1684[1]

Many of the small-paned windows were still of the old
hand-blown glass. There was some of the original hard-
ware, including the front-door key made of brass and $7\frac{1}{2}$
inches long.

Just down the hill was a barn, a spring house, and a smoke
house, also built in 1816 of massive magnificent stonework.
The tenant house, only five years old, stood on the site of
the original, which had burned down many years before.

The main house stood on a little knoll. A double avenue
of English boxwood, originally with a walk between (but
long since grown together) ran from the front porch down
the hill and then up another hill almost as far as the eye
could see.

[1] Strong, Solange, *Old Stone Houses of Loudoun County, Virginia*
Loudoun Times-Mirror Publishing Company, Leesburg, 1950.

Over and over I had been warned about the hazards of renovating old houses. One friend who saw Evergreen said bluntly, " It would be much cheaper to raze it to the ground and start over. No contractor would touch it except on a cost-plus basis."

" But I couldn't bear to see this house demolished. It's been lived in and loved for over a hundred and fifty years. No new house could possibly have so much charm."

" Charm be hanged. You women! You're heading for trouble and more trouble. Don't say I didn't warn you!"

Later that week, a Washington architect went out to the house with me. His reaction had a little of the same dire foreboding as that of my pessimistic friend.

" It has possibilities all right. So many, that as an architect they intrigue me. But you know how old houses are. You never know what you'll run into. This two-faced fireplace situation, for instance. . . ."

" Do you think we would run into trouble rebuilding that chimney?"

" There's no telling. The whole house might collapse. But I don't think so. We might have to put a supporting steel beam across these two rooms though—"

" Would you be willing to take on this job?"

" I'm game, if you're prepared to stand the strain and the risks involved."

Thus—gingerly—I acquired an architect. His first task, prior to making drawings, was to spend hours upon hours measuring. No two windows turned out to be the same size. No measurements could be taken for granted. Few lines were true. Often the tops of doors and windows were on such a slant that even the casual eye could see it.

When the architect's plans were completed, we pored over them. In addition to the living-room renovation, the dining-room fireplace—long closed—was to be reopened. The plans called for a picture window in the library facing on the front garden; three bathrooms, two of them on the second floor; a large farm kitchen, with a fireplace with a raised hearth, natural wood cabinets, and a Dutch door.

Each member of the family made suggestions. We took away and added, planned and replanned the kitchen, placed and replaced the downstairs powder room, closed up openings, added new windows. By February, four months before Mother and Dad were supposed to move in, the plans were complete on paper.

It took another six weeks to get bids. Finally the contract was let to a countryman, a local builder. I soon discovered why there is no high blood pressure in the country; it is because the pace is slow. It was the middle of May before any workmen appeared on the scene.

In the meantime, the gremlins designated to harass all new property owners descended on me in force. One day a neighbour's cattle got into the front lawn, soft from recent rains. Before the cattle were driven off, they had pockmarked the lawn with soggy hoof marks inches deep. We were months repairing the damage.

Then one night a drunken driver drove off the road over the embankment into the boxwood and rhododendron. The driver was not hurt but Evergreen's shrubbery was.

Meanwhile the grass was growing, the honeysuckle and the poison ivy were thriving, and the weeds on the hillsides were getting out of control. A power mower seemed indicated. Carefully I investigated the relative merits of various brands. The one I selected broke down the first day.

One night someone shattered several panes of glass in a front window. Heavy spring thundershowers forced water in under loosely hanging doors. Swallows came down the chimney into the house. All the mice and rats in the neighbourhood were using the deserted building as a favourite rendezvous.

The lesson seemed to be that the gremlins needed an overseer. A young Negro applied for the job. In April, Earl and Flossie and their three children moved into the tenant house.

Immediately the gremlins shifted the centre of their activity to the interior. The contractor would set out to replace a square yard of plaster, and an entire wall of plaster would fall. Window frames turned out to be rotten and had to be replaced. Often caulking would fall out the day after it was put in. It required some doing to chisel new openings in the thick stone walls. The termite man reported ominously that there was " termite activity underneath the house."

On the day after that, the county health authorities advised that a new drain field would have to be dug and a septic tank installed. The water people said that the spring would have to be cleaned and covered over, a new reservoir dug. They had a point, since a family of bats had taken up residence in the cool dampness of the spring house. I began to wonder if I'd made the worst mistake of my life the day I signed the paper for Evergreen.

The country contractor was afraid of rebuilding the living-room fireplace and had postponed it as long as possible. Finally, prodded by the architect, he started in. His plan was ingenius. He decided to leave the point of the two fireplaces as a supporting stone column and to rip out behind it. That done, he built the edges of the new fireplace to the second storey level. He then let the newly laid brick harden over the week-end before tearing out the supporting column.

" First thing Monday morning, we'll know," he told me. He shook his head dismally. " If this side of the ceiling is gonna cave in, that will end it."

On Monday I received no message that the ceiling had collapsed. On Tuesday came a letter from the countryman.

. . .

Dear Mrs Marshall :
    Since you have already noticed my worrying concern over the chimney and fireplace in the living room I can't help but to write and tell you it is up and safe. It is worked out to perfection in my book. If I stand

alone in the job I think it is wonderful. And I am pleased to the limit. I have smiled as I have never smiled before. Hoping you find it the same, I am very truly yours. . . .

Otto Kelley

I drove out as often as I could to see how the work was coming. With each trip I had to climb over more debris outside and in—tons of plaster, mountains of lath and ripped-out boards. The country workmen, always good-humoured, would exchange banter and community gossip, spit tobacco, lounge on the front porch over their lunch pails, and allow that " It's comin'—ma'am—slow, but sure. We'll git there yet. Don't you worry none, ma'am."

It was slow all right. Two weeks before my father was due to give his valedictory sermon to mark the end of his forty-six years in the ministry, the plumbing was still incomplete, the kitchen was scarcely begun, the plasterer was still busy, no interior painting had been done.

Moving day came. The van Dad had hired appeared in the driveway, and there was no alternative but to carry the household possessions to the loft of an outbuilding. Mother and Father planned to stay in Washington until their home was ready.

The work dragged on through the summer. By September, Mother was unable to stand the delay a minute longer. Dad could do whatever he liked, but she was going to move in. If she had to cook on a Sterno or a campfire and have workmen appear in her bedroom every morning at dawn— well—enough was enough!

The workmen—marvelling at her—good-humouredly swept out some of the debris and let her move. Then they went right on hammering and painting. It was October before the last of the workmen, by then attached to us like brothers, bade us a reluctant farewell.

During all the months of the renovation, I had been accumulating things for the farmhouse. The antique shops of Cape Cod had yielded some furnishings. A coffee grinder and a plaster figurine would one day be lamps. Three captain's chairs had been real bargains. A New England craftsman made me a coffee table with ceramic tiles set in the top—perfect for the library. The Forgue at Sandwich Village supplied tiny colonial and iron reproductions just right for the kitchen fireplace. A ship's bell would make a resounding farm bell.

During the fall, the Georgetown shops and some country auctions added more. Our Washington basement looked like a combination used-furniture store and warehouse. It became a problem to keep a path open to the washing machine.

Then the question was . . . how were we going to get all of the furniture out to the farm? I decided that a U-Drive-It truck was the sensible solution. Peter John, who had just got his driver's licence, said that he would be delighted to help. My brother-in-law planned to lend a hand loading the truck and driving it out to the farm.

Peter John and I appeared at the rental garage early the next Saturday morning. I told the young man behind the counter that I wanted to rent a truck.

"Yes, ma'am—what size?"

I turned to Peter for some help. He was thoughtful but silent. So I said, "I don't know exactly. What sizes do they come in?"

My tall son winced and gave me a withering look. Then he said knowingly, "We'll need about a ton and a half."

The man pulled a questionnaire form from under the counter.

"Okay— Now, madam, I'll have to ask you some questions. . . . Last name?"

"Marshall."

"First name?"

"Catherine."

"State in which you have your driver's licence?"

"District of Columbia."

"Married or single?"

"I'm a widow."

" By whom are you employed?"

" Well—I'm not exactly employed. I mean—I work for myself. What I mean is—well—I write books and things— sometimes."

" Mmm—seems a little odd. We don't usually—anyway, there isn't space here to put all that."

" Why not put the name of my publisher? That would look impressive—the McGraw-Hill Book Company."

" Okay—now—the name of your foreman?"

" Foreman? I've never had a foreman."

" No, I suppose not. Names of parents, if living?"

" Leonora Halestine Whitaker Wood and John Ambrose Wood."

That seemed to stop him cold. Suddenly the whole procedure seemed a little silly. . . . " Do you need the names of grandparents? Any genealogy? My great-grandparents came from—"

" No! No-o, but—colour of eyes and hair?"

Peter John chimed in crisply, " Blue—brown."

" Height?"

" You know, it's a funny thing, but I always have trouble remembering that. I think it's five-six. No, five-six and a half."

" That will do. Weight?" Here the young man's eyes swept me up and down.

" Oh, about one hundred thirty-three."

Suddenly, I felt facetious. " Look, if I should try a get-away with this truck, I'm sure you could use my bust measurement. It's—"

Peter John reddened slightly. " Mother, pl-e-ase!"

The young man said, "Now, we require a deposit, a minimum of twenty dollars. If you'll sign right here, please, I'll bring the truck around. You can wait there by the front door." And he disappeared into the gloomy, gasoline-smelling garage.

As soon as the man was out of sight, Peter John whispered, " Mom, what are we gonna do? You can't drive a truck.

And that man will be watching, so I can't drive it. That paper you signed said no one under twenty-one— Maybe we'd better call the whole deal off."

" Don't be silly." My tone carried more confidence than I felt. " Of course, I can drive it. A truck can't be so different from our Olds."

"But you're used to Hydramatic. It will be a gear-shift job and I—"

With a roar and an ear-piercing squeal of brakes, a monster of a truck appeared at the curb. Surely this couldn't be— But it was.

" Well, here she is, gassed up and ready to go. Now, if you'll just climb in the cab, I'll check you out."

Peter looked sheepish. " It *is* big—isn't it?"

" A ton and a half. That's what you said."

I climbed into the cab. It was like sitting halfway up the Washington monument. I could see over the top of every car on the street.

The young man began to explain the knobs, levers, and handles on the dash- and floorboard. In a bored monotone, he said that I should not pull this unless I wanted the truck to do so and so, and that I should turn this only after I had done something else. He mentioned something about a double clutch. I didn't know what a double clutch was. Finally he jumped down and, with a half-hearted wave of the hand, disappeared into the garage.

Peter John was still standing on the sidewalk. His face now wore a strained paternal expression. " I think, Mom, I'd better help you get this monster home. We can leave our car parked here awhile."

I tried not to show my relief. " I guess you're right."

So he climbed into the cab beside me and looked over the gadgets on the dash. " There's the starter, Mom—there. The clutch— Hey, don't forget the clutch."

The truck gave a lurch forward. " Easy, Mom, reach for the brake."

" I don't know where it is."

"Right there—*there!*"

We had several narrow escapes going down Sixteenth Street. I missed an Austin-Healey by a hair. The truck was so wide!

I noticed that Peter was biting his fingernails. "Man, would we have made mincemeat of that beautiful little car!"

A policeman at an intersection stared, but didn't blow his whistle. The driver of a Cadillac swore at me—in bellowing, stentorian tones. But fortune was with us. We made it back to our front door without passing any of our friends or acquaintances—we thought.

A month later a friend dropped by the house one afternoon. As she was leaving she said, "Apropos of nothing, awhile back I almost had an accident."

"You did? How was that?"

"One day I almost collided with a whopper of a truck weaving down Sixteenth Street. You know, it was the strangest thing—" here she looked at me curiously—"but I could have sworn that it was you driving that truck."

In one corner of the farmhouse attic, Mother found a pile of old books. Inside a nineteenth-century Latin grammar was a yellowed-clipping. There was no date on it, but it described a party once held at Evergreen. The society-page columnist of another century had been strictly the poetic type and had liked flinging words around. . . .

. . . The house with every window ablaze threw out its beacon light far over the surrounding hills to greet the gathering guests, making their hearts to feel a genial warmth, which increasing, only reached the climacteric of fervour when they merged into the illumination of chandeliers and mellow tinted radiance of happy faces . . .

The company consisted of about seventy-five guests, mostly young and susceptible, with a few couples of the younger married people of the vicinity. . . .

Supper was announced about eight o'clock. . . . We

dare not attempt to describe the supper. . . . But this
little secret we must tell. . . . We got it from the cook.
More than a dozen turkeys and chickens were sacrificed
and there was one cake for every four individuals. . . .

At a seasonable hour the guests departed and the
dying echoes of joyful sounds, with the silvery moon-
beams, wove into the silent night a mystical halo around
the festal scene.

Long live the happy couple who treated us so well,
and may their affectionate niece from the Buckeye State
visit them very frequently and occasionally between times.

Mother has always been the historian of our family. The
clipping was her first intimation that there were happy
ghosts at Evergreen. It gave her an insatiable curiosity
to know more about them. Mother has always had her own
techniques for historical research, which usually include
visiting local cemeteries, along with leisurely conversation
with local antiquarians.

Quakers from Bucks County, Pennsylvania, had settled two
villages in Loudoun County—Waterford, about 1733, and
Goose Creek (now Lincoln), two years later.

The Society of Friends, which from the beginning had
granted equal rights to women, sometimes found themselves
dominated by a woman. They might have known things
would get out of hand!

Thus, for many years, Hannah Janney was the preacher
of the Goose Creek meeting. In between having twelve
children, she taught and preached, visited and settled dis-
putes. Hers was the final word in the community.

The Friends advocated a strict, decorous life—no music,
no levity, plain clothes—no bright colours or ornaments.
But one member of the Goose Creek meeting had an irrepres-
sible daughter. She loved music and gay colours. Her father
cajoled and threatened, but it did no good. Still her feet
tapped out rhythms, her laughter rang out, and her love

for colour went unabashed. Finally her father disinherited her. The next day he had a visit from Hannah Janney.

"Isaac, I have just heard that thee has made thy will and disinherited thy daughter, Mary. Is that true?"

"Yes, that I have."

"Why did thee do that, Isaac?"

"I can't do anything with Mary. She dances instead of walking. She goes about the house singing. She will not wear the plain clothes. Over and over she has broken the disciplines. She is stubborn and contrary, set in her evil ways."

"Isaac, thee knows she gets her stubbornness honestly— from thee. Thee knows that the Friends' discipline provides that all children shall share equally in their father's possessions. Thee knows well that two wrongs will never make a right. I am here to tell thee, Isaac, that thee must change thy will."

"I won't do it."

"Yes, thee will, Isaac."

Isaac didn't give in without a struggle, but he was no match for Hannah. The will was changed. Hannah lived to be ninety-three, a dominant figure in the community to the end. She is buried in the cemetery around the bend from Evergreen.[2]

Yardley Taylor, the first builder of Evergreen and another member of Hannah's flock, was the first surveyor and map-maker in Loudoun County. With only a compass and a viameter attached to his buggy, he roamed every road, plotted every stream and every house. In 1853 he published his *Memoirs of Loudoun County, Virginia*. His book was published by Robert Pearsall Smith in Philadelphia, another Quaker and the son of Hannah Whitall Smith, the author of one of my favourite books—*The Christian's Secret of a Happy Life*. So the strands twine and intertwine.

[2] Nichols, Joseph, V., *Loudoun Valley Legends*, printed by Blue Ridge Herald Purcallville, Va., 1955. Used by permission.

Yardley had three sons. One of them, Richard Henry, set up an iron foundry and grist mill on the bottom land at Evergreen. He made the "Taylor plough"—especially designed to keep to a straight furrow. His farm bells and a frog doorstop can still be picked up in antique shops in the Leesburg area.

Richard Henry's buildings have long since disappeared. But when we, out of curiosity, dug on the site, we unearthed a small iron pot and some pieces of a Taylor's plough.

Another son, Oliver Taylor, had a green thumb. He turned part of Evergreen into the first nursery in the country. His boxwood—English and American—is now over a hundred years old. The trees he planted still stand—grafted walnut trees, from which the nutmeats come out whole; a row of red spruce to mark one boundary of the farm; the tall silver firs I had seen from the road that first day; rare Chinese cypress; chestnuts, Japanese maples, purple magnolias, and ginkgoes.

Local legend has it that, during an economic depression when Oliver was unable to sell his plants and shrubs, he set out all his leftover stock permanently on Evergreen land. It may be true because there is no end to the variety still there—forsythia, japonica, arbor vitae, double-flowered Japanese cherry trees, mock orange, yucca, rhododendron, quince, bamboo.

Eventually the plants fell into other loving hands when Sarah and Howard Hoge bought the farm in 1894. Howard was the new preacher for the Society of Friends at Lincoln and also, like Oliver, a horticulturist. He developed a thriving business from fifty acres planted in apple trees and became the first county agricultural agent and the first president of the Virginia Apple Growers Association.

His wife Sarah was noted for at least two things—her interest in the Women's Christian Temperance Union and her caramel ice cream. She loved to entertain, and always when the rhododendron was in bloom, the Hoges kept open house.

I have tracked down the recipe and have tried it. No wonder it became famous . . .!

CARAMEL ICE CREAM

1 quart or 3 pints of new milk
1 egg
Scant ½ cup flour
1 heaping cup of sugar
1 quart cream

Boil the milk. Beat the egg and flour together and add to the boiling milk. Put the sugar in a hot skillet. Stir and shake frequently until the sugar gets brown and liquid. Then stir it into the custard. Cool the mixture thoroughly. Put through fine sieve. Add the cream and freeze.

The caramel mixture may be made the day before the cream is to be used.

In the 1890s when only hand separators were used, milk was very rich. "New milk" then would be about the equivalent of half milk, half cream, today. "Cream" then would be called whipping cream today. Therefore, Sarah's ice cream was rich—rich—rich.

This is a more economical adaption of the recipe that I have worked out in my own kitchen:

CARAMEL ICE CREAM

1 pint half milk, half cream
4 eggs
½ cup flour
1½ cups sugar
1 can evaporated milk
1½ pints whipping cream
Pinch salt
1 teaspoon vanilla extract
⅔ cup water

Caramelize the sugar in a hot skillet, stirring constantly. Add the ⅔ cup water. Stir until sugar is dissolved and evaporated into a heavy syrup. Set aside to cool.

Separate the eggs. Beat the whites stiff, and set aside.

Add the flour and salt to the milk and evaporated milk. Beat in caramel mixture and beaten egg yolks. Cook mixture in top of double boiler, stirring constantly until custard begins to thicken and coats a silver spoon.

Fold in the egg whites. Cool, put through a fine sieve.

Whip the whipping cream and fold into custard mixture. Add vanilla. Freeze. This makes a gallon of ice cream.

One warning—this ice cream won't be as delicious as Sarah's unless it is made in a hand freezer. Old-fashioned ice creams have two characteristics not shared by most present-day ones—they are not slenderizing, and they will melt rapidly in the dish. This melting characteristic is not always true of some so-called ice creams today, to which gelatin, wax, or papier-mâché sometimes seem to have been added!

Since Sarah was once the president of the W.C.T.U., she might not like it that in Evergreen's new kitchen the old bricks for the fireplace came out of a Winchester brewery that was being demolished. But then again, since the brewery was demolished, that should please her.

On a moonlit night anyone with any imagination can see Evergreen's happy ghosts—Yardley Taylor driving his two-wheeled gig with the viameter attached along the dusty roads; Hannah Janney with that certain glint in her eye, keeping the menfolk strictly in line; the spirited Mary, laughing and dancing; Richard Henry, wearing his leather apron, the sparks flying from the anvil of his forge; Oliver wandering among his cherished plants; Sarah at her stove, stirring the burnt sugar for her caramel ice cream; and of course, on a certain silvery night, that company of the young and " susceptible" entertaining the niece from the Buckeye State.

Once the moving was completed and some of the house in order, Mother turned to the task of cleaning up the yard. The project with top priority on her list was the elimination of the poison ivy that grew everywhere.

One morning she noticed big creepers on the trunk of the gigantic ginkgo tree. The vines had been there a long time. They were twined and intertwined, a many stranded rope.

After digging up the roots, she began pulling at the rope of vines, hand over hand. Suddenly, something came crashing out of the tree, struck her shoulder a glancing blow, and fell at her feet with a thud. A white-faced animal struggled to its feet, stood its ground, and snarled at her.

Mother took one look, opened her mouth, and gave a yell that could be heard all the way to the house. It was the biggest possum she had ever seen. I'll always regret that I was not there to see the expression on Mother's face at the moment that she grounded her first possum.

Poison ivy was not the only weed waiting to be eliminated. By early spring, the hillsides were knee-deep in them, choking out the gnarled apple trees, all but smothering the shrubbery. Since as yet we had no farm machinery, Dad decided to use some gadgets of his own.

Always my Father has had a weakness for tools and gadgets; many times he has been tempted to spend too much of his ministerial salary on such things. Just after World War II, he had seen flame throwers advertised. It seemed that the War Department had been overzealous about flame throwers and had some extras. Father knew immediately that a flame thrower was just what he needed.

Mother was annoyed at the idea. "What on God's green earth do you want something like that for? You know perfectly well we haven't any money to spend on such silly things."

I remember that Father had looked wounded. He always

looks wounded when any member of the family questions his judgement about buying gadgets.

"The flame thrower is exactly what I need to get rid of the tall weeds in the corners of the yard. And I *am* going to buy it." With that he strode off and slammed a door.

Buy it, he did. What Mother didn't know was that the old flame thrower had been transported to Evergreen along with the rest of the household possessions. So now, we had the rare treat of seeing the great warrior stalking around the yard spurting flame in all directions.

The only trouble was that one day Father singed a clump of boxwood along with the weeds. Mother, outraged, insisted that the flame thrower be retired from active duty.

Then Father had another idea. . . . A neighbour had told him that there was nothing like goats for getting rid of weeds.

Mother protested that too. "That's downright ridiculous. Besides, goats are smelly."

"I found out about that too. It's only the males. The females aren't—smelly."

"But goats aren't discriminating. They'll eat the flowers too."

"That can be controlled. You have to buy a chain and tether them where you want them to eat."

The goats—a big nanny goat and her kid—long-legged, wobbly, and shy, rode back to the farm in the open trunk of Dad's car.

So far they haven't eaten any boxwood. The grandchildren think they're wonderful—especially the baby goat. They like to see her shyly stick her head around the corner of the barn.

By now, other animals have been added to the menagerie—Mike, a thoroughbred collie; a pair of Easter ducklings; and Dad's chickens and turkeys.

Mother had scarcely finished unpacking the dishes before father was in town pricing baby chickens and turkeys. What would a farm be without one's own poultry on the table?

Still he had been told that turkeys were hard to raise, so he decided to be conservative in his poultry project—a hundred chicks and twelve turkeys would be a start.

Earl had the chicken house cleaned and ready. Dad reasoned that if he let the turkeys roam over Evergreen's steep hillsides, they would develop too much muscle. He took completely to heart the philosophy that, if you want tender turkeys, "a turkey's foot should never touch ground."

Seven chickens died, only one turkey. The growing birds were stuffed with all the corn and feed they could eat. The bills for poultry feed were appalling.

But it was not long before fried chicken and wondrously plump and tender turkeys began to grace the table at Evergreen. By Thanksgiving, Father had developed a pattern for his chatter as he carved—the life story and vital statistics of the bird on the platter, plus, of course, the fact that its feet had never touched ground.

My brother Bob had listened quietly to Dad's turkey-raising tales through Thanksgiving dinner. Finally, thoroughly saturated, he said mildly, "Dad, do you have a pencil?"

"Sure. Why?"

"Let's see if we can figure out what your turkey-feed bill has been to date."

"Sure, son—now let me see. It's been. . . ."

When Bob and Father had finished their elaborate calculations, a conservative estimate was that the turkey we had just eaten had cost at least $1.75 a pound. The local grocery stores were selling turkeys at 59 cents a pound.

Father had other projects. I was continually finding old lists around the house, very impressive ones . . .

> Prune and spray old apple trees
> Deepen and widen the brook; plant willows, iris, mint, and watercress along its banks
> Screen in the back porch
> Build patio by kitchen door

Mend smokehouse roof
Build fences
Cut down locust tree

The locust tree was dead. Not only that, but its hollow trunk housed a hive of honeybees. Whenever Father ventured into the front yard, he was aggravated by the incessant buzzing of the bees around his head.

"We'd better put the tree cutting at the head of the list," Father told me. "The first strong wind will bring it down, and it might fall on the roof."

"Yes, but how are you going to do it?" I asked.

The problem was that there was only five feet between the tree and the front porch. On the other three sides were solid clumps of tall boxwood. Because that left nowhere for the tree to fall safely, felling it seemed to be a job for tree surgeons.

Father got estimates but whistled when he saw the figures. "It's outlandish! You'd think they planned to take that tree down an inch at a time. I'll show 'em! By golly, I'll do it myself!"

The first step was to get the bees out of the trunk. "Tomorrow morning we'll smoke 'em out," Father told Earl. "We can't work at getting the tree down with those infernal bees always in our hair."

Early the next morning a troubled Earl stuck his head in the kitchen door. "Missus Wood, de Rev'ent says we gotta smoke out dem bees. I's scairt of bees."

Mother thought fast. "Don't worry, Earl. I'll fix you up. I'll tell you what. You know that left-over wire screening in the corner of the tool house? Bring me a piece of that."

Earl produced the screening. Mother bent it in the shape of a helmet and put it over his head and face. Then she secured it around his neck with a long piece of cloth that terminated in a fetching bow at the back.

" Now put on these canvas gloves, Earl. Then I'll tie your sleeves tight at the wrists with a string."

Earl went toward the scene of action with his dusky face grinning through the screening. Father, waiting at the foot of the tree, took one look at Earl, at the bow at the back, and let out his most profane expressions. " Holy Jeehossifats, Earl! What happened to you?"

" Missus Wood, she fixed me up, Rev'en. Dem bees—dey's daidly."

Father handed Earl a thick stick with some rags tied over it. " Now, let's start the rags smoking. Then you climb up the tree and hold the smoking rags inside the hollow."

Earl, looking like something left over from a Hallowe'en party, struggled upward into the mighty locust. As he thrust the home-made torch inside the tree, the bees poured out in a torrent of angry buzzing. Helmet or not, Earl left the smoking rags in the hollow, slid down the tree trunk a lot faster than he had gone up, and made a dash for the safety of the porch.

Billows of black smoke were rolling out of every opening in the rotten trunk. The tree warriors were just congratulating themselves that the bees must certainly have departed for calmer fields when Mother, who had appeared on the porch to watch, yelled, " Dad, look! The tree's on fire—"

She was right. Tongues of flame were lapping around the great trunk. Father and Earl ran to get the hose. They connected it to the nearest outlet only to find that it was too short.

By then the situation was serious. The fire was being sucked up the hollow tree, chimney fashion, with flames shooting out at the top, dangerously close to the roof of the house.

But Mother had already gone to telephone the local fire department. Minutes later, the big trucks were clanging into the driveway, and the firemen soon had the flames extinguished.

That evening, Earl climbed the charred tree to scrape out handfuls of honey. " Rev'ent, it's de bes' honey I ever et," Earl said. " Dat smoke taste—dat's good."

Father looked gloomy. " I never ate smoked honey. You can have it. But I notice that the tree's still standing—and it has to come down."

A week went by. Daily Father grimaced at the blackened tree. Then Harlow, my brother-in-law, phoned and offered to help the following Saturday morning.

On the appointed day, I was there to watch. Father, Earl, and Harlow had gathered under the locust tree enough equipment to level all growing things in northern Virginia— a pile of rope, chairs, a crosscut saw, axes, whetstones, files, wedges, and a ladder.

As Harlow and Earl were busily engaged in hanging hand axes, saws, and lengths of rope to their belts, Father was giving them an unsolicited pre-flight briefing. " Now we'll do it this way—tie one end of the rope to the branch you're working on—just below the sawing point, of course. Then toss the other end over a limb above you, and one down to me here on the ground. I'll hold the rope taut. Then when you've sawed the limb through, I can let it down slowly —steering it clear of the boxwood and the porch roof."

It sounded good.

Earl and Harlow climbed aloft. Several of the smaller limbs were sawed off and successfully lowered to the ground. But then came a larger limb. As Harlow sawed, Father and I were getting increasingly uneasy.

Father yelled, " Hold up a minute, you two. That's a big one. I'm not sure I can hang on to it.' '

Harlow paused in his sawing and called down, " Why not find something to tie your end of the rope to?"

Immediately Father had an idea. He looped the rope under his arms and tied it securely across his chest. Then he backed up until the rope was taut. He reasoned that his 200 pounds would be ample counterbalance for the weight of the limb.

" Okay, boys, everything under control now—go ahead—saw."

As Harlow's saw cut deepened, the large limb began to sag, then suddenly it cracked and broke loose. Father wasn't ready. He tried to brace himself, but instead he was propelled toward the tree. Then he was standing on tiptoe. Then he was being lifted off the ground in little jerks.

I stood there, not knowing what to do. " Help, Harlow —help—Dad, he's—"

Father's booming voice rang out . . . " Help! Earl! Harlow . . .! Don't just sit up there— *Do* something . . .!"

Harlow and Earl started scrambling down. Father was dangling about four feet off the ground, fanning the air with his hands and feet. By then he had pulled out all the stops on his most unministerial vocabulary.

He was in no real danger, and the three of us were almost helpless with laughter. Finally Earl and Harlow got enough control of themselves to catch hold of Father's ankles. With much heaving and pulling, they got his 200 pounds back to earth.

Father, rubbing the rope burns on his chest and drawing himself up to his full six feet, said, " I fail to see what's so funny—"

I decided that it might be wise to ask for the services of the tree surgeon.

Bit by bit, step by step, project by project, the dream that I had that summer day in the Cape Cod kitchen is coming into being.

As I write, spring has come to Evergreen. Mike, the collie, roams the greening hillsides, sniffing the air. The baby goat is growing. The duck is sitting on fifteen eggs. The drake (typical male!) wanders around disconsolately, lonely, feeling sorry for himself. A few white-faced Herefords now graze the bottomlands where once Henry Taylor's forge stood.

Last year's corn has been sold at a good price. There is freshly turned sod in some of the fields. The old apple trees have all been pruned. New strawberry plants are thriving. Father reports that the egg production for March was 809 eggs, and that he thinks he may try raising a few more turkeys.

The last time I drove out to Evergreen I found Father busy building fences. He paused in his hammering long enough to comment, "Three years of solid work may make a dent in my work list. . . . Nothing like retiring to go to work!"

It sounded like complaining. But there was contentment on his face.

That same afternoon Mother and I stood on the front porch looking out over the sweep of lawn and shrubbery. The sun was going down. The tall pines cast lengthening shadows across the grass. The forsythia was almost gone; the Japanese quince and the crab apple were coming into bud. Late daffodils still bloomed, punctuating the far hillsides with golden exclamation points. The two of us had been silent, our eyes absorbing the beauty.

"You know," I said to Mother, "when I was a little girl in Mississippi I dreamed of this. Remember? The *Little Colonel* series, the Southern mansion, and all. Only this is so much more beautiful than anything I imagined."

Mother said, "It's the realization of my dreams, too, only in a slightly different way. All my married life, Dad and I have moved from one manse to another, improving and planting; then we've had to move on, leaving our plants for the next family.

"Now at the end of our ministry, it's as if the Lord is saying to us . . . ' Here it all is with dividends—all you've invested in love and energy—filled up, pressed down, and running over. I had it in mind all the time.' "

CHAPTER 16

You Can't Hold Back the Light

The back of the car was piled high with furnishings a boy would need for his room at prep school—a bookcase, a floor lamp, a desk light, sheets, blankets, towels, a cotton rug, some favourite pictures.

After we had crossed the Connecticut line into Massachusetts, the uneven contour of the land became rolling countryside, made lush by recent rains. Each mile was bringing us closer to the moment against which I had been steeling myself. Peter John was leaving home to take his last year in high school at the Mt Hermon School in northwestern Massachusetts.

"Sons are different," my friends had often told me. "You may as well face it. Once they leave home, that's it. You get no more than glimpses of them after that."

The blond boy who was driving was entertaining no such serious thoughts. He was listening to a baseball game on the radio.

My mind kept wandering from the battle between the Braves and the Giants, or was it the Indians and the Yankees? Much to Peter John's disgust, I could never keep those intrepid warriors straight. Instead I was remembering something I had seen many years before—the last page of my Baby Book written in my mother's round feminine handwriting.

That morning years ago, she had combed my long curls more carefully than usual, brushing each one round and round her forefinger. Then she had walked to the iron grillwork gate with me, kissed me good-bye, and watched me skip gaily down the street to my first day in the first grade.

She must have stood at the gate a long time, thoughts

stirring in her mind, as she watched that small retreating figure. Then she had turned back into the house and had written the thoughts down on the only blank page left in the Baby Book. . . .

> Today our dear little girl starts to school—no longer a baby. Seven years of childish joy, blessings, and love— the sunshine of her father's and mother's heart. Mingled with the pride and thanksgiving that fill my heart, there is an undercurrent of sadness. The little life will no longer be wholly under the home influence. . . . My prayer is that my child may always bless and beautify everything that she touches. . . .

The lines written on this final page were unabashedly sentimental. But why not? I understood now what Mother had felt on that morning long ago. Each generation of womankind has the same set of feelings. Life asks women to give and to give and then to give up, and to do both with equanimity and courage.

When that certain moment was upon us in our rooms in the inn the next day, I was not big enough to take it alone. But I knew where to go for help. Besides, don't all such moments need the benison of a benediction?

I tried to keep my heart from showing—not because I was afraid of the heart, but because I didn't want to embarrass Peter John.

"We should be pushing off for school," I said. "But first, would you indulge me in something? This is a significant day for us both. Would you be willing for us to have a prayer together and ask God's blessing on it?"

Peter nodded a little impatiently, so I made the prayer brief. The moment hung in space—hung, and passed. But there was the unmistakable feeling in the prayer that we were not two, but three—united across barriers that were no barriers.

Silently, Peter picked up his suitcases.

I was a little disappointed in the room at school—circa 1890, golden oak woodwork, the floors well worn by generations of boys' feet, battered furniture, two small windows almost covered with a summer's growth of ivy.

But Peter didn't seem to mind. He had just met his room-mate, Bruce, and liked him—as blond as he, also a senior. This room would be their digs—their very own. What did golden oak woodwork and worn floors matter?

Two other boys stuck their heads in at the door and introduced themselves. "We thought you might like some help in unpacking the car—"

The five of us made a series of trips between the car and the room, back and forth, up and down the wooden steps —so uneven and worn down in the middle. Soon everything was deposited in a heap in the middle of the room.

Then Bruce's parents appeared. His mother was small and pretty, dainty and feminine. After the introductions, she said, "Mrs. Marshall, you and I are going to have to go into a huddle about curtains and scatter rugs for this room—"

"It's a warm day," Bruce's father interrupted. "Why don't the five of us go down to the school store? We can get something to drink, and talk there."

So over sodas and Cokes, we had our impromptu conference. . . . "What do you boys want at the windows—curtains or short draperies . . .? I wonder if we couldn't speak to someone about getting the ivy clipped off the windows to let in more light . . .? What about bedspreads, scatter rugs . .? Your pictures will have to be hung from the moulding. The rules say no nails in the walls. . . . You have no easy chair in the room. Won't you need one . . .? So few clothes hangers—and no glasses in the bathroom. . . ."

As we walked back to the room, I noticed how Bruce's mother, all unconsciously, leaned on her husband's arm,

smiling up into his face. 'An intact family . . .,' I thought.
'How wonderful it must be. . . .'

Back in their room Bruce's mother opened one of his
suitcases and carried new shoes and galoshes to the closet,
piles of new underwear and pyjamas to his chest of drawers.

"I sat up till two last night sewing on name tags," she
said. "Can you imagine these boys actually getting their
own laundry together each week—and on time?"

"No—I can't. I suppose they'll learn."

She eyed the iron beds. "Bruce, can't I make your bed
for you one last time? You never get it smooth."

"Never mind, Mom, I'll do it myself—later."

She was acting out what I was feeling . . . the apron
strings almost severed, but the hands aching to perform a
last chore or two. Yet she had two other sons, and Bruce
was not the oldest. She had been through this before.

Peter looked at me. He knew too—knew beyond his
years. He said with hesitant dismissal, as if uneasy to have
me there longer, "I think you'd better go now, Mom."

So I shook hands with Bruce and his parents, stood
on tiptoe to pat my tall son on his cheek, and walked out
—down the worn, uneven steps.

As I drove through the winding avenue of trees to the
highway, I thought of our home—now an empty house—
waiting for me in Washington. I thought of it and turned
aside from the thought. Not yet—not quite yet.

Besides, I wanted to see how Peter's and Bruce's room
would look after they were unpacked and settled; then
during the months to come, I would be able to picture
Peter in that setting. But if I stayed a few more hours, I
mustn't seem to hover; the boys would never stand for that.

The things they needed—that would be a handy excuse.
When a woman is at loose ends, what does she do? She
goes shopping for someone she loves. In my mind I was
already making a list:

A lounge chair
More clothes hangers.

Two plastic glasses for the bathroom

In the village of Northfield, I spied a sign "Furniture and Appliances." It turned out to be a combination store, quite a combination. The local mortician also sold electrical appliances and furniture. The hearse was parked in the driveway.

On the second floor of the store was a maple armchair. "That will do. It's for my son at the boy's school. You do deliver, don't you?"

"Sure—this afternoon, if you like. Which building?"

"Why don't I meet you there? Could you make it one-thirty?"

The man agreed and I left to search out the hangers and the glasses. That done, I still had several hours before one-thirty.

How could I fill the time? I must replace the loneliness —if that's what was welling up in me—with action. So I drove on through the village towards the New Hampshire border. Were the strands of my life suddenly unravelling? Then I would tie the strands together. . . . There must be someone else to shop for. . . . My sister Em had been wanting some antique bone dishes. Perhaps some shop had not yet closed for the season. . . . I would like to find some copper utensils for Mother's farm kitchen at Evergreen. . . . And some maple syrup for Father. . . .

I drove on, watching the hills of Massachusetts stretching themselves to become the mountains of New Hampshire. But across the border no antique shops were open. I turned down a side road, wanting to explore, yet half fearful that I might not be able to find my way back.

The road wound and twisted. I passed no other cars. After several miles I saw a sign "Maple Syrup" in front of a white farm-house. As I drove into the yard, a little boy came running out to see who the visitor was.

"Do you still have any of that maple syrup for sale?"

"Come on in," he grinned. "I'll call Pop."

"I've sold almost all of this season's," the farmer said

when he appeared. "But if you don't need too much—?"

"How about a half gallon? Could you spare that?"

"Sure could. Make yourself at home. Chair right there. I'll fix the syrup for you."

This was the family dining room. The round table in the centre of the room was covered with pieces of tissue-paper dress pattern and cotton material. The two cupboards were filled with Early American pressed glass—a set of cranberry thumb-print tumblers and some ribbed opalescent like that Peter and I had once had so much fun collecting.

'The glass has probably been in the family always,' I thought. 'Antique dealers dream of finding places like this.'

The farmer came back with the syrup in two shiny cans, bearing professional-looking labels. About him and his family there was an air of sturdy Americana. This was New England at its best. No wonder this man's ancestors had made things hard for King George III's troops!

The friendly New Hampshire farmhouse had warmed me; the strange road I'd travelled into the mountains had given me a sense of adventure. I could feel my old zest for living seeping back; not even my loneliness could extinguish it.

When I got back to the school, I found the mortician-furniture dealer waiting. I showed him the room and he carried up the chair. The boys were nowhere to be seen, and I made no effort to find them.

The heap was gone from the middle of the floor. The beds were made—bumpy, but made. A pair of pyjamas was stuck under each pillow, half trailing out. Peter was using his book-case as a bedside table. The mementos of home he had insisted on bringing with him—two Toby jugs, some model cars, some favourite pictures and pennants—were carefully arranged.

His new alarm clock was on top of the bookcase; the Toby jugs and model cars on the first shelf. From the moulding his two favourite pictures had been hung by long wires—the wall plaque of Tam O'Shanter and Souter Johnny he had bought in Scotland and an informal *Life* magazine photograph of his father.

I pinned a note on the new chair, put some hangers and a plastic cup on each bed, gave one long last lingering look, and tiptoed out. This time I resolutely turned the car toward home.

My thoughts leaped across the miles to Washington. It's odd, I thought, how each life seems to be divided into eras or chapters. That morning of Peter's death had been the closing of one chapter, the opening of another. And now, this day—in which I've parted with my son—is another ending, yet another beginning.

What did the new era hold? Who could tell? I had no more idea than I had had at the grim moment when I had walked out of the hospital room in which Peter's body lay, had heard the door click shut behind me, and had walked down the chilly corridor. But underneath all fear of an unknown future had been the faith that " Surely goodness and mercy would follow me all the days of my life."

The faith had become a fact. There had been the mercy of the God who had taken the unpromising raw materials of grief and smashed hopes and turned them into astonishing good; there had been the goodness of all the friends whom He had sent into my life.

Now, as I drove homeward, through my mind there trooped a procession of those friends . . . A. D. so wanting to be with me in my hour of grief, slipping into the little hospital room—" Catherine, it was in those moments that I learned what Christ's power over death is. Glory filled that room. . . ." That Chinese woman whose name I never knew, sitting beside me in church the first Sunday after Peter's death, her love flowing, flowing. . . . Anita, tall and imperious, standing in the middle of my bedroom, saying, " I'll be damned if I'll feel sorry for you. . . ." Rebecca Beard, folding me in her ample arms as she asked for the touch of the healing Christ for the stricken spirit of one woman. . . .

I thought of Tom Wharton, his face alight with conviction
—"Catherine, you must insist that those sermons be printed
in Peter's own style. Any other way would be unfair to
him. . . ." I could hear again the ticking of the clock in
my doctor's office, and his quiet reasoning voice, "You're
flesh and blood, Catherine. Just thank God that you are . . .!"

I remembered that afternoon when I had stood in a
New England village post office and eagerly ripped open a
letter from a man I had yet to meet, Ed Aswell; of my
astonishment at the words I was reading—"There is not the
slightest doubt in our minds that this will be a good book
and a deeply moving one. . . . We are now prepared to
offer you a contract . . ." Then Ruth Welty's face leapt into
my mind. With her remarkable offer of editorial help, she
had certainly added to my reservoir of good will. . . . And
Jim Broadbent—that rugged Scot! I could still see the
pipe smoke wreathing his head, hear him reminiscing in his
buzz-saw accent about a boy with tousled hair who had
carried in his heart the dream of becoming a minister. . . .

Still they came on—so many friends—all the soldiers who
had written from Korea; the letters from Japan, Saipan,
and Formosa; from the British Isles, from Australia and
South Africa. . . . "Through the pages of this book, Christ
walked right into my living room. . . ." "This book was like
a shaft of brilliant sunlight on the dark path I was treading.
Thank you, thank you. . . ."

They had come from other unexpected quarters—like
Hollywood. There was Sam Engel. I could still see those
brown eyes behind the spectacles looking at me so unblink-
ingly—"Sure, Catherine, we need to pray about the movie.
You do it—now. . . ." And Marjorie Rambeau, hearing Peter's
sermon with her heart instead of her ears, rising in faith to
walk down that church aisle, not once, but fifteen times. . . .

I thought of the country contractor with his "worrying
concern" over the chimney at Evergreen; of my Dad with
the rope around his middle, dangling four feet off the ground,
yelling in his booming voice, "Help! Earl! Harlow! *Do*

something . . .!" And Mother standing on the porch at Evergreen, a snared dream in her eyes, saying so joyously, "Towards the end of our lives, here it all is with dividends— filled up, pressed down, and running over—"

During those years since Peter's death, I had found that life *is* people—wonderful people, dear people, God's people. Could it have been that I—who had so valued solitude that I had fled up the back stairs to find it—had had to be stripped, reduced to aloneness, to discover how much I needed people, wanted them? Out of loneliness I had found love. Out of the heart's need, I had crept humbly back to acknowledge the need and to rejoin the human race.

As I drove, darkness began closing in—not night, but a sudden summer thunderstorm. The rain fell in sheets. The car's wind-screen wipers struggled futilely to sweep away the torrents of water. Scissors of lightning slashed the sky with zigzag gashes. Then the storm was over as quickly as it had come.

A question nagged at my mind, wouldn't let go. The future? To what do you go home now?

At moments when the future is completely obscured, I thought, can any one of us afford to go to meet our to-morrows with dragging feet? God had been in the past. Then He would be in the future, too.

And with His presence had always come an end to taste-less living. Always He had brought adventure—high hopes, unexpected friends, new ventures that broke old patterns. Then out in my future must lie more goodness, more mercy, more adventures, more friends.

Across the hills light was breaking through the storm clouds. Suddenly just ahead of the car an iridescent rainbow appeared—hung there—shimmering. I hadn't seen a rain-bow for a long time.

I drove steadily into the light.

NAUGHT FOR YOUR COMFORT
TREVOR HUDDLESTON
'A noble book, a superb book, to be read by anyone who cares about the race or human relations.'   *Guardian*

THE TRUE AND LIVING GOD
TREVOR HUDDLESTON
'A prophetic testimony to a living God . . . by one of the great figures of our age.'   *Church Times*

THE SCREWTAPE LETTERS
C. S. LEWIS
'A brilliant exposition of Hell's latest novelties and of the divine platitudes that are Heaven's unanswerable answer.'
Punch

LETTERS TO MALCOLM: *Chiefly on Prayer*
C. S. LEWIS
C. S. Lewis's sane and brilliantly imaginative approach to Christianity put this discussion of the problems of private prayer on to the best seller lists in 1964.

COME OUT THE WILDERNESS
BRUCE KENRICK
'This is a truly *remarkable* book compelling and convicting. I can compare it in fact only with that of Trevor Huddleston's *Naught for Your Comfort*. There are few books one would dare to put into anyone's hands and say "This is Christianity." But here is one.'   *Bishop of Woolwich*

GOD'S FROZEN PEOPLE
MARK GIBBS and T. RALPH MORTON
'Puts down in plain English some clear and revolutionary thinking about the role of the laity . . . reads like an exciting novel.'   *Archdeacon of London*

LETTERS AND PAPERS FROM PRISON
DIETRICH BONHOEFFER
These documents, smuggled out of prison under the nose of the Gestapo, have a clear and shining unity.

THE PLAIN MAN LOOKS AT HIMSELF
WILLIAM PURCELL
A book of self-examination for the ordinary Christian.

THE PLAIN MAN LOOKS AT THE BIBLE
WILLIAM NEIL
'A good popular guide book to the Bible which is well worth reading for its own sake.' *Church Times*

THE IMITATION OF CHRIST
THOMAS À KEMPIS
A new translation into modern English, enhanced by the poetic quality of the language.

THE GOSPELS IN MODERN ENGLISH
J. B. PHILLIPS
'Familiar works acquire a new point and freshness.' *Scotsman*

LETTERS TO YOUNG CHURCHES
A new translation of the Epistles
J. B. PHILLIPS
'It would have saved me a great deal of labour if his book had come into my hands when I first seriously began to try to discover what Christianity was.' *C. S. Lewis*

A MAN CALLED JESUS
J. B. PHILLIPS
Contemporary in their language, ageless in their meaning, these 26 short plays by Religious Fontana's best-selling author describe the life of Jesus. J. B. Phillips' sales to date 1,480,000

THE DIVINE PITY
GERALD VANN, O.P.
'A searching discernment, an interpreter's skill, wise comment on human nature, make him profitable reading for both Catholic and Protestant.' *British Weekly*